MW00582756

Coercion and the State

AMINTAPHIL
The Philosophical Foundations of Law and Justice

Series editor
Mortimer Sellers, *University of Baltimore*

David A. Reidy • Walter J. Riker
Editors

Coercion and the State

 Springer

David A. Reidy
University of Tennessee
Knoxville, TN
USA

Walter J. Riker
Vanderbilt University
Nashville, TN
USA

ISBN 978-1-4020-6878-2   e-ISBN 978-1-4020-6879-9

Library of Congress Control Number: 2007942722

Printed on acid-free paper

9 8 7 6 5 4 3 2 1

springer.com

We dedicate this volume to our wives, Kathy and Dawn, with love and gratitude

Contents

Contributors

Scott A. Anderson is Assistant Professor of Philosophy at the University of British Columbia, and a Visiting Fellow at the University of Chicago Law School, 2007–2008. He works in ethics, social and political philosophy, and the philosophy of sex and gender, with a special interest in coercion.

Emily R. Gill is Caterpillar Professor of Political Science at Bradley University. She is the author of a number of articles on various aspects of liberal political theory, including democratic theory, pluralism and groups, citizenship, and feminist theory, and the book *Becoming Free: Autonomy and Diversity in the Liberal Polity* (2001).

Carol C. Gould is Professor of Philosophy and Political Science and Director of the Center for Global Ethics and Politics at Temple University. She is the author of many articles in social and political philosophy, feminist theory, and applied ethics, and has edited or co-edited eight books. She is the author of *Globalizing Democracy and Human Rights* (2004), *Rethinking Democracy* (1988), and *Marx's Social Ontology* (1978).

Kenneth Henley is Professor of Philosophy at Florida International University. He has published articles on political and legal philosophy and ethics in various books and journals. His most recent work concerns the rule of law and the International Criminal Court, sovereignty, and the limits of legal positivism as evinced by the British extradition case of Augusto Pinochet.

Monica Anne Hlavac is a Ph.D. candidate in Philosophy at Duke University where she is working on a dissertation on the legitimacy of the human rights regime.

Bruce Landesman is Associate Professor of Philosophy at the University of Utah. His special interests include ethics, political philosophy, applied ethics, and Marxism. He is the author or co-author of a number of articles, including several on professional responsibility.

Steven P. Lee is Professor of Philosophy at Hobart and William Smith Colleges. He has written widely on issues in moral philosophy, especially on the ethics of war. Recently, he has edited the previous volume in this series, *Intervention, Terrorism, and Torture: Contemporary Challenges to Just War Theory* (2006).

Burton M. Leiser is Emeritus Professor of Philosophy at Pace University in New York. He received his Ph.D. in Philosophy from Brown University, his J.D. from Drake University, and degrees from the University of Chicago and Yeshiva University. He is the author or editor of a number of books in philosophy and law, most notably the three editions of *Liberty, Justice, and Morals: Contemporary Value Conflicts* (1986).

Joan McGregor is the Lincoln Professor of Bioethics and Professor of Philosophy at Arizona State University. Her research interests include cultural issues that arise in biomedical contexts, the patenting of human biological materials, and coercion. She has authored a number of papers and the book *Is It Rape? On Acquaintance Rape and Taking Women's Consent Seriously* (2005).

Alistair M. Macleod is Emeritus Professor of Philosophy at Queen's University, Canada, where he teaches moral and political philosophy. In addition to *Social Justice, Progressive Politics and Taxes* (2004), his recent publications include papers on free markets and democracy, invisible hand arguments, the war on terrorism, and human rights.

David A. Reidy is Associate Professor of Philosophy at the University of Tennessee where he is also Chair of the Legal Studies Program. He is the author of many articles, and the editor of several volumes, on the work of John Rawls and in political and legal philosophy more generally. His most recent book is the monograph *On the Philosophy of Law* (2007).

Walter J. Riker is Lecturer in Philosophy at Vanderbilt University. He received his Ph.D. in Philosophy from the University of Tennessee. He works in political and legal philosophy and applied ethics. He has previously published in *Social Philosophy Today, Southwest Philosophy Review*, and, most recently, *Political Studies*, where his essay, "The Democratic Peace is Not Democratic: On Behalf of Rawls's Decent Peoples," appears.

Wade L. Robison is the Ezra A. Hale Professor of Applied Ethics at the Rochester Institute of Technology. He received his Ph.D. in Philosophy from the University of Wisconsin-Madison, with a minor in law. He has published extensively in philosophy of law, on David Hume, and in practical and professional ethics. His book *Decisions in Doubt: The Environment and Public Policy* (1994) won the Nelson A. Rockefeller Prize in Social Science and Public Policy.

Don E. Scheid is Professor of Philosophy at Winona State University. He received his Ph.D. in Philosophy from New York University and his J.D. from the University of Utah. He has taught at Bowdoin College, University of Illinois-Urbana, and the University of Utah. His main areas of interest are moral and political philosophy and the philosophy of criminal law.

Christine T. Sistare is Professor of Philosophy and Chair of the Philosophy Department at Muhlenberg College, where she also co-directs the Philosophy & Political Thought Program. She is the editor of *Civility and Its Discontents* (2004), co-editor of two other AMINTAPHIL volumes (1997, 2000), and the author of *Responsibility and Criminal Liability* (1989), as well as many articles in philosophy of law and ethics.

Helga Varden is Assistant Professor of Philosophy at the University of Illinois at Urbana-Champaign. She has published several papers in political philosophy, including "Kant's Non-Voluntarist Conception of Political Obligations" in *Kantian Review* and "A Kantian Conception of Rightful Sexual Relations: Sex, (Gay) Marriage and Prostitution" in *Social Philosophy Today*.

Chapter 1
Introduction

David A. Reidy and Walter J. Riker

Coercion is a complex phenomenon. It occurs in both interpersonal and institutional or political contexts. In this volume we are primarily concerned with coercion in institutional or political contexts (paradigmatically, coercive state action). Nevertheless, coercion in interpersonal contexts is not absent from the discussion, and for good reason. Insofar as the concept of coercion is put to work in both interpersonal and institutional or political contexts, a complete and coherent conceptual analysis (as well as a complete and coherent evaluative theory) will have to range over its use in both kinds of context.[1] Further, while the capacities of institutions and bodies politic to act are dependent on complex systems of rules in ways the capacities of individual persons to act are not, thus giving rise to the distinction between interpersonal and institutional or political contexts, it remains the case that institutions and bodies politic cannot act save through the agency of individual persons. Interpersonal coercion is thus often ingredient in or mixed with institutional or political coercion. So, no discussion of coercion in institutional or political contexts can proceed fully divorced from discussion of it in interpersonal contexts. A parallel point holds for discussions of coercion in interpersonal contexts. Because institutional or political coercion often provides background conditions favorable to interpersonal coercion, no discussion of the latter can proceed fully divorced from the former.

Still, interpersonal contexts and institutional or political contexts are distinct to some degree. And one must start somewhere. Without asserting any reason for thinking one is more basic or fundamental than the other, we simply take coercion in institutional or political contexts as our point of departure or focus, with the hope that our so doing will in no way prejudice or hamper efforts to arrive at a philosophically satisfying and normatively sound account of coercion in interpersonal contexts.

Communities or associations of various sizes and sorts can and do coerce their members to maintain order and to make possible the goods at which they are aimed. Families and schools often coerce children for the sake of their moral and

---

[1] One helpful review essay on coercion is Scott Anderson's "Coercion," available online in the *Stanford Encyclopedia of Philosophy* (http://plato.stanford.edu/entries/coercion).

D.A. Reidy and W.J. Riker (eds.), *Coercion and the State*.
© Springer Science + Business Media B.V. 2008

intellectual development. Churches and religious communities often coerce believers for the sake of their spiritual salvation. Clubs and other voluntary organizations often coerce members to insure fidelity to organizational norms and ends. And of course states often coerce both individuals (citizens and non-citizens) and institutions (corporations and other states). Police forces arrest and judges convict, fine and incarcerate individuals. Officials sanction and sometimes dissolve corporations. And they quarantine those deemed a sufficient threat to public health, peace and order, whether due to mental or physical disease. They police borders and sometimes detain or deport non-citizens. Finally, states sometimes go to war, overtly or covertly, to force other states to behave in ways deemed more acceptable. Coercion is, then, an ubiquitous feature of our institutional, political world. Further, it would seem to play a needed and important role in realizing and maintaining that world as orderly and humane. Hence, it would seem at least sometimes and in some institutional and political contexts to be justified.

Yet, despite the significant utility gains it often promises, coercion remains problematic in institutional and political contexts. For one thing, it does not always deliver, indeed, does not always promise, significant utility gains. For another, it sometimes so offends against freedom, equality, independence, respect or some other value affirmed by those acting within the relevant institutional or political context that it cannot be morally redeemed by utility gains, even if they are significant gains. So, while coercion would seem at least sometimes and in some institutional or political contexts to be justified, it would seem also at least sometimes to be unjustified. That, in any case, seems a very common and likely sound intuition.

This intuition is compatible with two understandings of coercion. On the first, coercion is understood as a morally neutral phenomenon that may turn out to be morally acceptable or not in light of considerations external to it. On the second, it is understood as a morally non-neutral phenomenon, as always *prima facie* unjustified in itself, though sometimes also morally redeemable in light of considerations external to it. Importantly, on neither understanding is coercion something we ought to accept or acquiesce to without justification.[2]

Of course, before we can identify the conditions under which coercion is justified in institutional or political contexts, we need first to be able to recognize coercion for what it is in those contexts. And this is no easy task. The conceptual work key to improving our understanding of and ability to identify coercion begins, at least in a contemporary philosophical idiom, in the late 1960s, with Robert Nozick's

---

[2] This does not imply that the aim of such justifications is or should always be to convince the coercee that the (proposed) coercive act is justified. It is probably futile to aim such justifications at the children, the mentally incompetent, and the criminal elements of society that exist among us. Nevertheless, the coercer must always have good reasons to use coercive force against the coercee. Just who should judge the adequacy of these reasons, and how they should do it, are open questions that some of the authors in this volume seek to answer.

well-known essay, though of course it begins more generally with Aristotle's discussion of voluntariness in the *Nichomachean Ethics*.[3] The chapters in Part I mainly
continue and contribute to this conceptual work. The chapters in the remainder of
the volume, those in Parts II, III, IV, and V, mainly continue and contribute to the
normative and evaluative work that follows once we have come to a correct understanding and learned reliably to identify instances of coercion. They examine coercion in the contexts of both the domestic state and the international order.

One unresolved conceptual issue is whether or not coercion can result from
direct uses of force, or results only from certain conditional threats. Aristotle holds
that acts to which an individual contributes nothing, but is instead moved from
without, as when someone is carried off by others or by the wind, are paradigm
examples of coercion.[4] One of the problems with this sort of view, we can call it a
"force view" of coercion, is that the coercee does not actually perform an act. How
can a person be said to have been coerced into doing something when she does not
actually *do* anything? A signal merit of the kind of view put forward by Aristotle,
however, is that it seems to capture our understanding of coercion in certain paradigm cases. When we see the police arrest a criminal and forcibly take him off to
jail against his will, we typically see a paradigmatic instance of coercive state
action.

Nozick offers an alternative to force views such as Aristotle's. On Nozick's
view, coercion results only from certain conditional threats. It occurs when (a) one
person P threatens another person Q, (b) thereby altering Q's perceived rational
self-interest, (c) all in order to alter increase the likelihood that Q will do what P
wants her to do, and (d) Q acquiesces as a result of P's threat. On Nozick's view,
we can call it a "conditional threat view," the paradigm instance of coercion is not
the direct use of force or violence. It is rather the successful direction of an agent's
will or choice through the manipulation of the alternatives she faces.

On Aristotle's view, when a person gives in to conditional threats and does what
the person making the threat wants her to do, she acts voluntarily, for her act is
"worthy of choice at the time when [it is] done."[5] Aristotle concedes that there is
an "element of the involuntary" in cases like this. And so he is willing to allow that
the person who acts as she does because she faces a certain conditional threat may
be less morally responsible for her action than she would be were she to so act
absent the threat. But he insists that she is not forced, not coerced, to do anything.
Her action is voluntary, regardless of how the situation in which she chooses and
acts came to be.

Nozick agrees that acquiescing to a conditional threat is voluntary. But he argues
that the agent who voluntarily acquiesces to a conditional threat is still coerced. The

---

[3] See Robert Nozick, "Coercion," in *Philosophy, Science and Method: Essays in Honor of Ernest Nagel*, S. Morgenbesser, P. Suppes, and M. White, eds. (New York: St. Martin's Press), pp. 440–472; and Aristotle, *Nichomachean Ethics*, many editions, 1109b26–1111b10.

[4] *Nichomachean Ethics*, 1110a8.

[5] *Nichomachean Ethics*, 1110a10.

issue, as he sees it, is not whether the person subject to a conditional threat has good reason to act, or voluntarily acts, as the person making that threat desires. The issue is rather whether the person making the conditional threat intends by so doing to direct the threatened person's will or choice by altering in an illicit way the options she faces.

One feature of conditional threat accounts of coercion like Nozick's is they seem to leave the door open to the possibility of coercive offers. After all, offers are often made for the purpose of directing the will or choice of another by altering the options she faces. Of course, it would be silly to suppose that all offers are coercive. My employer surely did not coerce me into taking my current job by making me a better salary offer than competitors. But what then makes some offers coercive, assuming some are? Suppose you come across a drowning person, offer to save her only if she agrees to a certain number of years of indentured servitude to you, and she agrees. Did you make a coercive offer? Was she coerced? Alternatively, suppose you come across a deathly ill person, offer her life-saving medicine if she agrees to pay you its very high but market price, and she agrees. Did you make a coercive offer? Was she coerced? The offer in the drowning case feels like a covert or closet conditional threat, and hence a coercive offer. The offer in the illness case feels more like a genuine and thus non-coercive offer. But what is the basis of the distinction being felt here? The three chapters of Part I take up these issues.

In Chapter 2, Scott Anderson defends what he calls an "enforcement" approach to coercion. The enforcement approach holds that coercion is best understood as one agent enforcing decisions about the actions of another against that other, where the use of physical force or violence is the paradigmatic means of doing so. On this approach, police coerce a suspect when they arrest, handcuff, and physically take her to jail, against her will. Unfortunately, he says, this approach has been super-seded in recent years by the "pressure" approach. The pressure approach holds that coercion is best understood in terms of conditional threats and that the exercise of force on another is not essential to coercion. Indeed, direct uses of force (as in the police example above) may not even count as acts of coercion on this approach. Despite the current popularity of the pressure approach, Anderson argues that we ought to turn our attention back to enforcement.

The enforcement approach deserves special consideration because it better gets at what is fundamental to coercion. For example, conditional threats only work where one agent has, and is known to have, the ability and the willingness to enforce a decision against another with force or violence. The content of a condi-tional threat does no work unless the person threatened has reason to believe, usu-ally provided by the background context, that the threat will be enforced. Thus, the pressure approach depends on or requires an appeal to the more basic enforcement approach.

In Chapter 3, Burton Leiser takes up the pressure or conditional threat approach. He holds that "coercion occurs when one person threatens to visit some evil or unwanted consequence on another unless that other does or refrains from doing some act in accordance with the coercer's demands." He then usefully distinguishes coercion from similar concepts such as compulsion, bribery, seduction, and blackmail.

Leiser argues that whether a particular person was coerced or not is always a matter of objective fact the truth of which is independent of that person's feelings of having been coerced. While I may have in fact been coerced when I feel coerced, I am not in fact coerced because or whenever I feel coerced.

On Leiser's view, the law is coercive because it attempts to persuade people through the promise of sanctions to do (or refrain from doing) what the legislature commands. There is no pretense that every potential criminal will be deterred by such threats, but this is irrelevant to the question of whether the law is coercive. Coercion depends on the existence of a credible threat of punishment. However, not all threats should be understood as coercive. For instance, the Arab states surrounding Israel mounted a war against it as soon as Israel announced its birth, but they did not intend to coerce Israel. Rather, they intended to destroy the new state. Leiser draws a parallel between this case and the current situation between Islamic extremists and the West. Leiser concludes his paper with discussion of some difficulties involved in the exercise of coercion on the international scene (a matter taken up in detail by the chapters in Part V), given that there is often no common authority powerful enough to make threats sufficiently credible to coerce bad actors.

The enforcement and pressure approaches to coercion outlined above associate coercion with violence or threats respectively, so they typically deny that offers can be coercive. The idea is that offers tend to make people better off than they were before, whereas coerced persons are made worse off than they were before. In Chapter 4, Joan McGregor argues that some offers are coercive, and ought to draw moral censure as a result, despite the fact that they might leave the person who accepts the offer better off than she would have been had no offer been made. McGregor develops her argument using as a key example offers to the poor and uneducated to participate in clinical medical trials.

Clinical trials with human subjects represent an important source of knowledge about medical drugs and practices. Nevertheless, this research must not be done without the informed consent of subjects. This is made clear in the *Nuremberg Code* (1949), in the World Medical Association's *Declaration of Helsinki* (1964), and, more recently, in the guidelines produced by the World Health Organization's Council for International Organizations of Medical Sciences (1982). What worries McGregor is that an "undue influence" exerted by offers to participate in clinical medical trials may undermine consent, and thereby render such offers coercive. Her analysis focuses attention on the unequal bargaining positions of the medical researchers and participants respectively in clinical trials that take place in poor, third-world countries. Medical practitioners control access to medical care that the poor, sick and uneducated people in the third-world desperately need. This situation amounts to a very unbalanced playing field. Offers to participate in clinical medical trials made under these conditions simply take advantage of these vast power inequalities. When medical practitioners make offers under these conditions, they willfully threaten the volitional aspect of informed consent. According to McGregor, an individual's decision to take part in a clinical medical trial under these conditions should not be seen as voluntary. When medical practitioners take advantage of their relative bargaining power to undercut the volitional component of consent, their offers ought to be seen as coercive. This analysis applies generally to all vulnerable parties, such as children, prisoners, economically or educationally disadvantaged persons, who are at a significant bargaining disadvantage relative to those who control clinical medical trials.

The chapters in Part II consider different attempts to defend morally at least certain exercises of coercive state action. States standardly claim final and exclusive authority over the morally defensible use of coercive force within their territories. But what could ground this authority? If might does not and can not make right, then the final and exclusive authority of the state over coercive force can not be grounded in its power. But what then?

This question is especially vexing in the context of modern, pluralist liberal democracies. In states of this sort, citizens think of themselves as politically free and equal. And they disagree reasonably, and know they disagree reasonably, over comprehensive moral, religious and philosophical doctrines. Three things follow. First, each may demand of every other a public moral defense of the state's authority over coercive force. Second, appeals to allegedly morally significant hierarchies established by nature are unlikely to succeed as a public moral defense of this authority. Third, appeals to allegedly true comprehensive conceptions of a good life or the good society, as established through moral, religious or philosophical inquiry, are similarly unlikely to succeed. But what then is one to appeal to in order morally to defend the state's authority over coercive force?

One possibility is justice: the authority of the state to regulate and deploy coercive force is predicated on or derived from the justice of its aims or ends. But there are a couple of problems with this view. First, it accords the state too much authority, or an authority with too wide a scope. The authority of the state to coerce, at least in any modern liberal democracy, is always constituted and therefore limited by the conditions of its constitution. Not every just aim or end is one that may be legitimately secured by the state through coercive state action. And not every exercise of coercive force is subject to state authority. Further, even if the authority of the state was not so constituted, there would still be good moral reasons to refuse to the state a blank check when it comes to authorizing coercion in the name of justice. Finally, in modern pluralist liberal democracies, citizens reasonably disagree over what justice requires in a wide range of cases. Many will regard some laws and policies as either less than just or as unjust. Assuming any moral defense of the authority of the state over coercive force must be public and to each and all, appeals to justice then are likely to leave the state with too little authority. So long as some citizens not unreasonably regard a law or policy as unjust, there can be no moral defense of the state's authority to coercively enforce it. But this cannot be right. So, the moral defense of the authority of the state over coercive force must appeal to something more or other than justice. But what?

In Chapter 5, Alistair Macleod argues that since coercive institutional arrangements can be seen as morally defensible or not, their defensibility cannot depend on their coercive character. Whether an institution exercises coercive force is a matter empirically ascertainable and logically distinct from whether its exercise of coercive force is morally defensible. Macleod then notes an asymmetry between coercion in institutional or political contexts and in interpersonal contexts. In interpersonal contexts, we typically talk about coercion when one person forces another person to do something that would normally be considered wrong or immoral or at least undesirable. And in interpersonal contexts, to be coerced typically is to be at least partially absolved of responsibility for one's actions. However, in institutional or political contexts, say, when the state coerces a citizen, the person coerced is not typically being forced to do something that would normally be considered wrong or immoral or undesirable. Further, to be coerced by the state, to comply with its demands out of fear of its power to sanction, is not typically to be absolved, even partially, of responsibility for one's conduct. Inquiry into the full implications of this asymmetry Macleod leaves for another day. He draws on it to motivate his special focus on institutional or political coercion.

Macleod wonders how we might morally defend the coercive aspect of coercive institutional arrangements. He considers both thin and thick versions of arguments that appeal, first, to justice, and, second, to democratic processes. A thin argument from justice posits that coercive institutional arrangements are morally defensible, as coercive, if and only if they meet the demands of formal justice. A thick argument from justice posits that they are morally defensible if and only if they deliver to all citizens or subjects an equal opportunity to live satisfactory and fulfilling lives. On the thin argument from democratic processes, they are morally defensible so long as all members of society are genuinely allowed to vote. On the thick argument from democratic processes, they are morally defensible so long as all voters enjoy meaningful and fair value for their equal right to vote. Macleod rejects both thin arguments as inadequate and then considers whether the two thick arguments, one appealing to substantive egalitarian justice, the other to a rich ideal of democratic political processes, ultimately converge.

In Chapter 6, Walter Riker articulates and defends a deliberative democratic account of the state's authority over, and to engage in, coercive action. Riker argues first that for several reasons the moral defense of the state's authority to coerce must appeal to more than considerations of justice. Riker himself offers a defense that appeals to deliberative democratic political processes as a form of public reason-giving between free equals that commands respect in and of itself and thus lends a moral status to political outcomes and state actions aimed at enforcing them that would otherwise be absent. Deliberative democratic accounts of the sort Riker presents seek to legitimate coercive state action by grounding it in rules or reasons that all citizens understand and could reasonably accept. Coercive state action grounded in rules or reasons that all citizens could reasonably accept is more than a mere exercise of force against citizens, it is an exercise of force in the service of a shared and public reason.

This ideal of state action limited by a shared and public reason (an ideal drawn from the liberal tradition) has been criticized in recent years because of widespread and quite reasonable doubts, given the depth of reasonable disagreements between citizens, about the possibility of finding any rules or reasons that they could all reasonably accept. Riker argues that criticisms of this sort miss the mark. Kant, Hart,

Soper, and Rawls all appeal to shared and public reasons to legitimate coercive state action. Yet they are each realistic about the inevitability of dissensus in political life. Their appeal to shared and public reasons to legitimate coercive state action is not an appeal to the moral force of consensus or agreement. It is rather an appeal to the moral force of reciprocity in political life, to reciprocity of reason-giving in the process of public justification and to reciprocity of advantage in the process of material production and exchange. Still, Riker concludes, deliberative democratic accounts of the legitimate authority of the state to coerce are not free of difficulty. Riker concludes by pointing toward some of these remaining difficulties.

In Chapter 7, Christine Sistare turns the tables in order to consider the legitimacy of coercive citizen action against the state rather than coercive state action against citizens. While liberal legal and political theorists typically recognize civil disobedience as sometimes morally justified, they also typically limit civil disobedience to nonviolent means and insist that those engaged in civil disobedience be willing to accept their legally valid punishment. All violent modes of resistance to injustice are theorized as species of rebellion or revolution. Sistare argues for a more nuanced analysis here, in particular one that acknowledges as sometimes morally defensible violent modes of resistance, violent civil disobedience, short of rebellion or revolution. She develops her argument through an extended analysis of John Brown's violent struggle against slavery. Brown did not intend to overthrow and replace the US government or to set aside the US Constitution. He is not properly or best understood as a revolutionary. Brown instead wanted to realize the founding principles and promise of the US government and Constitution. Like other abolitionists, he took seriously the expectation of the signers of the Constitution that slavery would eventually wither away. When it did not, when it instead appeared to be spreading and rooting itself more deeply in the American polity, Brown took up arms. Sistare argues that Brown's resort to violence was a reasonable, even morally required, response to the compelling evidence that ordinary political processes could not contain and bring about the end of slavery. Brown acted consistent with, indeed as required by, the natural duty to promote justice. Sistare's analysis raises deep questions about the moral authority of citizens to engage in violence, short of rebellion or revolution, so as to advance the cause of justice.

When we think of coercive state action we typically think of the state enforcing what H.L.A. Hart called the "primary rules" of its legal system, rules that require and forbid certain kinds of conduct. But as Hart emphasized, all modern legal systems contain also "secondary rules." Secondary rules are a diverse class of rules that include those "power-conferring" rules that enable persons, if they follow the rules, to bring about legally recognized changes in their status—for example, to enter into a contract or to become married. Because secondary rules do not require anything of anyone (no one is required to enter into contracts or become married) and are not enforced in the same way as primary rules (if you fail to make a valid contract because you violated the governing secondary rules, you are not punished or sanctioned, you simply have no valid contract), it may appear that they do not constitute a site of coercive state action. Yet, through its secondary rules the state can extend or withhold important benefits to classes of persons, perhaps thereby indirectly coercing them into behaving in one or another preferred manner. The chapters in Part III focus on contemporary marriage law in the United States and whether, by virtue of its failure to extend the status and benefits of marriage to same sex couples, it constitutes coercive state action, and if so, whether it is morally defensible.

In Chapter 8, Emily Gill argues that because the issue of same-sex marriage is, for most citizens, an issue inextricably bound up with religious commitments, it cannot be examined apart from issues of religious liberty and anti-establishment. She begins by examining the claim that the citizens of a liberal democracy ought not be constitutionally prevented from enacting laws or policies that express their religious commitments. A familiar objection to citizens enacting laws or policies that express their religious commitments is that citizens who find that their religious commitments are not so expressed will feel demeaned within and excluded from, less than full members of and as alienated from, the political community. This objection presupposes, of course, that all citizens have a fundamental interest in being visibly and publicly affirmed and included within or by the state. Whether all citizens have or ought to have this interest is unclear. The matter is disputed. One might be tempted to conclude here that there ought to be, then, no constitutional prohibition of citizens adopting laws and policies that express their religious commitments. The matter ought to be left to democratic political processes. So, if citizens wish to restrict marriage to heterosexual marriage solely to express their religious commitments, they ought to be free to do so through democratic political processes. Sure, some citizens may as a matter of fact feel excluded or demeaned. But this contingent fact about only some citizens is not sufficient to justify a constitutional limit on the democratic authority of citizens generally.

Gill rejects this line of argument, but not because she thinks that all citizens have or ought to have a fundamental and general interest in being visibly and publicly affirmed and included within or by the state, and not because she thinks there is any way to settle the issue of the legal recognition of same-sex marriage without some group feeling that is has been visibly and publicly demeaned or excluded within or by the state. Gill rejects this line of argument because in the case of marriage both critics and proponents of the legal recognition of same-sex marriage agree that state recognition or approval of marriage is a great good. On this particular issue, there is a shared and important interest in being visibly and publicly affirmed and included within or by the state. Thus, this is an issue that is ripe for constitutional resolution. In a liberal polity, the good of having one's marriage visibly and publicly recognized or approved by the state ought to be extended, constitutionally, to as many couples desiring marriage as possible. Regardless of the sentiments or judgments of the majority of Americans, those seeking legal recognition for same sex marriage are presently subject to morally indefensible coercive state action.

In Chapter 9, Kenneth Henley agrees with this conclusion and extends the analysis. He argues that excluding same-sex couples from the legal institution of marriage constitutes today coercive state action in the spheres of conscience and religious belief. This coercive state action is, Henley maintains, illegitimate because there are no sound secular or shared and public reasons for discriminating against same-sex couples. Same-sex couples are excluded from marriage for purely religious reasons. Thus, current marriage law is properly viewed as coercive state action aimed at a sexual regimentation justified only by religious reasons. Laws preventing same-sex marriage might have once been a part of a complex system of rules geared toward enforcing very widely-shared social (if also Christian) norms of conduct regarding sex, procreation, gender, marriage and much else. But regardless of what might have been at some earlier time, the laws preventing same-sex marriage now stand out as an anomaly. Contemporary resistance to same-sex marriage is little more than a hopeless attempt to reinstate a lost system of sexual regimentation that now cannot but be seen for what it is (and was), a peculiarly religious system. Henley concludes that we ought to secure the legal recognition of same-sex marriage.

Recent events have highlighted one kind of coercive state action that in years past might have received less attention: coercive state action in the service of national security. The chapters in Part IV consider issues raised by coercive state actions of this sort, and in particular by indefinite or other legally atypical detentions of suspected terrorists.

Nearly everyone agrees that individual persons and states have a right to self-defense. They need not remain passive in the face of aggression by others. But this right to self-defense is not a right to do just anything to thwart aggression. There are limits. For example, in the context of national defense, what a state can do in self-defense is constrained by the rules or norms of just war. They govern when self-defense is allowed, what it allows, and what is required once aggression has been successfully thwarted. Several of these rules or norms have been challenged in recent years on the ground that given the new threat posed to states by global forms of terrorist aggression, new rules or norms are called for.

One new rule or norm advanced by the United States would allow states to indefinitely detain or coercively restrain certain suspected terrorists, without charging them with any crime and with no prospect of any trial. This rule or norm has generated significant controversy. In Chapter 10, Don Scheid offers a limited defense of it. He rejects the idea that indefinite detention is always and everywhere morally indefensible. He argues instead that under certain conditions indefinite detention of some suspected terrorists may be justified. After rejecting a few commonly made arguments for indefinite detention, Scheid argues that the indefinite detention of some terrorist suspects—"mega-terrorists" who are willing to use weapons or methods of mass destruction and cannot be deterred by threats of punishment—can be justified by way of an analogy to more familiar instances of presumably morally defensible preventative detention—the involuntary institutionalization of the mentally ill or of chronic sexual offenders.

Of course, if the argument for the indefinite detention of suspected "mega-terrorists" is by way of analogy to other morally sound instances of preventative detention, then its practice will likely have to be revised so as to mirror the various procedural safeguards essential to the moral soundness of those other instances of preventative detention. Scheid concludes his essay by considering a range of procedural safeguards, adjusted to the relevant circumstances (international "mega-terrorists" and national security), that would secure, if they were adopted, the practice of indefinite detention against moral criticism.

In Chapter 11, Wade Robison considers one such procedural safeguard, namely the Writ of Habeas Corpus, a fundamental and constitutional check on the power of the state to coercively detain persons. The Writ has been an object of controversy recently. Should it be available to suspected terrorists? To non-citizens coercively and indefinitely detained? Is its availability subject to utilitarian calculations? Robison argues that the Writ is one of several fundamental constitutive conditions of both citizenship and official political authority in our republican system. It simultaneously empowers citizens to challenge and disempowers officials from initiating certain coercive state actions. Because it functions as a constitutive condition of official authority, it ought to be available not just to citizens but also to non-citizens subject to official attempts at coercive state action. And it ought not to be subject to the sorts of utilitarian calculations that might justify indefinite detention. That is, it ought to constrain or frame those calculations.

In Part V, we move beyond the context of the domestic nation state and into that of the international order. The chapters in Part V consider the nature and potential justifications of various forms of coercion found within the global or international context: coercive action by one state against one or more others, coercive action undertaken by international or by nonstate actors, and (the possibility of) coercive action undertaken by something like a world state. Coercion is at present largely undertheorized in the global or international context. Nevertheless, three issues seem to deserve immediate attention.

The first involves the coercive intervention by one state into another on humanitarian grounds. When and why is this justified? There are obvious good reasons for one nation to use military force to seek to end abuses of human rights inflicted upon citizens of another nation by their own government. However, traditional considerations of just war theory, including the principle of state sovereignty, seem to morally forbid such interventions, and also to give abusive governments some right to defend themselves against such humanitarian efforts. The second concerns the rise in power, and thus capacity to coerce, of various new actors in the global or international context. Transnational or international global governance institutions like the World Bank or United Nations often either exercise or aspire to exercise coercive force. So too do multinational corporations like Nike or Royal Dutch Shell. How should we think about the coercive force wielded, now or in the future, by these actors on the global or international stage?

The third issue that commands immediate attention is whether we have arrived at a time in which some form of global authority, authorized to regulate coercion within and between states and to coerce noncompliant states, some form of a world government or state, is a moral necessity. If so how ought we think about this global authority? What is its scope and its relationship to existing systems of state authority? And how might we make the transition from the status quo to the envisioned new world order without morally indefensible coercion?

In Chapter 12, Steven Lee addresses the issue of humanitarian intervention (HI), the use of military force to promote human rights in a foreign country where they are routinely violated. Lee rejects the "standard approach" to HI. It takes as its point of departure just war theory and its principles of state sovereignty, nonintervention, and national self-defense. It seems both to morally forbid HI and to morally allow states potentially subject to HI to defend themselves through force. This is exceedingly counter-intuitive (think of cases like Rwanda), and so Lee concludes that we ought to reject the standard approach to HI.

Lee then articulates and defends an alternative approach according to which HI is thought of not as a unique form of coercion by states discontinuous with their legitimate coercive activity within their own domestic spheres, but as a familiar form of coercion by states continuous with their legitimate coercive activity in the domestic sphere. In particular, on Lee's view, if coercive state action in the domestic sphere is morally defensible when it promotes or secures human rights, justice and democracy there, then it may be morally defensible also when it promotes or secures these things in the international order. HI is simply a natural extension or implication of the principles that support domestic coercion. These principles then serve also to limit the scope of HI.

In Chapter 13, Carol Gould discusses coercive power of the sort that is wielded by transnational agents, for instance, multi-national corporations and non-state global governance institutions, in transnational contexts. She argues that too often this power amounts to a "power over" people's lives. "Power over" refers to the way that some agents are able to control the behavior of other agents, or the way institutions can control the behavior of individuals. Gould argues that this power over others ought to be transformed into a "power to" get certain things done. In the transnational context, Gould says, "power to" should be understood as shared social power to achieve important social goods across international boundaries. Three required transformations are necessary to turn "power over" into "power to" in the transnational context. First, decision-making in economic, social, and political institutions, including cross-border ones, needs to be democratized. Second, regional human rights protections must be implemented. Third, transnational solidarity must be cultivated.

In Chapter 14, Monica Hlavac defends a developmental approach to judging the legitimacy of global governance institutions (GGIs), such as the World Bank, the World Trade Organization, and the International Criminal Court. Many now worry about the legitimacy of GGIs, but there is little systematic theorizing on the subject of legitimacy in this context. Some recent critics of GGIs have proposed highly idealized lists of conditions that they claim all GGIs ought to meet. Some of these proposals focus on substantive legitimacy-making conditions, such as environmental protection or respect for human rights, while others focus on procedural conditions, such as accountability, fairness, equality, and inclusiveness. Hlavac rejects these proposals, largely because of what she refers to as "the problem of normative unclarity." Simply put, it is not yet clear how we ought to understand the relationship between GGIs and those most impacted by their activity. Further, given the diverse goals and functions of the various GGIs discussed in the literature, it is not clear that any one account of legitimacy could apply to all GGIs. Thus, the substantive and procedural conditions emphasized in extant accounts of GGI legitimacy are unlikely to prove adequate to assessing the legitimacy of the full range of GGIs we encounter today.

Hlavac proposes instead a developmental approach to GGI legitimacy. This approach recommends one minimal, initial, and provisional condition for legitimacy— robust transparency. This minimal, initial, provisional condition of GGI legitimacy requires that GGIs ensure that all parties likely to be affected by the GGI's activities have access to information about the GGI's goals, practices, research, and so on. With improved transparency should come increased participation in GGI activities by those impacted by them. This should also help to dispel the current normative unclarity regarding GGIs. As those impacted by GGIs begin to participate more fully in GGI activities, a richer array of locally specific norms regarding the relationship between particular GGIs and those they impact is likely to develop. With a clearer view of the normative relations between GGIs and those they impact, we can then begin to build additional conditions into legitimacy standards tailored to particular GGIs.

In Chapter 15, Bruce Landesman examines the divide between cosmopolitans and liberal nationalists regarding the extent to which any morally defensible coercive international authority might range over global or international economic relations. Cosmopolitans hold that fundamental principles of economic justice apply directly to individuals across the globe and that a morally defensible international authority will possess the power coercively to secure redistributions of wealth and income between states or between individuals in different states. Liberal nationalists hold that fundamental principles of economic justice apply only to individuals within particular states and that a morally defensible international authority will have little or no power coercively to secure redistributions of wealth and income between states or between individuals in different states. Landesman sees merit in both views. To sort out his intuitions, he examines Michael Blake's recent defense of the liberal nationalist stance. According to Blake, economic relations of relative inequality are morally significant in the context of the nation state because the nation state is a bounded system of coercion. Economic relations of relative inequality are not morally significant in the context of the international order because it is not a bounded system of coercion. In the international context, only absolute levels of economic well-being (for example, that all persons enjoy a certain absolute minimum of basic material and economic resources) are morally significant. Landesman is not convinced.

Landesman rejects Blake's claim that it is systems of coercion that make inequality a matter of justice. Rather, Landesman says, inequality is a matter of justice because it results from human conventions that can be altered by human choices. This does not mean that inequality occurs intentionally. What it means is that we can recognize the norms and conventions (for example, the structure of property rights) that lead to inequality in our world, and we can alter or reject these norms and conventions if we ultimately decide that this is the just thing to do. Of course, that we can alter these norms does not mean we have a reason to alter them. Ultimately, Landesman's disagreement with Blake comes down to the fact that Landesman thinks relative economic inequality prima facie unjust in and of itself, regardless of context, and Blake does not.

Landesman also rejects Blake's claim that the global or international order is not a bounded system of coercion, or is far less so than the domestic order secured by a nation state. Blake notes that on the global stage only states are coerced directly; individual persons are coerced only indirectly as members of states. Landesman does not see why this matters. Coercive actions against states in the international order can just as effectively maintain, produce, and even worsen inequalities, not only between those states, but also between individuals in them, as any direct exercise of coercion by a state against its own members. Landesman concludes that relative economic inequalities are a matter of justice both domestically and globally or internationally. As such, they are proper or legitimate subjects to be taken up by a morally defensible international authority with the power to coerce.

In Chapter 16, Helga Varden inquires into the case for an international or cosmopolitan authority with the power to coerce. Following Kant, she argues that the goal of international relations in not merely the absence of war, but the condition of perpetual peace: a peace consistent with each person's human right to freedom. According to Varden, perpetual peace requires a public international authority that regulates a cosmopolitan legal order. This cosmopolitan authority is charged with developing and enforcing international law. A public cosmopolitan authority is the only kind that can enable rightful relations between states, because only a cosmopolitan authority can put all states under universal laws, publicly and impartially enforced. Only a cosmopolitan authority can replace the inevitable and dangerous conflicts of private judgments of right within an international order of sovereign states with a unified and unitary system of public judgments of right, a system within which coercive force in the international order is always backed by a shared and public reason(s). Of course, Varden sees, as did Kant, that moving from the existing international system of states to a cosmopolitan system of public global right is itself problematic. She concludes by discussing why Kant, she and we might favor the development of regional federations, for example the European Union, as a step toward the regulative ideal set for us by the ideal of cosmopolitan right.

As the chapters in this volume show, there remain substantial theoretical and practical disagreements over the nature of coercion, and the scope of its justified use, in institutional or political contexts. Still, the authors here seem to share an understanding of the important role coercion must play in our efforts to realize and maintain a humane and stable social order, both at home and around the world. Thus, notwithstanding the significant contributions made by the contributors to this volume, philosophically informed and normatively sensitive reflection on coercion in institutional and political contexts will remain a pressing task for this and future generations. We suspect that the possibility of our achieving our common human good may well depend on it.

Part I
What is Coercion?

Chapter 2
How Did There Come To Be Two Kinds of Coercion?

Scott A. Anderson

Political theorizing throughout the modern era uses the term "coercion" and its cognates (compulsion, force) in so many ways that one may despair of finding neat conceptual boundaries for it. Historically, as now, "coercion" appears to be a catch-all term, rather than one that clearly demarcates, say, acts of domination from acts of badgering or arm-twisting. Typically, however, it is used to capture a way that agents with considerable power can constrain the wills, actions, opportunities, bodies, and lives of others. Throughout this literature, coercion generally refers to the sort of power that states possess against their inhabitants, war victors hold over the vanquished, or even a church hierarchy holds over priests and laity, and husbands have sometimes wielded over their wives. These uses suggest a sort of irresistible power, which can operate through various mechanisms, including physical force and violence, threats, positional authority, and social pressure. Until relatively recently, few theorists paused to give a careful analysis of its meaning or conditions; more typically, they have taken for granted that the term is understood, and that the sort of power it invokes is evident when in use.

There is an interesting story to be told about how the concept of coercion became a philosophical topic of its own. However, I will focus here on the slightly different, later story, of how in the course of philosophical investigation, theorists came to find and distinguish two kinds of coercion, and then to attend to one to the virtual exclusion of the other. In the process, I will offer some reasons for thinking that the bifurcation of this topic is significant, and in some ways problematic. After elaborating the distinction between the two kinds of coercion, I will show that the recognition of a categorical distinction in kinds of coercion is historically locatable. I will consider some of what can be said for and against the distinction, but I will be principally interested to trace how it entered, virtually unnoticed, into theorizing about coercion. I conclude by highlighting a few of the difficulties that arise if one does not attend to this history.

Contemporary philosophical writing on coercion as a special subject begins virtually from scratch with essays by Robert Nozick in 1969 and Harry Frankfurt in 1973, and a collection of essays on the subject in the NOMOS series, published

D.A. Reidy and W.J. Riker (eds.), *Coercion and the State.*
© Springer Science+Business Media B.V. 2008

in 1972.[1] These pieces, especially the ones by Nozick and Frankfurt, generated numerous responses and a discussion that continues today. While Nozick and Frankfurt both conceive of coercion principally as involving threats by one agent against another, Michael Bayles writes in the NOMOS volume that there are two kinds of activities to which the term "coercion" applies:

> At least two kinds or varieties of coercion may be distinguished. In one type physical force is applied to cause behavior in another person. For example, one may clasp another's hand and force his finger to squeeze the trigger of a gun. Such "occurrent" coercion takes place infrequently.... In a second variety, dispositional coercion, one man (the agent) threatens another (the victim) with a sanction if the latter fails to act as requested.[2]

While Bayles holds that the former, force-involving form of coercion is less common, interesting and important than the dispositional sort, he nonetheless thinks it falls within the bounds of the larger concept. Later writers, such as H. J. McCloskey, explicitly deny this:

> I suggest that the core notion of coercion is that of power exercised by a determinate person, persons, or organizations(s), by the use of threats backed by sanctions in terms of evils to be imposed, benefits withdrawn or not conferred.[3]

Responding to the view that some uses of force are also "coercion," McCloskey writes,

> When subjected to force, one does not act at all; rather one is acted upon; things are done to one or *via* one. ... The person who is subject to force, the physical force of another, or to natural forces, has things happen to him. ... By contrast, the coerced person acts. He does what he does as a result of coercion.... [H]e chooses to do it.[4]

If McCloskey is right about this, then Bayles and a few like him are wrong about how to use the term "coercion." What McCloskey and Bayles apparently agree about, however, is that there is a kind of categorical difference of some importance between threatening to impose evils or to withdraw benefits, and the direct use of force to constrain activity.

In the literature on coercion since Nozick, McCloskey's association of the term "coercion" exclusively with the making of threats is clearly the majority view

---

[1] Robert Nozick, "Coercion," in *Philosophy, Science, and Method: Essays in Honor of Ernest Nagel*, Sidney Morgenbesser, Patrick Suppes, and Morton White, eds. (New York: St. Martin's Press, 1969); Harry Frankfurt, "Coercion and Moral Responsibility," in *The Importance of What We Care About* (New York: Cambridge University Press, 1988); J. Roland Pennock and John W. Chapman, eds., *Nomos XIV: Coercion* (Chicago, IL: Aldine-Atherton, 1972).

[2] Michael Bayles, "A Concept of Coercion," in J. Roland Pennock and John W. Chapman, eds., *Nomos XIV: Coercion* (Chicago, IL: Aldine-Atherton, 1972), 17.

[3] H. J. McCloskey, "Coercion: Its Nature and Significance," *Southern Journal of Philosophy* 18 (1980), 340.

[4] *Ibid.*, 336.

among theorists who have analyzed the concept.[5] That is, coercion is these days widely regarded as necessarily involving the following elements:

1. The coercer communicates some sort of proposal,
2. whereby the coercer aims to alter the costs/benefits of action for the coercee,
3. whereby the coercer aims to affect the course of action that the coercee intentionally undertakes.

Such a communication will suffice to coerce if the proposal is a threat and if the threat meets certain further conditions, such as that it is credible, significant, immoral, and/or that it renders him unable to resist, and/or succeeds in bringing the coercee to act.[6] There has been considerable debate over what precise qualifications must be added to generate necessary and/or sufficient conditions for coercion; these debates are, however, premised on the view that coercion quintessentially works by altering or constraining the *will* of the coercee, and not just her body.

Whether or not one accepts Bayles' or McCloskey's views regarding the status of force as a "kind" of coercion, the view that these are distinct categories of activities, and that threatening is the principal, paramount form of coercion, is a relatively recent narrowing of the concept. Prior to the late 1960s, those who bothered to say what they meant by coercion would rarely draw any sharp distinction between threatening to use force and using force directly as forms of coercion. For instance, Hans Kelsen directly connects the coercive order of the state to its use of force:

> As a coercive order, the law is distinguished from other social orders. The decisive criterion is the element of force—that means that the act prescribed by the order as a consequence of socially detrimental facts ought to be executed even against the will of the individual and, if he resists, by physical force.[7]

---

[5] The denial that direct force is a mode of coercion is explicit in Hans Oberdiek, "The Role of Sanctions and Coercion in Understanding Law and Legal Systems," *American Journal of Jurisprudence* 21 (1976), 82; Mark Fowler, "Coercion and Practical Reason," *Social Theory and Practice* 8 (1982), 329; Michael Gorr, "Toward a Theory of Coercion," *Canadian Journal of Philosophy* 16 (1986), 383; Joel Feinberg, *Harm to Self* (New York: Oxford University Press, 1986), especially chapter 23; Onora O'Neill, "Which are the Offers *You* Can't Refuse?," chapter 7 in R. G. Frey and Christopher Morris, eds., *Violence, Terrorism, and Justice* (Cambridge: Cambridge University Press, 1991); Mitchell Berman, "The Normative Functions of Coercion Claims," *Legal Theory* 8 (2002), 45. It is implicit but unmistakable in Nozick's account and in most of the considerable number of theorists who have taken their bearings from him (see note 15 infra). Felix Oppenheim, in *Dimensions of Freedom* (New York: St. Martin's Press, 1961), offers a forerunner of Nozick's approach. For those who accept force as a kind of coercion, see Virginia Held, "Coercion and Coercive Offers," in Pennock and Chapman; Martin Gunderson, "Threats and Coercion," *Canadian Journal of Philosophy* 9 (1979), 247; Grant Lamond, "Coercion, Threats, and the Puzzle of Blackmail," in A. P. Simester and A. T. H. Smith, eds., *Harm and Culpability* (Oxford: Clarendon Press, 1996).

[6] There may be other sets of sufficient conditions as well; for instance, it is sometimes argued that offers of benefits can sometimes also be coercive. On coercive offers, see Joan McGregor's contribution to this volume.

[7] *The Pure Theory of Law*, trans. Max Knight (Los Angeles, CA: University of California Press, 1967), original German 1st ed. 1934; 2nd ed., 1960, 34.

Kelsen goes on to count as coercive acts those acts of state involved in detaining those suspected of crimes, detaining for protective custody, detaining of the insane, detaining in internment camps potential enemies of the state, and the confiscation or destruction of property.[8] Christian Bay writes,

> When a person wants to do something (or remain passive) and is forcibly restrained (pushed), we speak of 'coercion.' The same word is used also if he is still able to do what he wants but has to suffer as a consequence a severe punishment or the loss of a very important reward.[9]

Dennis Lloyd writes in a collegiate primer on law:

> [I]s law really conceivable, or at least possible in any practical sense, when it is not ultimately backed by effective force? Certainly the force of law is and seems always to have been linked with rules which are capable of being enforced by coercion; the hangman, the gaoler, the bailiff, and the policeman are all part of the seemingly familiar apparatus of a legal system.[10]

And lastly, in a somewhat extended discussion of coercion, J. R. Lucas writes that,

> [W]e are concerned with the *enforcement* of decisions: we are considering the conditions under which decisions will be carried out regardless of the recalcitrance of the bloody minded. We therefore define *force* in terms of bloody-mindedness, of what happens irrespective of how recalcitrant a man is, of what happens to him willy-nilly. Force, then, we say, is being used against a man, if in his private experience or in his environment either something is being done which he does not want to be done but which he is unable to prevent in spite of all his efforts, or he is being prevented, in spite of all his efforts, from doing something which he wants to do, and which he otherwise could have done by himself alone. A man is being *coerced* when either force is being used against him or his behaviour is being determined by the threat of force.[11]

And:

> [I]mprisonment is the paradigm form of coercion.... Even if it were not regarded as a penalty, it would still be effective in frustrating the efforts of the recalcitrant to prevent a judicial decision being implemented.[12]

The works from which these remarks are taken are more general in nature than those that have recently focused on coercion, mostly remarking upon the nature of coercion only in passing. Thus they perhaps should be regarded as offering recitations of received wisdom and terminological usage, rather than considered opinions.

---

[8] *Ibid.*, 40–41.

[9] *The Structure of Freedom* (New York: Atheneum Press, 1965 (originally published 1958)), 16–17. Also, "[C]oercion in this study means (a) the application of actual physical violence, or (b) the application of sanctions sufficiently strong to make the individual abandon a course of action or inaction dictated by his own strong and enduring motives and wishes." *Ibid.*, 93.

[10] *The Idea of Law* (Middlesex, England: Penguin, 1970), 35 (first published in 1964). In his index, the entry for coercion says, "See force, sanction."

[11] *The Principles of Politics* (Oxford: Clarendon Press, 1966), 57 (Lucas' emphasis).

[12] *Ibid.*, 60.

Nonetheless, the divergence of recent philosophy from the earlier common wisdom is unmistakable, and would appear to be noteworthy, even if it has largely gone unnoticed. We may therefore ask two parallel questions: why did these earlier theorists treat force and threats of force as jointly exemplars of coercion? And why have later theorists pulled apart the making of threats from the use of force, and treated the former alone as definitively coercion? I'll give a too brief discussion of the first question en route to a lengthier, more detailed and critical discussion of the latter.

The quotes from the theorists just canvassed suggest that coercion occurs equally when force is used directly to alter or constrain action as well as when one tries to inhibit or induce action by threatening to use force as a sanction. A good way to make sense of the parallel here is to see both activities as uses of force: one immediate, one latent. In both cases, the principal effect is to constrain possibilities for action, either immediately or in the future. While force can be used to manipulate a body into various movements and positions (Bayles gives the example of forcing a finger to "squeeze" a trigger), uses of direct physical force are much more apt for inhibiting action by limiting the possibilities for action. Activities such as killing, disabling, incarcerating, shackling, tackling, blocking, drugging, and stunning are all means of making many otherwise possible actions impossible. These may all be called "broad spectrum" techniques in that they can prevent whole ranges of actions, in addition to preventing specific actions; being subjected to them can imperil one's ability to do many things one might want to do. Similarly, credible threats of one of these sorts of force likewise raise the possibility that whole ranges of potential actions—perhaps all action, if the threat is of death—will become impossible. One who is able and willing to use such force can leverage this power by conditioning such threats on the target's failure to meet the threatener's demands. So with both direct and threatened uses of force, a powerful agent uses that agent's demonstrated ability and willingness to use force to constrain another's possibilities for action, either directly or prospectively, and does so either for the sake of such constraining itself, or to channel the target's choices of actions in a direction the powerful agent prefers.

My positing a likeness of direct uses of force to threats of force is likely to be resisted for several reasons, and I will not be able to give an adequate defense of this picture here. However, I can bolster this understanding of the relationship of force to coercion in a couple of ways. One important thing to consider is the aim of the discussion in which the analysis of coercion figures. One of the key purposes of political theory is to evaluate and justify certain forms of political arrangements, and in particular to explain what if anything justifies the existence of governments and the awesome powers that they typically wield. One frequent justification is that the ability and willingness of some agents to use overwhelming force (or like power) against others gives rise to a need for mutual, rationalized protection provided by an even more powerful, omnicompetent agent. Weber and others go so far as to suggest that a state's legitimacy depends on its ability to monopolize the means of force and violence within its borders, since individuals must attend closely to the matters of who has the ability to coerce them, and what those agents want. But individuals would hardly need protection against threats of violence if these were never executed. The power involved in coercion stems from the willingness and ability of some to take violent, forceful means against others; similarly, worries about state behavior stem from what states actually do to people, not just what they threaten to do. Both the state's justification and its need for justification stem from this common kind of power.

Yet, it may be suggested, the state need not resort to uses of force and violence just to coerce, at least not in general. After all, states wield many sorts of powers besides those that require impositions of force on their subjects. Many lesser threats and constraints, such as parking fines and license revocations, help generate compliance with lesser edicts. While this is true, it does not undercut the special relationship of force to power suggested above. I can bring this out by noting that, unless very special circumstances apply, the claim that X coerced Y implies a sort of "all-things-considered" assessment of the power relations between X and Y: such a claim will be undermined if, for instance, Y has equally or more potent means by which to preempt or fend off X's threat, or with which to retaliate against X after the fact. Force and violence are key—perhaps *the* key—variables in this assessment. While one might be able to coerce without possessing a significant advantage in terms of force and violence (e.g., as blackmail is said to do), it is hard to see how one could coerce while being at a significant disadvantage with respect to these means. That's why it's hard to see how, barring very special circumstances, one could in any meaningful sense coerce one's government to do what it otherwise opposes. (A person might be able to persuade, cajole, trick or otherwise lead the state to do his will, but hardly ever to force it to do so.) As Lucas suggests above, incarceration is the lynchpin of modern state-organized systems of coercion: it is a technique by which the state can forcefully and humanely stop those who would disrupt its orderly operations. Such an advantage in force and violence is one of few trump cards—and perhaps the only one—that can give an agent, including states, a monopoly on the power to coerce.

The power to aggregate, maintain, and direct the means of force and violence against others is the sort of power that makes rogues, mafias, and states significant actors in political philosophy, and draws our attention to how best to regulate them. Unless scofflaws are checked by some system that can impose its will upon them regardless of their inclinations, they will generate social chaos and lead private individuals to make coercion a private matter again. The state's monopoly on the justified use of force and violence gives it the power needed to check scofflaws, and upon this power and others like it the rest of the state's powers depend.

Thus it seems to me that theorists have had good grounds to regard direct uses of force and threats of force as both within the extension of the concept "coercion," and perhaps definitive of it. At the very least, there is use for a concept that refers to this sort of power, and the term "coercion" has for a long time been routinely used to refer to such power. Yet recent analytic philosophy of coercion has come to associate "coercion" either exclusively or primarily with the use of threats.[13] It is to the merits of this view I now turn.

---

[13] Or, more generally, conditional communicated proposals, which may include some "offers" as well as threats.

Despite the discussion above, I suspect that it will seem to most readers obvious that making threats—even threats of force—and using force for any purpose are distinctly different activities, and should be conceptualized as such. The following seem to me the strongest considerations in favor of this view.

1. Successful threats can sometimes be bluffs; that is, one can sometimes coerce another without the ability or willingness to exercise the kind of power one advertises. Not so with direct force.
2. While some threats are of force/violence, and others perhaps akin to force/violence, many potentially coercive threats fall far short of force/violence.
3. As McCloskey argues, there is an intimate, ontological connection between coercion and coerced acts. Direct uses of force against a body do not generate particular actions by the receiving party, and hence the question, "what was she coerced into doing?" receives no answer.
4. Following on 2 and 3, the forensic issues that arise about actions in response to threats are distinctly different, and more difficult, than the issues that arise in the wake of direct uses of force.

Good bluffs make adventitious use of power lodged somewhere, in someone, and thus demonstrate that the sort of power one needs in order to coerce is not necessarily fully within the control of the coercing agent. Yet while (1) raises many interesting issues I cannot address here, to my knowledge there is no extended treatment of coercion by bluffing in the philosophical literature, so this likely has not motivated the change in analysis. The three remaining considerations combine to form a more likely impetus to a different approach to coercion from the one I've described.

The emphasis of recent philosophy of coercion on threats, altered actions, and particular cases seems to derive at least in part from a very different interest in coercion than that motivating the classical political theorists. Rather than conceiving of coercion as a decisive, possibly sustained use of power, theorists have more lately conceived of coercion as a quality manifested in certain actions which respond to some considerations rather than others. There are several possible motivations for this turn, besides those mentioned above, but this conception appears to be most valuable as an analytic tool for answering questions about an agent's responsibility or culpability for particular actions, or for determining whether one agent has treated another properly and/or has respected her autonomy. The focus of attention correspondingly shifts from what the *coercer* does, and how, to why the *coercee* does what she does.

Perhaps the best and most prominent example of this analysis of coercion is Alan Wertheimer's *Coercion*,[14] a book which sorts through numerous cases and develops a sophisticated set of tests for whether an action should count as coerced.

---

[14] Alan Wertheimer, *Coercion* (Princeton: Princeton University Press, 1987).

But even if Wertheimer and others are motivated by different questions than their predecessors, it's not apparent, I think, that Wertheimer or any of other recent theorists understood that they were *reconceptualizing* coercion, diverging from earlier thought about it. Nor does it seem that the implications of this divergence have been well or widely understood. Intended or not, the seeds of this reconceptualization can be found in the earliest and most influential writing in the recent philosophy of coercion—Nozick's "Coercion."[15] It is helpful to give some detailed attention to how this essay, seemingly unawares, redeploys its predecessors' thinking about coercion in ways that sharply alter the understanding of coercion's nature. After taking up this task, I will conclude by highlighting some of the implications of these alterations for what we can say about coercion.

Nozick begins his essay noting that it is an exploratory study for a longer work on "liberty."[16] He quickly offers the following five "conditions for coercion" for an act by a coercer (R) against a coercee (E):

[P]erson R coerces person E into not[17] doing act A if and only if:

1. R threatens to bring about or have brought about some consequence if E does A (and knows he's threatening to do this).
2. A with this threatened consequence is rendered substantially less eligible as a course of conduct for E than A was without the threatened consequence.
3. R makes this threat in order to get E not to do A, intending that E realize he's been threatened by R.
4. E does not do A.
5. Part of E's reason for not doing A is to avoid (or lessen the likelihood of) the consequence which R has threatened to bring about or have brought about.[18]

After some minor refinements and the addition of two further conditions (needed to handle some improbable counterexamples), these five conditions are taken as granted, with the balance of the essay devoted to working through definitional problems with the key concept in these conditions: *threat*.

In light of claims about "coercion" in earlier political philosophy, Nozick's approach is noteworthy for narrowing the scope of the term to include only threats. It also departs from its predecessors by making judgments about whether coercion has occurred depend principally on three factors: the coercer's issuance of a conditional

---

[15] A measure of the influence of this essay is that at least ten subsequent theorists have published works containing recognizable reproductions or variants of Nozick's list of conditions; many more give substantive responses to his essay. See my "How the Coercer Got Away: Evaluating Nozick-style Accounts of Coercion," unpublished manuscript.

[16] Nozick, 440.

[17] Although this is stated as a prohibition, Nozick explicitly intends to cover prohibitions and affirmative directives. Nozick, n. 3.

[18] Nozick, 441. This list substitutes my preferred variable names for Nozick's, and his amendments in 1', 2', and 5' on 442 for his 1, 2, and 5 on 441. I have also ignored several later technical adjustments to these conditions that are unimportant to the issues here.

threat; a specification of the intentions and beliefs of the coercer; and a specification of the resulting actions, intentions, and beliefs of the coercee. In emphasizing these elements, Nozick's account ends up treating the power implied by the coercer's threat—the basis of its credibility—as a kind of unanalyzed given. Or, more precisely, the credibility of the coercer's threat—and hence its power—is left to depend on whether in fact the coercee gives it credence. Nozick's account gives no place to the actual, historically demonstrated powers of the coercer or relevantly similar agents. Hence broader power relations between coercer and coercee are obscured by turning them into facts about the psychological states and communications of the two agents involved.

Although this approach is strikingly different from the thinking on coercion evident in earlier political writers, Nozick does not begin *ex nihilo*. He says he obtains the raw materials for his five conditions from two now classic works of legal and political scholarship: H. L. A. Hart and Tony Honoré's *Causation in the Law*, and Hart's solo work, *The Concept of Law*.[19] The two works differ in purpose. *Concept* offers a foundational account of the nature of law through consideration of the workings of society and state, given our typical psychological and moral strengths and weaknesses. *Causation*, by contrast, is more of a manual for jurists, specifically those in an English or North American legal framework, who are presented with concrete cases requiring forensic investigation and resolution according to the established laws of the land. The two works differ accordingly in their interest in and remarks about coercion. Given Nozick's stated aims, apparently realized in *Anarchy, State, Utopia*, one might expect his essay to have more in common with *Concept* than with *Causation*. Yet the style of Nozick's analysis and the resulting theory of coercion are much more in keeping with the aims and thinking in *Causation* than that in *Concept*.

The part of *Concept* Nozick draws upon most directly would appear to be a passage in which Hart describes how coercion works in a situation of a gunman robbing a bank clerk.

> [T]o secure compliance with his expressed wishes, the [gunman] threatens to do something which a normal man would regard as harmful or unpleasant, and renders keeping the money a substantially less eligible course of conduct for the clerk. If the gunman succeeds, we would describe him as having *coerced* the clerk, and the clerk as in that sense being in the gunman's power.[20]

This passage bears more than a passing resemblance to Nozick's conditions 1 and 2, which highlight the coercer's threat and its effect on the coercee's incentive structure.

Superficially, *Concept* seems to understand coercion in a way that is congenial to recent theorists. For one thing, Hart's main foil here is John Austin's "command

---

[19] H. L. A. Hart and Tony Honoré, *Causation in the Law* 1st ed. (Oxford: Oxford University Press, 1959); H. L. A. Hart, *The Concept of Law* (Oxford: Oxford University Press, 1961).
[20] Hart, 19. See also 80.

theory" species of "positivist" legal philosophy, which treats the state as something like a gunman writ large. So Hart labors to show that coercion could hardly be the only or principal source of law's authority. Rather, the well-functioning state requires broad voluntary compliance with its orders, since it's nearly impossible for a state to impose its will coercively on all of the people who might otherwise be tempted to defy it. Thus, while not abandoning earlier theorists' claims that coercion is necessary for law's legitimacy, Hart may be said to downplay it somewhat, and to emphasize other at least necessary conditions for the state to achieve power, legitimacy, and widespread voluntary compliance with its directives. Also, as in the example above, Hart seems to associate coercion closely with threats, and not with uses of force *per se*, and repeatedly interchanges "coercion" with orders backed by threats of sanctions, perhaps even excluding any other understanding of the term.[21] So in this regard, Nozick and later writers are consonant with at least Hart's dicta.

However, Nozick focuses on what Hart says about a threat's effect on its target's incentive structure, but neglects Hart's sketch of the relative powers of the agents involved. This seems to me an important interpretive choice. The difference in power created by the gunman's weapon is not extraneous or incidental to Hart's use of this example to explain coercion. To see why, it helps to consider briefly Hart's understanding of the role of law in protecting individuals from scofflaws and deviants. Although Hart denies that law is *merely* a set of orders backed by threats, he explicitly argues that what he calls "municipal law" (i.e., that of the state) necessarily requires the employment of coercive sanctions in order to establish rules for public safety and stability, and thereby make voluntary compliance rational. In a key passage, Hart discusses the minimum features necessary for a legal system to give its subjects a reason to comply with it, compatible with their mutual, peaceful coexistence. After noting that, in general, a large majority of people in society is likely to uphold its codes voluntarily, and only a small minority likely to defect from them, he then writes:

> Yet, except in very small closely-knit societies, submission to the system of restraints would be folly if there were no organization for the coercion of those who would then try to obtain the advantages of the system without submitting to its obligations. 'Sanctions' are therefore required not as the normal motive for obedience, but as a *guarantee* that those who would voluntarily obey shall not be sacrificed to those who would not. To obey without this, would be to risk going to the wall. Given this standing danger, what reason demands is *voluntary* co-operation in a *coercive* system.[22]

Hart's invocations of "organization," "guarantees," and a "coercive system" is significant. For people to be able to risk voluntary cooperation with others, and with state orders in general, they require security against recalcitrant members of society.

---

[21] "[W]e shall use the expressions 'orders backed by threats' and 'coercive orders' to refer to orders which, like the gunman's, are supported only by threats." Hart, 19.

[22] *Ibid.*, 193 (Hart's italics).

Such security does not come merely from giving scofflaws incentives or ordinary motives to comply, but from the existence of an organization that can impose sanctions that keep malefactors in check, whether they wish to follow the state's orders or not. Regardless of whether the term "coercion" is properly limited to threatening activity, the real import of coercion, for Hart, is in the larger organization or system of coercion which both threatens and then follows through with physical sanctions.

This is even clearer in a different context late in the book. In arguing that there is such a thing as international law, Hart confronts a "sceptic" who reminds that in the international context there is both a need for and an absence of a sovereign to coerce compliance with crucial laws.

> The sceptic [about international law] may point out that there are in a municipal system ... certain provisions which are justifiably called necessary; among these are primary rules of obligation, prohibiting the free use of violence, and rules *providing for the official use of force* as a sanction for these and other rules.[23]

Hart replies by distinguishing the situation of states vis-à-vis one another from the situation of individuals living in social groups. It is his characterization of the intra-state context that is of interest.

> In societies of individuals, approximately equal in physical strength and vulnerability, *physical sanctions* are both necessary and possible. ... [N]o mere natural deterrents could in any but the simplest forms of society be adequate to restrain those too wicked, too stupid or too weak to obey the law. Yet because of the same fact of approximate equality and the patent advantages of submission to a system of restraints, no combination of malefactors is likely to exceed in strength those who would voluntarily co-operate in its maintenance. In these circumstances ... sanctions may successfully be used against malefactors with relatively small risks, and the threat of them will add much to whatever natural deterrents there may be.[24]

For Hart, then, what makes "municipal law" coercive may include the fact that it amounts to orders backed by threats, but it is crucial that these threats carry not just any old sanction. In fact, they need to be systematic, organized, and backed by physical force, and must provide guarantees for law abiding citizens that their rectitude will not bring doom or devastation. It seems fair to say, then, that for Hart the coerciveness of the state encompasses more than its use of threats, and requires at least mention of its willingness and ability to use such superior power to make good on its threats. It is precisely this aspect of Hart's interest in coercion that Nozick leaves out of his own account.

Turning now to Nozick's other source, his conditions 3 and 5 appear to be adapted from the analysis in a section of *Causation* that deals with what we might

---

[23] *Ibid.*, 213 (emphasis added).
[24] *Ibid.*, 213–214 (emphasis added).

call cases of "undue influence."[25] Condition 4, the "success condition," is also implicit in the discussion of these cases. In Nozick's account, these conditions describe intentions/mental states of the coercer and coercee, and also require that the coercee's reasons for action stem appropriately from the coercer's activities.

It's fairly clear why, when confronted with a possible case of coercion, *Causation* should urge jurists to attend to the beliefs and intentions of the threatening and threatened parties. One of its main concerns is to help jurists determine the etiology of certain actions, in order to determine facts such as whether there was a *mens rea* in a crime or genuine consent to an agreement, or for assigning responsibility for actions that have been improperly influenced. In such investigations, an investigator may need to grasp both the typical and the actual beliefs or intentions of the parties involved, or an agent's reasons for action, or the effects one agent might have on another's incentive structure.

> Of course generalizations about the way in which either the person in question or other persons respond, e.g., to threats, or by what reasons they are or are not actuated, have an important place in such cases. They may be used as *evidence* that a person in saying he acted from a certain reason was not speaking the truth (or was forgetful), because it was 'out of character' for him or is rare for anyone to act for such a reason.[26]

With respect to *Causation*'s concerns, coercion is just one way that agents may unduly influence each other; it treats threatening as one kind of "interpersonal transaction," other forms of which include physical compulsion, hypnosis, and fraud.[27] What these have in common is that, under some circumstances, they may suffice to shift responsibility for an action or event from the shoulders of the proximately causal agent onto those of an actor more remote from the event of interest. Thus threatening, and its psychological aspects, are of interest to *Causation* insofar as they raise questions about who is responsible for what, in cases before the bar. In adopting *Causation*'s approach here, Nozick's account may be specially suited to help answer these sorts of questions.

Causation, however, does not aim to provide a general account of coercion, and even the passages in *Causation* which Nozick draws upon for his conditions 3 and 5 do not mention threats, threatening, consequences, or anything that would be specific to coercing. Given Nozick's appropriation of *Causation*'s analysis, our

---

[25] What I describe here as cases of "undue influence," Hart and Honoré call more neutrally "interpersonal transactions." They write that when such a relationship between actors is claimed,

> Four common features demand attention in the various relationships of this type. ...
>
> (ii) [Nozick's 5] the first actor's words or deeds are part of the second actor's reasons for acting ...
>
> (iv) [Nozick's 3] except in the case where the first actor has merely advised the second act [sic], he intends the second actor to do the act in question.

Hart and Honoré, 49–50.

[26] Hart and Honoré, 53.

[27] See, e.g., *ibid.*, 48–54, 134–135, 172–178.

question is whether the psychological aspects of threatening and being threatened are especially germane to a more general account of coercion's nature. Views here will differ, but there are at least some reasons to doubt that they will. For one thing, people are likely to become accustomed to many standing threats (such as the criminal law), and thus likely to feel no special pull once they have adapted to their yoke. Second, the account would seem to make ignorance a defense against coercion: if one is unable or unwilling to recognize that a threat has been made against oneself or one's interests, then one becomes uncoercible. What is ordinarily a form of extreme weakness would become a source of indomitability. Finally, while sometimes psychological factors will be important in the outcome of a coercive situation, this is not always true: consider the bouncer who threatens the unruly patron with "move or I'll move you," or the gunman who is determined to gain his victim's wallet the easy way or the hard way. Just as in Aristotle's case of the seamen jettisoning their cargo, some outcomes are not made voluntary just because a person's will is their proximate cause; the fact that their cargo was lost at sea did not result from the seamen's choice to dump it.

Conclusion

The import of this history can be judged, albeit obliquely, by considering the results that recent philosophy of coercion has reached. For instance, with respect to freedom, recent authors have concluded that "choices made in contexts of coercion do not differ from choices made in ordinary circumstances in ways that justify classifying the former as unfree."[28] Another has argued that, with respect to responsibility, "the question of whether or not a person is morally responsible for a coerced act is *logically independent* of the question of whether or not she was coerced."[29] Another concludes that the enforcement of just law is typically *not* coercive.[30] These and other strikingly innovative views have been defended by well-placed philosophers in well regarded journals. Notably, the above mentioned writers' views on coercion can be traced directly to Nozick's article. If one does not attend to recent intellectual history when considering these views, it could lead one to suppose that the notion of coercion being discussed is the same as the one that has been prominent throughout the history of western political philosophy. And this could lead to unfortunate confusion.[31]

---

[28] Michael J. Murray and David F. Dudrick, "Are Coerced Acts Free?," *American Philosophical Quarterly* 32 (1995), 118.

[29] Denis G. Arnold, "Coercion and Moral Responsibility," *American Philosophical Quarterly* 38 (2001), 61 (my emphasis).

[30] William Edmundson, "Is Law Coercive?," *Legal Theory* 1 (1995), 81. Though Edmundson endorses this view, he recognizes its novelty, calling it a "repugnant conclusion."

[31] For more detailed arguments about the difficulties with "Nozick-style" accounts of coercion, see my "How the Coercer Got Away," note 15, *supra*.

Chapter 3
On Coercion

Burton M. Leiser

1 Introduction

Does the law coerce people into behaving as they do? If so, by what right do legislators and other authorities engage in such coercion? Perhaps they should merely entice us into what they think is acceptable behavior and leave it to us to decide. And what does it take, or what should it take, to prove that a person has been coerced—e.g., in a case of alleged date rape? Are the alleged victim's feelings enough?

In order to understand the nature of coercion as clearly as possible, I will begin this paper by offering a definition of it and comparing it to related concepts, such as compulsion, bribery, seduction, and blackmail. Along the way, I will seek to determine the essential components of coercion and the ways in which it differs from those others.

An important question concerns the subjective, as opposed to the objective components of coercion. If a person *feels* coerced, is that sufficient to establish that she has been coerced?

In addition to the law and governmental forms of coercion, there are some well-known private forms of coercion. What is their place in the scheme of things?

I will suggest that some kinds of demand are not conceptually consistent with the concept of coercion that I have outlined, although they appear to be coercive.

And finally, I will ask whether the apparent analogy to domestic law in the so-called law of nations is a legitimate use of language and the extent to which international law can be properly said to exist.

2 Defining Coercion

Coercion occurs when one person threatens to visit some evil or unwanted consequence on another unless that other does or refrains from doing some act in accordance with the coercer's demands.

D.A. Reidy and W.J. Riker (eds.), *Coercion and the State.*
© Springer Science+Business Media B.V. 2008

The word *person* in this definition refers either to natural persons—i.e., particular individuals—or to artificial persons, in the Hobbesian[1] sense—i.e., collective or corporate actors such as corporations, churches, labor unions, or governments. Thus, one individual, *A*, may threaten another, *B*, with significant harm if *B* fails to act in accordance with *A*'s commands. *A*'s threat, *t*, constitutes an attempt to coerce *B* to behave in a certain way. A few examples:

- *A* holds a gun to *B*'s head and says, "Your money or your life."
- The European Union withholds promised funds from the Hamas-led Palestinian Authority (PA), declaring that unless Hamas accedes to certain demands, such as that it recognize Israel's right to exist and agree to abide by all agreements entered into between the PA and Israel, the funds will not be forthcoming.
- The Roman Catholic Church threatens to excommunicate anyone who divorces his or her spouse.
- A religious community threatens to shun anyone who commits adultery.
- A university threatens tenured faculty members with instant termination if they become involved in amorous relationships with their students.
- A municipality passes an ordinance imposing a fine of two hundred dollars on anyone who parks in bus stops.

Note that whether the alleged coercer has actually engaged in an act of coercion is a matter of objective fact. It does not depend at all upon the feelings of the alleged coercee, as we will see shortly. Moreover, there is a clear distinction between *attempted* coercion and *actual* coercion. An attempt by *A* to coerce *B* into acting in a certain way may succeed or fail. If it succeeds—that is, if *B* acts in accordance with *A*'s demands because *B* is intimidated by *A*'s threats, then *B* has in fact been coerced. However, if *B* does not comply with *A*'s demands, then *B* has not been coerced, although *A* *attempted* to coerce *B*. Thus, in the first example above, if *B* complies with *A*'s command and gives up his money, *B* has been coerced by *A*'s threat. However, if he does not, then he has not been coerced to give up his money, and *A* has engaged in attempted coercion. A Catholic who divorces his wife despite the Church's threats to excommunicate him has not been coerced, despite the Church's attempt to do so.

This definition of *coercion* is morally neutral. It makes no prejudgment as to whether a particular incident of coercion or attempted coercion is right or wrong, justified or unjustified. It is of no moment whether the coercer is an individual or a collective, such as a state. Those issues are separate and distinct from the question whether a particular set of events constitutes coercion or not.

There is a peculiarity about *coercion* that is worth noting here. The word rarely crops up in ordinary discourse, and generally appears only *after* an incident has occurred, as an attempt to explain, justify, or excuse one's conduct. Thus, a robber

---

[1] Thomas Hobbes, *Leviathan*, Part I, chapter 16.

does not set out to coerce his victims. He sets out to *rob* them. The municipality does not pass an ordinance to coerce drivers. It passes an ordinance to prevent parking in certain spaces. The word *coerce* appears only *after* the event. The robber's victim explains that he handed over his money only because he was coerced into doing so, making it clear that his action was not motivated by generosity or charity or as a fair exchange, but by fear of the consequences of not complying with the robber's demand. This is a perfectly rational explanation of his behavior, and not at all an admission of guilt. Similarly, one who was criticized by his passenger for having passed up a handy parking space at a bus stop might offer as an "excuse" or an explanation for his behavior the fact that the law prohibited doing so and that he was coerced by the threat of a steep penalty from violating the ordinance. In the same way, a devout Catholic might explain to his mistress that the Church's sanctions against divorce prevented him from dumping his unloved wife and marrying his beloved mistress, its coercive penalty being more than he could risk in light of his devotion to the Church, his children, and his community.

If an attempt at coercion is to have any chance to succeed, the threat t that is made by the coercer A must be credible, at least to the person B (or the persons, if that is the case) who is being coerced. If the threat is not credible, if B either does not believe that A has the power or the will to carry out the threat, or believes that the threat itself is inconsequential, then it is not likely that B will be intimidated by the threat, and the attempt at coercion will fail.

Although coercion and compulsion might be thought to be comparable, they are quite different. A person being coerced has a choice between acquiescence or resistance to the coercer's demands, even though the unpleasant consequences of failure to acquiesce might be highly probable or even a dead certainty. One who is compelled to act in a certain way has no choice, but because of some physical or psychological force over which he has no control, must behave as he does. Thus, for example, an alcoholic acts under a psychological or physiological compulsion when he reaches for a drink, but cannot properly be said to be coerced into doing so. Similarly, one who is forced into a prone position by having his arm twisted behind him has been compelled to assume that position, but was not coerced into doing so.

Only human agencies can engage in coercion. Inanimate objects and natural events might cause people to engage in certain forms of behavior, but it would be odd to say that one was coerced into doing what one did because of them. An impending landslide, flood, volcanic eruption, or fire might *compel* one to flee from the site, for example, but it makes no sense at all to say that they had *coerced* him into doing so. A person who is swept off his feet by a raging current and deposited several hundred yards downstream has been compelled, but not coerced, to land where he did. Animals other than humans might be capable of compelling one to act in one way rather than another, but they can't coerce such action. A snarling pit bull or lion or a swarm of bees might *compel* me to retreat to safety, but none of them can properly be said to have *coerced* me into doing so.

Coercion entails an attempt by one person to overpower the will of another, not by reason or rhetoric, but by threats and intimidation. If a person acts because of some power that is not under her control, where she has no choice but is compelled[2] to do what she does, then her will is not implicated and it is inappropriate to use the word *coercion*. A good example is the following lead paragraph from an AP dispatch from Baghdad dated September 21, 2006:

> Insurgents are now using unwitting kidnap victims as suicide bombers—seizing them, booby-trapping their cars without their knowledge, then releasing them only to blow up the vehicles by remote control....

These unfortunate victims are *not* suicide bombers, since *suicide* implies deliberate self-destruction, and these individuals have no idea that they are being used as human bombs deployed to destroy others while being destroyed themselves. Their destruction is brought about, not through their own volition but through others over whom they have no control.

The actual application of force by the coercer against the person who is being coerced is not necessary for coercion to have taken place. Indeed, such force may preclude the possibility of coercion being meaningful. A person who is forcibly prevented from violating a particular command by being forcibly seized and sequestered in a jail cannot be said to have been coerced. He has been *compelled* to act or not act in a particular way; but since his will has not been involved, it would be inappropriate to say that he was *coerced* into doing so.

Although coercion generally entails a threat of some negative or painful consequence, closely related concepts involve just the opposite. One who engages in enticement or seduction holds out the promise of profitable or pleasurable rewards for compliant behavior. One who has been lured into the arms of an attractive young woman can hardly complain that he was *coerced* into the pleasures of intercourse with her. Special terminology is reserved for other inducements that people offer to one another. Bribery, for example, consists of offering a reward for behavior that one would otherwise be reluctant to do or that the person being bribed knows she is morally or legally forbidden to do. It doesn't seem to be a form of coercion, though the relationship is very close. On the other hand, blackmail does; and it seems that the reason that blackmail is a kind of coercion is because the blackmailer's threat is precisely that she has the power to bring some significant evil upon her victim unless the victim complies with her demands.

Some forms of coercion seem quite benign, while others are not. A mother who threatens her children with dire consequences if they don't go to school would seem to be fully justified in doing so, for she would merely be fulfilling her maternal duty

---

[2] It is instructive to consider the origin of the word *compel*, from the Latin *pellere*, to push or drive, as the wind *impels* or drives a boat onward, or as an object is *propelled* forward, not necessarily of its own volition (for it may have no volition at all), but by a force that acts upon it in such a way as to cause it to move. The origin of *coerce* is more complex. It derives from the Latin *arcere*, from which we get such words as *ark* (a container for secret things) and *arcane*, and suggests that one who coerces reaches deep into the recesses of the mind of the one who is coerced and moves him to do what the coercer wants him to do.

to see to her children's education. Whether coercing a child to go to school or do his homework is wrong and constitutes a violation of the child's rights is another matter, which I leave to those who think they are experts in that field.

On the other hand, we would condemn a mother who used identical tactics to persuade her children to steal jewelry for her, for what she was trying to induce them to do was unlawful, and for that reason her attempt to coerce them into doing so would also have been unlawful.

3   Coercion as an Objective Fact

Coercion is an objective fact. However one might feel about an incident after it is over, those feelings are not determinative of whether coercion was actually involved. One who has succumbed to the blandishments of an effective advertisement, bought an expensive item, and thereafter suffered from buyer's remorse cannot complain that she was "coerced" into the purchase. Whether the merchant chooses to allow her to return the item or not, the customer's mere *feeling* that she was helpless before the clever advertising program and had no choice but to lay her credit card on the counter and sign the charge slip is insufficient to establish that she was coerced.

Adhesion contracts are a different matter, for the very point of such a "contract" is that one of the parties was tricked into "consenting" to its provisions, or was in a situation where meaningful choice was impossible. For example: A young client of mine became seriously ill, was transported to the emergency room of a local hospital, and was admitted to the hospital, where she remained for a number of days during treatment of her illness. At the time, she was in dire straits. Before admitting her, the hospital personnel presented her with a number of documents that she was required to sign. One of those documents was a form releasing the hospital from liability for the loss of any valuables the patient had brought with her unless they were placed in a safe deposit box on admission. Later, the patient discovered that the designer jeans and watch she had been wearing had been stolen. The hospital denied liability for her losses, offering the release form in its defense. On behalf of my client, I argued that she was coerced into signing the release, for if she had not done so, she would not have been admitted to the hospital despite her grievous illness. Under those circumstances, she had no meaningful choice about the matter, the hospital management had an unfair advantage, and there was no real meeting of the minds. Consequently, the "contract" was void. (I also noted that it would have been rather odd for the hospital to insist that she deposit her jeans in the hospital's safe.) In short, a contract or agreement that one party is coerced into making— whether it is written or oral—is no contract at all. Similarly, the recent incident in which two journalists being held captive by Muslim terrorists were coerced into converting to Islam at gunpoint resulted in no conversion at all, though some Muslims insist that once a conversion has taken place, even under such circumstances, it is valid and enforceable under Islamic law.

Discussions of coercion in date rape are often hopelessly confused. The harm that is inflicted on young women in cases of date rape cannot be overestimated. An incident of date rape can have lifelong psychological repercussions on the victim. However, fuzzy thinking or imprecise use of language does not further understanding of the issue. Rape is generally defined as sexual intercourse to which one of the parties, most often the woman, did not consent. The counseling service of a major American university offers the following advice to women "survivors" who harbor guilty feelings or remorse after they have had sexual relations with an acquaintance:

> Survivors, living and learning in this culture, may also accept "explanations" of "why it isn't rape," although they have been inwardly traumatized. The important thing to remember is that if there are feelings of violation, if a person's lifestyle and self-esteem are negatively affected by the incident, or survivors believe they have been raped, then it is rape.[3]

I do not want to trivialize the harm done to the victims or the gravity of the situation either for the alleged victims of date rape or for the alleged perpetrators of it. But conceptually it is difficult to distinguish date rape from the business transaction discussed above. The buyer who feels cheated by the seller must do more than relate her feelings if she wants to prove that she was cheated or that she was coerced into the purchase at issue. Suppose a financial counselor, like the university counselors, advised:

The important thing to remember is that if there are feelings of having been cheated, if the buyer's lifestyle and self-esteem are negatively affected by the transaction, or the buyer believes she has been cheated (or coerced), then she has been cheated (or coerced).

The purchase may have been a very large one entailing a major commitment of resources over a long period of time; but unless the buyer can prove that the seller made false promises to her or misrepresented the merchandise or compelled her through some improper stratagem to make the purchase, her mere *feeling* that she has been cheated or coerced into making the transaction is not enough to establish that she has in fact been cheated or coerced. Similarly, the alleged victim of date rape's mere *feeling* that she was raped is not enough to establish that a rape in any ordinary sense of the word has occurred.

4   Threats, Sanctions, and the Criminal Law

A *threat* of some sort is a necessary condition for any instance of coercion to exist. But what is a threat?

---

[3] State University of New York at Buffalo Web Site, Counseling Services, http://ub-counseling.buffalo.edu/violenceoverview.html.

As I suggested in the definition of *coercion* I offered in Part II above, where *A* is attempting to coerce *B* to do whatever it is that *A* wants *B* to do (or refrain from doing), *A* threatens to inflict some harm or other unwanted evil on *B* if *B* does not act in accordance with *A*'s demands. This suggests that the evil that *B* might suffer will be visited upon him in some way through the agency of *A*. To be sure, the word *threat* is often used metaphorically to refer to natural events that have nothing to do with human agency: earthquakes, tidal waves, floods, volcanic eruptions, and the like. It is not uncommon to hear weather forecasters talk about a "threat of tornadoes." But this metaphorical use of the word is not relevant to the threats that are involved in coercion. No rational person is likely to heed a potential coercer's threat to send a lightning bolt or a tornado in his path; but he might give some credence to a threat to fire him, harm his children, break his leg, or execute him.

For such threats to be effective, the coercee must believe that the coercer means to carry them out and that he has the capacity to do so. A coercer who has gained a reputation for not following through on his threats, or who is perceived to be weak or powerless, is not likely to succeed in persuading the coercee to follow his commands.

Criminal law is designed precisely to be coercive: to persuade people through the promise of painful sanctions to do what the legislature commands or to refrain from doing what it forbids. I pay my taxes before the deadline for payment has passed because I know that if I fail to do so, I will ultimately have to pay far more, and that the government will not only be aware of my delinquency, but that it has the power to force me to pay up. Even though I am often tempted to drive at unlawfully high speeds and to double park on busy city streets, the threat of heavy penalties or the loss of my license to drive is generally enough to make me comply with the law, or at least to stick closely enough to its commands so as not to attract the attention of the highway patrol.

Sanctions are specifically intended to be coercive. Although criminal sanctions may have an added retributive purpose, they are most often designed to deter potential offenders from violating the law by making the cost of the offense so much greater than any benefit that they might gain from committing the offense that they would refrain from doing so. It is presumed that most potential offenders are rational enough to make the calculation that the legislature intends to induce them to make, foresee the likely consequences, and refrain from the forbidden conduct. There is no pretense that *every* potential offender will do so or that *all* crime can be deterred by the threat of such penalties. Other methods, including such precautions as fences, barricades, safes, and protective clothing, which may be non-coercive, as well as educational programs designed to persuade potential offenders that the law ought to be obeyed, may be employed. But in the end, punishment is intended to be coercive. The threat of punishment offers the potential offender a choice between obedience to the law and unpleasant, undesired, and costly consequences. Such sanctions are never sufficient to deter every potential offender, but if they deter the ordinary person, their purpose has been served and their imposition justified.

Other means of coercion exist within civil societies—means that can be invoked by private citizens organized into groups. They can have a powerful impact on individuals, corporations, and governments, and can lead to significant changes in their policies and behavior. A labor union can threaten to strike and bring a corporation or a government to its knees. A group of indignant people mounting a boycott can destroy a company's business unless it complies with their demands. Demonstrations, rallies, and other public manifestations can bring enormous pressure to bear on their organizers' targets. Such tactics generally follow failed efforts to bring about the desired changes through negotiation and reason. A singularly successful example is the Montgomery, Alabama, bus boycott. Initiated by poor black workers who chose to walk many miles to work in all kinds of weather, and face threats of being terminated from their employment rather than ride segregated buses, they coerced steadfast segregationists and city officials into treating them with the dignity they rightly felt they deserved.

Strikes and boycotts are purely coercive, leaving little if any room for compromise. Once resort has been made to them, they can easily get out of hand and extremists may take the reins. To their targets, organizers of strikes, boycotts, and mass demonstrations say, in effect: "You must either comply with our demands or we will continue to organize, strike, and demonstrate; we will expand our base and bring you into such disrepute that you will no longer be able to do business as you have been doing. We believe that our cause is just even though you don't, and we are prepared to continue our campaign until you come to our point of view, or at least comply, in your behavior, with our demands, whether you like it or not."

Such tactics have worked repeatedly through the years, often on a very large scale. Strikes and picket lines have brought important improvements to the wages and benefits of workers from companies that might never have offered anything comparable. On the other hand, some strikes have backfired, as for example the strike of air traffic controllers throughout the United States in the early 1980s, which was brought to a swift and decisive end by President Ronald Reagan, who fired all of the striking controllers and replaced them with eager new recruits.

5   International Forms of Coercion

The international campaign of divestment against the racist system of apartheid in South Africa had a significant impact on South Africa's economy, but it is reasonably clear that the economic and other sanctions (e.g., social, sports, and cultural sanctions that placed South Africa and its people in virtual isolation from the rest of the world) ultimately won the day. A change of regime occurred, apartheid was abolished, and truth and reconciliation commissions effected a radical transformation of the nation's government. The fall of a long-established and deeply entrenched authoritarian regime and its replacement by a relatively democratic government that adopted radically different racial policies did not occur because reason prevailed and negotiators and mediators were successful in bringing the parties to a meeting of the minds, but because the economic and social pain of the international boycott had become too much to bear, and because the pressure threatened to become even greater.

5.1 Threats That Are Not Coercive

5.1.1 Israel and the Arabs

The Middle East provides a number of cases of international measures that appear to be coercive but may not be so. Of these, the most interesting, for our purposes, is the continuing threat, starting at Israel's birth in 1948 and even before, by Arab states and terrorist organizations to destroy the State of Israel and its Jewish citizens. The Arab states surrounding Israel[4] mounted a war against it immediately upon the announcement of Israel's birth. Their intention was clearly *not* to be coercive, as we have been using that term, but simply to destroy the new state and, as their leaders often reiterated, to cast the Jews into the sea.[5] For coercion to be meaningful, there must be a threat and a condition that would satisfy the coercer and thus head off the threat. But no conditions are laid down that the people of Israel might comply with to head off the disaster that is promised. At times, in order to gain tactical or negotiating advantage, various Arab leaders have enunciated conditions that appeared at the time to be sincere overtures for a peace agreement. The negotiations between Israel and the Palestine Liberation Organization (PLO) under Yasser Arafat, brokered by various American presidents and secretaries of state, are excellent examples. Even after all the conditions for agreements had been reached, the Arab side always came up with additional conditions that Israel could not accept without ceasing to exist. A couple of alternatives did exist: (1) Israel could close up shop and its people could emigrate anywhere in the world that would take them, or (2) Israel could recognize a "right of return" of millions of so-called Palestinian refugees who could then swarm into Israel, constitute themselves into a ruling majority, and fashion an Islamic state like those that dominate the rest of the region from Morocco to Afghanistan and beyond. No state in history has voluntarily allowed itself to be annihilated. If Hobbes was correct in his belief that the fundamental principle upon which every state is founded is its own preservation and the preservation of its subjects' lives, then Israel's leaders would have been grossly

---

[4] Egypt, Syria, Lebanon, Jordan (then known as Transjordan), Yemen, Saudi Arabia, and Iraq.

[5] See, for example, a report in the New York Lebanese newspaper, *Al Hoda* (June 9, 1951), quoting the Secretary-General of the Arab League, Azzam Pasha, who "assured the Arab peoples that the occupation of Palestine and Tel Aviv would be as simple as a military promenade. ... He pointed out that they were already on the frontiers and that all the millions the Jews had spent on land and economic development would be easy booty, for it would be a simple matter to throw Jews into the Mediterranean. ... Brotherly advice was given to the Arabs of Palestine to leave their land, homes and property and to stay temporarily in neighboring fraternal states, lest the guns of the invading Arab armies mow them down." See also Sheikh Abd Al-Muhsin Al-'Abikan, advisor to the Saudi Justice Ministry, in his weekly television program on religious rulings (September 11, 2004): "President Jamal 'Abd Al-Nasser [told] the UN forces in 1967, 'Get out and we will throw them into the sea. We will throw the Jews into the sea.' ... I heard him when I was small. He said in his speeches, 'Let's throw them into the sea.'" Memri Special Dispatch 956, August 12, 2005.

delinquent if they had accepted either of these alternatives. Of course, there was always a third alternative: annihilation of both the state and its population by a massive invasion from all over the Muslim world, the ultimate jihad. No one in his right mind would accept any of these alternatives, for they were all suicidal. Consequently, the "offers" made to the Israeli people have not been offers at all, and those who have made them have not been sincerely interested in reaching an agreement with Israel or its citizens. Coercion is not at issue, for there has been no meaningful choice. Instead, from the very outset, most Arab leaders, including both political and religious leaders, have sought the extinction of the State of Israel and the extermination of its people. One would not have had to be a survivor of the Holocaust, or the son or daughter of a survivor, to see that the only meaningful response was to embark on a war of survival whenever the threat became too immediate.

5.1.2 Islamic Extremism and the West

The current conflict between the non-Muslim West and Islam is rather similar. With some notable exceptions, Islamic leaders, whether clerical, political, or terrorist, have declared war on the West. They are fighting this war on a number of fronts, some much more overt than others. Al Qaeda and its offshoots are the most overt, using suicide bombers to great effect in the United States and Europe (e.g., the bombings in Spain, London, and elsewhere in Europe) as well as in Iraq, Afghanistan, Egypt, Indonesia, Argentina, and elsewhere. They ruthlessly employ more subtle methods to bring about their ultimate goal. The forced conversion of captive journalists is symbolic of their ultimate aim: the conversion of the entire world to Islam and the establishment of a universal caliphate, either by persuasion or by force. Their goal is the establishment of shar'ia law throughout the world and the disappearance of any competing system of law or way of life anywhere on earth. There is no room, to their way of thinking, for any religion but Islam, and whatever is required to establish the reign of Islam over all the earth, including the physical extermination of anyone or any group of people who stands in the way, they deem to be perfectly legitimate. Once again, this is not a case of coercion in any meaningful sense of the word. There is no appeal to reason, no argument presenting alternatives. It is perhaps a paradigm case of an *argumentum ad baculam*, in which one says that you ought to do as I say because I can beat you senseless if you don't. It is simply a threat—and a very meaningful threat at that, given recent history—that if you don't comply completely with our demands, we will not hesitate to kill you and destroy everything and everyone precious to you.

6 International Law, International Institutions, and Coercion

We have enough experience with criminal sanctions to know with reasonable certainty that they work much of the time. Nevertheless, recidivism is common enough, and beyond that, some potential offenders are so intractable as to be immune to the threat of any sanctions that anyone can dream up. Domestically, however, there is generally some authority capable of enforcing the commands of the law and maintaining sufficient order to enable a civil society to exist.

On the international scene, it is more difficult to enforce such sanctions because there is no common authority with power enough to make them work and because different actors have disparate interests and ideologies, making the coordination of strategies and the achievement of consensus on a single policy almost impossible except in the most unusual circumstances. Nevertheless, where such consensus exists, as in the case of South Africa discussed above, sanctions have a reasonable chance of working. Unfortunately, such examples are hard to find, as the conditions for success are so rare.

The principal problem is that there is nothing resembling a world government, though some feeble institutions exist. The United Nations is in place and does a reasonably good job organizing humanitarian missions—though other organizations, like the Red Cross, seem on the whole to do a better job of it. The UN secretariat—essentially the administrative arm of the organization—is lacking in credibility, largely because of the corruption and scandals that perennially infect its operations, but also because it has proven itself to be so inept at accomplishing what it has been charged to do, especially when those failures reach to the very heart of the organization's mission. The UN failed, for example, to act decisively to stop the genocide in Darfur. Similarly, in June 1967 the UN peacekeeping forces in Sinai were ordered out by President Nasser of Egypt, who made it clear that his purpose was to launch a war against Israel. The "peacekeepers" promptly folded their tents and departed, abandoning their peacekeeping function the moment there was a threat of war.

The problem reaches beyond the UN administration, however. The General Assembly, which meets every September in New York, has no legal power at all. In general, it serves no useful function, unless an expensive annual conclave of kings, presidents, and prime ministers that enables them to blow wind at one another is considered to be useful. It has no legislative power, but devotes its time to churning out wordy resolutions that are swiftly forgotten and have no discernible effect on anyone or anything. This is perfectly appropriate, since those resolutions are usually passed by automatic majorities of mostly inconsequential states whose delegates seem to enjoy their ability to sound important and pronounce authoritatively on issues that they think will affect other states.

The Security Council, which was invested by the UN's founders with great power, is rarely able to exercise that power because of the political games played by the five permanent members. Its resolutions are usually hedged about with so many escape clauses and couched in such ambiguous language that they have very little credibility and even less practical effect.

The World Court or International Court of Justice, ICJ, has virtually no power at all. The ICJ is a court whose main attribute is the beautiful building in The Hague that has been bequeathed to it. Most courts that deserve the name have some other attributes that are generally considered to be essential, but the court in The Hague has none of them. It has no compulsory process. That is, it has no sheriff who has the power to haul defendants and witnesses into the court at the point of a gun if they choose not to cooperate. So there is no compulsory process such as other courts elsewhere must have if they are to function. It has no real jurisdiction, for states can opt out of its jurisdiction whenever they choose—and they often do. Indeed, the court's charter is quite specific about this. It says that when one state brings a complaint against another, the court has jurisdiction only if the state against which the complaint is raised submits to the court's jurisdiction. But that doesn't stop the court from hearing the case without the defendant. It can not only hear the case in the defendant's absence and without the defendant raising a defense, despite the Court's Charter, which provides that the defendant state has a perfect right to refuse to acquiesce in the court's jurisdiction. Nothing in the Charter empowers the court to hear the case if the defendant refuses to participate. But the court can go even further, and pass judgment on the absent defendant over whom the court has no legal jurisdiction after it has heard only one side of the case in the defendant's absence. Nevertheless, this is all an exercise in futility, since the absent defendant has no duty ever to appear before the court, the court has no power to bring the defendant in and no power to impose sanctions on the defendant. And once the flurry and sputtering are over, everyone can go about his business as if the court did not exist—which is probably just as well.

Other international courts, often temporary and of more specific and limited jurisdiction, are little better. The world was recently treated to the sad spectacle of the International Criminal Tribunal for the former Yugoslavia, the ICTY, trying Slobodan Milosovic for several years. The main purpose of the trial seems to have been to give Mr. Milosovic an opportunity to harangue the members of the court and the public with his "defense." The trial dragged on for so long that the defendant ultimately died—probably convinced that death was better than the boredom of his never-ending trial.

Thus, the coercive power that ordinarily constitutes the *raison d'ètre* of the law seems to be lacking in the international sphere. There is no legislature worthy of the name (unless one imagines that philosophers of law writing windy tomes have the power to influence affairs in the rough-and-tumble world of international politics in peace and war), no executive capable of carrying out or enforcing the "law of nations," and no court with the ability to adjudicate real cases and controversies in the absence of the parties' consent. This is almost enough to make one wonder whether international law exists at all. But of course it does, at least in some metaphorical sense.

7 Conclusion

We have come a long way in these few pages. I have moved from a relatively simple definition of "coercion" to distinguishing it from compulsion. I have suggested that coercion entails an interaction between two or more persons in which one acts upon the will of the other in such a way as to make him choose between two undesired consequences. I noted that other concepts are related to coercion (e.g., bribery, seduction, and blackmail) but are different from it in certain important respects. And I noted that some forms of coercion are commendable while others are just the opposite.

I distinguished between certain voluntary transactions over which one party might suffer remorse and suggested that genuine coercion has an objective component and that a purely subjective feeling of remorse is insufficient to establish that one has been coerced.

Turning to the law, I concluded that the law—especially the criminal law—is essentially a coercive device designed to regularize human conduct through the threat of evil consequences to those who fail to follow the rules. I also looked at private coercive sanctions, such as strikes and boycotts, against both private entities and public ones.

Turning to the international scene, I examined the Arab campaign against the State of Israel and concluded that in essence, it cannot be called coercive, at least as far as Israel itself is concerned, since it is essentially intended to leave the people of Israel no choice; for a choice between death by force of arms and national or personal suicide is no choice at all. I suggested that the Islamic campaign against the West is similar, in that it is tantamount to a demand that the western world surrender all that is meaningful to it or suffer extinction by the sword or other weapons. Such threats are not coercive, for they leave one with no rational choice but to fight back.

Finally, as to whether institutional means of coercion exist with respect to international law, I concluded that for all practical purposes, despite the best intentions of the founders of the United Nations, they do not, and consequently international law is not law properly so called, but merely the collection of those customs that nations generally agree upon from time to time—and I would add that those customs exist only so long as nations in general agree to follow them and do follow them.

Chapter 4
Undue Influence as Coercive Offers in Clinical Trials[1]

Joan McGregor

Coercion has been conceptually connected with threats. Under the standard account of coercion, threats propose to make the victim "worse off" than his or her baseline, or where he or she was before the proposer intervened in the victim's causal nexus. This model of coercion that focuses only on the notion of threats does not go far enough to capture cases where the victim's vulnerability is taken advantage of to accomplish the coercion. In the kinds of cases I have in mind, no threats are used or needed. Clinical trials conducted in developing nations, for example, are at risk of taking advantage of the vulnerabilities of the subjects that can rise to the level of coercion. In this paper, I will consider the question whether in some instances clinical trials with vulnerable populations involve coercion that is accomplished not with threats but rather through offers.

There is widespread agreement that protection of the welfare and rights of research subjects, wherever they live, must be of the highest priority and not subordinated to the ends of research. Research subjects should not have their interests or welfare compromised for the ends of others. This protection of research subjects has been delineated as a human right in the *Nuremberg Code*; it requires the informed voluntary consent of all participants in experimental research.[2] The *Declaration of Helsinki*, drafted originally in 1964 by the World Medical Association, enumerated a list of duties and responsibilities compliance with which is expected of all physicians engaged in experimental research with humans and it specifies minimum rights for individuals participating in experimental research. Foremost among them is that there be informed consent. The World Health Organization (WHO), the health and human rights arm of the United Nations, established the Council for International Organizations of Medical Sciences

---

[1] I would like to thank the participants to the AMINTAPHIL conference on Coercion in St. Louis in October 2006. I would particularly like to thank Kenneth Kipnis who commented on this paper at the conference and the editors of this volume.

[2] "Trials of War Criminals Before the Nuremberg Military Tribunals under control Council Law No. 10," (US Govt. Printing Office 1949) reprinted in Judith Areen et al., *Law, Science and Medicine*, 2nd ed. (Eagan, MN: Foundation Press, 1996), pp. 996–998, Art. 1 [hereinafter Nuremberg Code].

(CIOMS) and released guidelines for researchers conducting experiments on human subjects in an international setting in 1982. The CIOMS guidelines serve as a guide for other countries seeking to institute their own regulations regarding research with human subjects. The guidelines require that the ethical review committees, e.g., Institutional Review Boards (IRBs), be "no less exacting than they would be in the case of research carried out in [the sponsoring] country."[3] These are the international standards addressing the ethics of the use of human subjects in research and they clearly enumerate a basic right to consent to research. The United States has a set of federal regulations for protecting human subjects, called the "Common Rule" (45 C.F.R. Part 46) which includes similar protections.

Consent is the central focus of these research guidelines. Consent can turn an action that is impermissible, touching someone else's body, into something that is permissible. Because of this "magical" power of consent, there is a tremendous amount of attention paid to the conditions surrounding the performative utterance of consent. Drawing on the wisdom of John Austin, consent is something we *do* with words.[4] Consent changes the rights and obligations of the actors. Nevertheless, it can fail due to certain infelicities. It can "misfire" and not alter the moral world for a variety of reasons, for instance, if consent was not freely given. Coerced consent is consent that has misfired.

Research with human subjects is an important vehicle to gain knowledge about drugs, medical therapies, and other therapeutic products. No one doubts whether there should be research trials with human subjects, nevertheless, research trials must ensure that subjects' participation is not secured by force, coercion, or deception. In the Nazi internment camps, many inmates were compelled to be research subjects, literally forced to submit to unspeakable atrocities under the guise of medical research. Those practices were clearly unacceptable no matter how beneficial the outcomes of the research purported to be. (Interestingly, the physicians who were tried for crimes against humanity at the Nuremberg trials continued to justify their actions on the basis of the benefit to scientific knowledge.) Threats to potential subjects to secure participation, for example, when prisoners are threatened with longer prison terms if they didn't agree to participate in experimentation, are also unacceptable as methods of securing human subjects for research. It is not a justification for coercion that the trial does not pose significant risks to the subjects. Coerced or deceived consent does not respect the subject's freedom to decide on his or her own what risks to assume. Overt force and coercion as was practiced in the Nazi experiments is quite obviously immoral and should not be practiced. Another

[3] "Proposed International Guidelines for Biomedical Research Involving Human Subjects," reprinted in *Ethics and Research on Human Beings: International Guidelines*, Z. Bankowski & R. J. Levin, eds. (Geneva: Proceedings of the 26th CIOMS conference, World Health Organization, 1993) Guideline 15.
[4] Austin, JL. *How to do things with Words* (Cambridge: Harvard University Press, 1975), pp. 16–45.

process flaw in securing human subjects for research is the use of deception. For instance, the type of deception that was practiced in the Tuskegee study, where a large group of uneducated black men were told that they were getting treatment for their disease but in fact were not, similarly undermines freedom. Beyond those blatant forms of undermining the freedom of human subjects, viz., force, coercion, and deception, there are the more subtle forms of undermining the freedom of the subjects of research and thereby causing consent to misfire. Because they are more subtle, their existence is more controversial.

Federal regulations that protect human subjects (known as the Common Rule) specify that research involving human subjects must have informed consent. Informed consent is undermined when there is coercion or "undue influence." (CFR 46.116). The Common Rule, further states that

> When one or all of the subjects are likely to be vulnerable to coercion or undue influence, such as children, prisoners, pregnant women, mentally disabled, economically or educationally disadvantaged persons, additional safeguards have been included in the study to protect the rights and welfare of these subjects. (46.111.b)

The Common Rule admonishes researchers to guard against "coercion" and "undue influence," since both can affect the voluntariness of the agent and thus the legitimacy of the consent. Tying coercion and undue influence to vulnerable populations is important. Vulnerable populations can include those with cognitive disabilities or deficiencies, children, the mentally disabled, and those vulnerable because of their circumstances, economic or educational deprivation or lack of other resources. All find themselves vulnerable in relation to the researcher because of his or her authority and knowledge and what he or she can offer them. Members of vulnerable populations are in a relatively weak bargaining position, a position of powerlessness, relative to the researcher. Consequently, the researcher can exploit his or her superior power and bargaining position.

In this paper, I want to explore the Common Rule's notion of "undue influence" as a form of coercion. I will argue for an understanding of undue influence in clinical trials as "coercive offers." The notion of vulnerable populations will play a central role in this analysis. Recently there has been controversy about the meaning and usefulness of the 'undue influence' criterion of the Common Rule. Ezekiel Emanuel, bioethicist for the NIH, in a number of recent articles on the undue influence criterion argues that the standard of undue influence is worthless, or, if not entirely worthless, redundant.[5] I think that his account is wrong and will show the important work (and often unnoticed work) that the criterion does (or should do). Emanuel's critique is that the notion of undue influence of research subjects is really about excessive and unreasonable risks that subjects might take on when the monetary incentive to participate is great. The proscription against undue influence in the Common Rule does not, according to Emanuel, do any extra work that

---

[5] Ezekiel Emanuel, "Undue Inducement: Nonsense on Stilts?," *American Journal of Bioethics*, v. 5, n. 5, 2005, p. 9.

couldn't be done by having Institutional Review Boards (IRBs) more closely scrutinize the risk/benefit ratio of research protocols and exclude research that is excessively risky.

Emanuel's analysis of undue influence is incorrect in several respects. The trouble starts with his four necessary elements of undue influence: (1) A good is offered in order to do something; (2) the offered good is excessive and thus irresistible; (3) this leads to poor judgment on the part of the offeree; and (4) that poor judgment leads to a high probability of a serious risk of harm. Only the first condition from his list, that a good is offered in exchange for something, is necessary for undue influence. The other conditions are too vague to be useful or are clearly not necessary conditions. Consider an example of an "undue influence" outside the research setting, the example of an impecunious mother with a very sick child and a lecherous millionaire.[6] The millionaire proposes to the impecunious mother that he will pay for the medical treatment that her child needs if she will become his mistress. Condition one—she is offered a good in exchange for doing something—is satisfied. How helpful are Emanuel's other conditions, for instance, the second condition—is the offer excessive? The notion of "excessive" is extremely dependent on the context. Having the millionaire pay for the surgery for her sick child is irresistible for this woman because she doesn't have other means to pay for it. Is Emanuel's third condition satisfied, namely, does Ms. Impecunious exercise poor judgment when she decides to take the lecherous millionaire up on his offer? If what is meant by exercising poor judgment are choices that go against one's self-interest, it is not clear that her choice to accept the offer is an exercise of poor judgment. In this case, whether it is in her interest or not depends on which interests one chooses to focus. From the perspective of her child's welfare, it is in the mother's interest to accept the offer; on the other hand, from the perspective of avoiding unwanted sexual interactions it is not. Many of our choices force us to pick from divergent interests. Accepting a job advances my interest in making a living but goes against my desire to be lazy and sleep late. Ms. Impecunious's choice to accept the offer would be a rational one, nevertheless, given her goal of getting medical treatment for her child.

The fourth condition is that the offered good leads to poor judgment in assessing the seriousness of the harm that may result from the proposal. Not all cases of undue influence involve serious harm. And what is considered serious harm will to some extent be a function of the agent's circumstances and values. For example, if Ms. Impecunious was a prostitute, she might view the proposed exchange of surgery for sex as not harmful since she willingly exchanges sex for money as her livelihood. Or consider a research case: Maternal-fetal HIV transmissions trials were carried out in developing nations in the 1990s. The study design involved the use of placebos even in the face of evidence that AZT significantly reduced vertical transmission of HIV. Pregnant women in Africa and other countries were asked to

---

[6] This example comes from Joel Feinberg.

consent to participate in these experiments even though that study design would not have been acceptable in industrialized nations. Were those women unduly influenced into participating in those trials given their miserable circumstances and their weak bargaining positions relative to the Western researchers? We will return to that question.

What's missing in Emanuel's approach is the wisdom of the Common Rule's attention to vulnerable populations and their susceptibility to undue influence. The Common Rule acknowledges that many people, because of their external circumstances or internal conditions are vulnerable, leaving them in a disadvantaged position for entering research trials. These vulnerabilities leave them in a relatively weak bargaining position. Their consent to participate may be less than fully voluntary because of the combination of external and internal conditions, for example, their lack of alternatives, their lack of understanding of the conditions of the clinical trials, their lack of power and status in society which may make them overly deferential, or fearful, or trusting. Questions of undue influence are distinct from questions of risk (although cases of undue influence may induce someone into a risky trial). Risks versus benefits of the study can be assessed independently to some degree of the particular circumstances of potential participants and should be done by IRBs. Without considering the specifics of given individuals' situations or characteristics, IRBs can assess the risks and benefits of a clinical trial. This is not fully accurate since if a country is in the midst of a deadly outbreak of a virus without treatment options, for example, they would be willing to take risks that outside of that epidemic would not be warranted.

The Common Rule specifies that the researcher must guard against coercion and undue influence (I would include deception as well) of the subjects since they can affect the voluntariness of the agent, thereby vitiating informed consent. These criteria concern the autonomy of the potential subject not her welfare (although these can and do often go together).

Stepping back a bit, recall what coercion is about. Coercion is a central issue in moral, political, and legal philosophy because it undermines the freedom of the victim and renders his or her consent invalid. Undermining freedom without justification (or adequate justification) is not morally acceptable, particularly in societies that value individual autonomy. Coercers ensure that their victims "choose" the option that they, the coercers, want. Because the coercer effectively forces the coerced to choose the option that the coercer wants, because the coerced does not really consent, we judge the choice to be other than free. By proposing only unwelcome options, the coercer places the coerced between "a rock and a hard place," forcing a choice between the lesser of evils.[7]

---

[7] Joel Feinberg used the idea of "unwelcome" alternatives. See his *Harm to Self* (New York: Oxford University Press, 1989), especially chs. 23–24.

A few important facts about coercion:

1. Some instances of coercion are morally acceptable or justified instances and others are not. Enforcement of just laws is a prime instance of justified coercion. The law threatens that if you do x (some unacceptable action) then the law will punish you.
2. Not all coercive threats coerce. For some people, a coercive threat may work and coerce them. For others, it may prove irrelevant to their motivation; they may have other sufficient reasons to act as the coercer desires. I do not murder people who frustrate me. But this is not because of the coercive threat of the law. I have independent and motivationally sufficient reasons for not killing. Alternatively, a murderer may acknowledge the law's threat, but perform an unlawful action anyway. He may be motivationally immune to the law's threat; the sanction may be too weak or the probability of its imposition too slight or his will to kill simply beyond the reach of reasons.
3. Coercion does not take away choice. The victim is not literally precluded from choosing the option that the coercer doesn't want. Even in the most extreme case of "your money or your life", people have not given over their money to the robber. Coercion, then, is distinct from compulsion, which literally forces the victim to do what the compeller wants. Dragging someone handcuffed along the street leaves the victim with no choice, not an unpleasant one. Physically forcing a woman, with overwhelming physical strength, to have intercourse, is compulsion; whereas threatening her life if she fails to submit to intercourse is coercion.[8]
4. The coerciveness of the threat or the effect on the victim and the differential between the threatened sanction and the sought after act are relative to the victim's position and preferences. This is pretty obvious in the law-breaking example. For many repeat offenders, the coerciveness of the law is minimal. For others, the threatened sanction is sufficient to coerce them to obey the law (even though they don't want to do so).

A more general point about factors that affect voluntariness is that voluntariness lies on a continuum. An act may be fully voluntary, less than fully voluntary due to external or internal forces that affect the voluntariness of the action, or fully involuntary. As noted above, coercion does not literally preclude the actor from acting in a particular way. Instead, it alters the options available so that the coerced is left with only harmful or unwelcome options from which to choose. It makes the choice to do what the coercer wants less than fully voluntary. The threshold between voluntary and nonvoluntary actions depends on the context, normative and otherwise. Coercion cannot render an act of murder nonvoluntary and therefore excused. But it can render lesser crimes nonvoluntary and thus excused. And standards for legally valid consent vary with the context. Feminists complain that criminal rape

---

[8] See Anderson's and Leiser's contributions to this volume.

laws typically set the standard for consent too low, especially when compared to other areas of the law where the moral stakes are presumably not as high.[9]

Coercive proposals are standardly understood to include only threats. Threats are easily detected since they propose to make the victim "worse off" than his or her normal (*ex ante*) baseline.[10] The proposal, "Your money or your life" proposes to make the person "worse off" than she was before the proposal was made. Before the proposal, the person could have both his money and his life; after the proposal that option is closed. Or the proposal, "Have your villagers participate in the clinical trial or we will shut down all the medical services to your village" makes the villagers "worse off" than before the researchers' arrival. The standard analysis of coercion starts with distinguishing whether the proposal is a threat or an offer. Threats propose to make people worse off relative to their normal or expected baseline if they fail to go along with what the coercer wants; offers propose to make people better off relative to their normal or expected baseline. Threats provide fewer options and worse ones and offers propose more options, thereby presumably opening up freedom.

This distinction between threats and offers is not accurate or helpful. First, many offers can be translated into threats and vice versa (an offer that you can't refuse, for example, "If the villagers agree to participate in the research trials, the village will continue to have medical services."). Second, identifying the appropriate baseline, the normal or expected course of events, needed to distinguish threats from offers is difficult and controversial. The richer the baseline, the more threats we will see. If we build into our baseline accepted normative requirements (for example, that everyone ought to have access to medical services), then pointing to a possible future violation of those requirements will constitute a threat (for example, suggesting that someone might lose access to medical services if she doesn't do x). On the other hand, the more impoverished the baseline, the more we limit the baseline to only what can be anticipated as a descriptive matter of fact in light of natural causal

---

[9] See my *Is it Rape?* (Ashgate Publisher, 2006).

[10] See the literature on coercion: Bayles, Michael D., "A Concept of Coercion," in Pennock and Chapman eds., *Coercion* (Chicago, IL: Aldene-Atherton, 1972), pp. 16–29; Benditt, Theodore, "Threats and Offers," *The Personalist*, v. 58, 1979, pp. 382–384; Feinberg, Joel, *Harm to Self*. (New York: Oxford University Press, 1989); Frankfurt, Harry, "Coercion and Moral Responsibility," in *The Importance of What We Care About*. (New York: Cambridge University Press, 1988); Gorr, Michael, "Toward a Theory of Coercion," *Canadian Journal of Philosophy*, v. 16, 1986, pp. 383–406; Gunderson, Martin, "Threats and Coercion," *Canadian Journal of Philosophy*, v. 9, 1979, pp. 247–259; Haksar, Vinit, "Coercive Proposals," *Political Theory*, v. 4, 1976, pp. 65–79; Held, Virginia, "Coercion and Coercive Offers," in Pennock and Chapman, *supra*. McGregor, Joan, "Bargaining Advantages and Coercion in the Market," *Philosophy Research Archives*, v. 14, 1988–1989, pp. 23–50; Nozick, Robert, "Coercion," in *Philosophy, Science, and Method: Essays in Honor of Ernest Nagel*, Sidney Morgenbesser, Patrick Suppes, and Morton White, eds. (New York: St. Martin's Press, 1969), pp. 440–472; Wertheimer, Alan, *Coercion*. (Princeton: Princeton University Press, 1987); Zimmerman, David, "Coercive Wage Offers," *Philosophy and Public Affairs*, v. 10, 1981, pp. 121–145.

laws, the fewer threats we will see. On an impoverished baseline of this sort, a passing boater who proposes to save a drowning swimmer for $50,000 would make an offer rather than a threat and therefore could not coerce the swimmer into paying the sum to save his life. Of course, if we suppose that drowning swimmers have a right to unconditional rescue by passing boaters, then we we'll see a threat and coercion, rather than an offer, in this case. If we must distinguish threats from offers, we must settle on one or another conception of the relevant baseline. But notwithstanding a good deal of philosophical work on this front, the discussion continues without resolution.

Apart from the problem of distinguishing offers from threats, why suppose that only threats coerce? Proposals that make the recipients "better off" than their *status quo ex ante* (however we determine the baseline) may share characteristics of coercion, for example, by being the only eligible option for the recipient in a miserable situation. Offers make their recipients better off than their normal course of events, but when recipients of those proposals are in miserable circumstances with no other options and the proposer *takes advantage* of those situations, they can have a similar effect on the victim as a threat. It is important to notice that the more miserable a person's situation is, the easier it is to offer to make them better off (no matter how stingy, unfair, or exploitative the offer) and get them to do what you want. The consequence of the view that only threats can be coercive is that the worse off people are, the more vulnerable they are, and the harder it is to coerce them since it is difficult to make them worse off than they already are. This seems a perverse conclusion. Vulnerable populations we should think of as more susceptible to coercion, not less so. Getting the Congolese prisoner who is fed only twice a week by the warden to participate in a nontherapeutic and risky medical trial does not require the threat of harm if he fails to participate. The offer of four meals a week in exchange to agreeing to participate would suffice. People in miserable, vulnerable situations can be influenced, induced, "forced" with minor offers, to do all kinds of things. Would it be a fully voluntary choice to participate in research in the Congolese prisoner example?

Linking the 'undue influence' condition and the notion of vulnerable populations in the Common Rule acknowledges that the "worse off" people are (worse off in different senses), the easier it is to make them "better off" relative to their baseline and, thereby, *unfairly take advantage* of their miserable situations. That advantage taking can result in coercive offers, offers that they "can't" refuse given their miserable situation and thereby undermine the legitimacy of their consent. Ms. Impecunious is a prime example of this; the lecherous millionaire used her vulnerability to "force" her to do what he wants, leaving her with one eligible option. This goes on in many arenas. Poor workers in the developing world accept positions working long hours, with little pay, in dangerous conditions, but those job "offers" make them "better off" than their *status quo ante*. People who are in desperate situations can be made "better off" by offers that would be unacceptable to people whose normal course of events are not desperate or deprived in some way. Contrary to what Emanuel said about undue influence requiring "excessive" amounts of monetary compensation, people in miserable circumstances don't require excessive goods to be "induced" to go along.

Clinical trials in developing nations are open to the charge of exploiting the vulnerable by taking advantage of their lack of options and their dependency on researchers for medical care. Depending on how bad the agents' circumstances are, the clinical trial (the "offer"), may be their only option, raising then the specter of coercion. This is the problem of undue influence. The proposal to enter the trial, with the promised good, no matter how meager the good is or how risky or unfair the trial is, may still make her "better off" relative to her miserable baseline. Under standard coercion analysis, these proposals would not therefore be coercive since the person is being made "better off" than before the trial.

Undue influence might be referred to as "coercive offers." [11] They are *offers* because they propose to make the person "better off" relative to his or her baseline, they hold out a good or option for the recipient that wasn't there before, but they are *coercive* since, given the recipient's lack of options, the proposal is likely to present the only eligible choice (all victims of coercion have a choice, nevertheless, the consequences of not going along with the proposal is the greater evil), the proposer takes advantage of that person's vulnerability, and offers them an unfair deal. For extremely impoverished people with no medical alternatives, the offer of any medical treatment even in trials where they have a 50% chance of getting no treatment (a placebo trial) is better than their current alternative of no medical treatment. Not just any offer that an agent "can't" refuse because of lack of options is going to be coercive. When the proposer takes *unfair advantage* of the person's vulnerability and offers her an unfair deal because of that person's lack of options, then it is coercive. They are coerced to accept the unfair offer given their miserable circumstances. Offers of money or other resources for impoverished people with little or no alternatives may have them seeing only the promised reward—without regard to the conditions on getting it. Combine those conditions with populations who are illiterate and deferential to the role of the authority of the medical professional and you have a situation that is ripe for coercion.

The Common Rule acknowledges that threats can coerce and thereby undermine the voluntariness of research subjects but it also recognizes that participants can be unduly influenced, coerced, with promises of goods, particularly when they have severely limited options. The undue influence condition guards against the taking advantage of the vulnerable. It addresses two moral issues—the issue of undermining voluntariness due to the weak bargaining position of vulnerable populations, and the issue of the unfair sharing of the burdens of research since the vulnerable are more likely to be induced into research, thereby shouldering the *burdens* of research, without receiving its benefits. This is one of the reasons that medical research carried out in developing nations is morally problematic since it is often unlikely that the research subjects or their community will share in the medical benefits of research.

The better off/worse off distinction relative to a baseline, used by most accounts of coercion, ignores the power relationships that occur when there are radically

---

[11] See my "Bargaining Advantages and Coercion in the Market," *supra*, pp. 23–50.

disparate bargaining strengths between the agents.[12] In assessing the coerciveness of the relationship between a researcher and a research subject, one must first attend to the relative strengths of the bargaining positions between the parties involved. Coercion involves exercising power over another; in the research context, it involves exercising superior bargaining power.[13] Lack of bargaining power comes in many forms: lack of knowledge and abilities to gain information, of economic resources, of medical resources, and of status or power due to socially enforced gender, class, or racial roles. In the research domain, other factors play a role. Researchers have authority in their positions as medical or scientific professionals and potential subjects believe (often erroneously) that researchers would only propose to them medicines that are for their benefit. This is the "therapeutics misconception"; the belief that a medical practitioner would only give you something that was for your therapeutic benefit. Since vulnerable persons are more prone to the therapeutic misconception, researchers must be more vigilant about the possibilities of subjects entering trials based on false or misleading information. Generally vulnerable populations are more susceptible to a range of pressures or misconceptions.

Two conditions for having bargaining power sufficient to coerce another are that the weaker party is *dependent* in some way on the stronger party (e.g., there are no other options or potential exchange partners), and the stronger party has influence over whether some significant *evil* occurs to the weaker party (such as loss of life, health, security).[14] If the stronger party takes *advantage* of these conditions of the vulnerable person, by offering a worse deal than he would otherwise, then this is not just exploitation but coercion.

As researchers move clinical trials to developing nations, where there are large numbers of diseased persons with few medical alternatives, high illiteracy levels, and little by way of governmental regulation of trials, there is the likelihood that the populations will be vulnerable and susceptible to undue influence to enter clinical trials. The concern over participants' consent should not be limited to the problems of deception or misconception. It should extend to the problem of undue influence and coercive offers. Otherwise there is a risk that participants' consent will be compromised by offers that unduly influence their choice to participate.

Consider two cases of clinical trials done in developing nations in the last decade that generated heated debates about the legitimacy of the consent in the trials.

Pfizer went to Cato, Nigeria after a meningitis epidemic started in 1996 to test the effectiveness of Trovan, a broad-spectrum antibiotic, on sick children. The drug Trovan had not been approved for use on children. The epidemic provided Pfizer with an opportunity to test out its oral antibiotic on hundreds of dangerously sick children. [15]

---

[12] *Ibid.* 24.

[13] *Ibid.* 25.

[14] *Ibid.* 34.

[15] A group of parents of the children in Nigeria sued Pfizer; Ajuda Ismaila ADAMU et al. v. Pfizer No.04 Civ. 1351(WHP) USDC, S.D. New York, November 8; and see "Pfizer Faces Criminal Charges in Nigeria," by Joe Stephens, *Washington Post*, Wednesday, May 30, 2007; p. A10.

At least 15 maternal-fetal HIV transmissions trials were carried out in developing nations in the 1990s. Nine were sponsored by CDC or NIH. The study design involved the use of placebos even in the face of evidence that AZT significantly reduced vertical transmission of HIV and was the standard of care in developed nations. Many children whose mothers were enrolled in these trials were put at risk of HIV infection.[16]

The news reports on the research design of the HIV trials that were conducted in Africa and other developing countries raised public awareness about the ethical problems inherent in conducting clinical trials in these countries.[17] Those clinical trials were designed to examine whether a smaller dose of AZT than had already been shown effective in reducing the transmission rate from mother to child, a protocol called 076, would reduce the vertical transmission of HIV. The trials were randomized clinical trials (RCT) with the control arm being given placebos and the active arm given AZT in a significantly reduced dose compared to 076. One of the central criticisms of the design of these studies was that since it was known that AZT (076) would reduce vertical transmission, it was unjustified to give the control group a placebo—an inert substance. There was an efficacious treatment at this point—a *standard of care*—and these trials did not give the control arm that treatment.[18] It was argued that these pregnant women were unduly influenced to enter these trials since it was unlikely that they understood the significance of the placebo arm, believed they were getting treated for their disease, and had no other options for medical treatment for HIV.

Many charged that the HIV trials violated international guidelines, including the *Declaration of Helsinki*, which sets out ethical guidelines for clinical trials in an international setting. In particular they argued that the trials violated the human rights of the subjects because the research design went against international norms, specifically the norm of what was morally acceptable to give to control groups. The *Declaration of Helsinki* states that "[i]n any medical study, every patient—including those of a control group, if any –should be assured of the *best proven diagnostic and therapeutic method*."[19] It is unacceptable for an enrolled subject to get no effective treatment for her illness when there is a known efficacious treatment. Were this allowed, subjects would be harmed by participation in the study. This makes placebo trials acceptable only where there is no proven efficacious standard of care.

---

[16] Joe Stephens, "The Body Hunters: Exporting Human Experiments: Where Profits and lives Hang in the Balance: Finding an abundance of Subjects and Lack of Oversight Aboard, Big Drug Companies Test Offshore to Speed Products to Market," *Washington Post*, Dec. 17, 2000, p. A1.

[17] Peter Lurie and Sidney Wolfe, "Unethical Trials of Interventions to Reduce Perinatal Transmission of the Human Immunodeficiency Virus in Developing Countries," *New England Journal of Medicine*, v. 337, n. 12, 1997, pp. 853–856; for a defense of the HIV trials see Harold Varmus and David Satcher "Ethical Complexities of Conducting Research in Developing Countries," *New England Journal of Medicine*, v. 337, n. 14, 1997, pp. 1003–1005.

[18] It should be noted that the pharmaceutical companies normally provide the drugs without charge for clinical trials.

[19] *Declaration of Helsinki*. October 2000. 52nd World Medical Assembly. Edinburgh. Available at http://www.wma.net/e/policy/b3.htm. Emphasis added.

These women, however, were in a vulnerable position without medical and financial options; they were HIV positive and pregnant and were offered services and medicines to enter this clinical trial. How many of them understood the details of the research design is unclear.

Defenders of the African HIV trials argue that these trials provided access to valuable medicines that the people of those countries wouldn't have had without these trials. They argue that if we don't use people in developing nations in clinical trials we are denying those people the possible benefits of the drug. African nations have tremendous need for drugs to treat HIV and AIDS and they wouldn't have access to the drugs at all without the trials. They also point out the *standard of care in these countries* was *no treatment* for pregnant women with HIV. Defenders of the HIV trials assume that if research subjects are *not* made worse off then the design is morally acceptable.[20] That takes us back to the view that coercion is only possible in cases where the participants are made worse off.

As noted earlier, individuals in miserable circumstances can be made unfair offers, even incredibly unfair offers, that will make them better off than their *status quo ex ante*. This happens when A, the proposer, takes opportunistic advantage of B's lack of options and pressing need, to get B to choose the option that A wants. The worse off B's circumstances are, the easier it is to make him "better off," since almost any deal will improve his *status quo ex ante*. The most desperate people will be made "better off" relative to their baseline by the most unscrupulous proposals. Opportunistic exploiters can coerce, by offering the vulnerable person a miserable option as their only option.

Consider the details of the Pfizer case: Was there undue influence of subjects who agreed to be participants in the Nigerian meningitis case? Pfizer came into a country that was facing a horrendous childhood epidemic and set up a clinic.[21] Pfizer's staff set up next to Médecins Sans Frontières (MSF) and MSF claimed that Pfizer took away their local medical staff. Desperate parents brought their sick children in for treatment. The parents alleged later, when many of their children died or suffered severe disabilities, that Pfizer did not adequately inform them that they were enrolling their children in a clinical trial as opposed to merely receiving standard treatment from these Western physicians. There were neither signed informed consent forms from the families nor any evidence that they had been verbally told that they agreed to be part of a clinical trial. In this case, Pfizer, by quickly moving into this epidemic situation to test their drug on very sick children, displayed the nature of an opportunistic exploiter. Pfizer knew that confusion reigned and seized the chance to use those desperate conditions for its own advantage, to quickly get subjects for a clinical trial of its new drug. Parents had the

---

[20] See Ruth Macklin, "Bioethics, Vulnerability, and Protection," *Bioethics*, v.17, n. 5–6, 2003, p. 140.
[21] In the United States it is difficult to imagine that a clinical trial during an epidemic with children would ever be approved, particularly when there was an available treatment.

alternative of the MSF, but Pfizer was clever about culling enough children for its own purpose and thereby preventing those families from availing themselves of the treatment from MSF (who was giving the standard of care).

But what about the argument that the drug researchers are making the sick in developing nations "better off" than they would be otherwise? That claim may or may not be true in the Nigerian case. Other groups were there to give aid, such as MSF, and but for the intervention of Pfizer, MSF might have helped more sick children with better treatments—in this case with injectable antibiotics. But does it matter that without the intervention the sick would be worse off? In the HIV vertical transmission cases it is true that most of the women in the trial did not have medical alternatives. Without the clinical trial they would not have been treated with any drugs to prevent the transmission of HIV to their newborns. This fact is significant to many theorists.[22] But what is the relevance really? The fact that a proposal makes someone better off than his *ex ante* position does not morally sanitize the exchange. We have noted earlier that the worse off someone is, the easier it is to offer to make him or her better off. If we exclude as possible exploitation and coercion cases where individuals are made better off, then the hardest people to coerce or exploit would be those who are the worst off. The people who are "worse off," who suffer from the worst poverty and disease, who are the most vulnerable, will be the most difficult to coerce! That can't be right. We certainly would not want to say that just any research proposal that makes people "better off" relative to their *ex ante* baseline is morally permissible because it does not run the risk of undermining the subjects' consent. The better off/ worse off standard relative to the baseline of the individual is problematic since there are so many people, particularly in the developing world, who are in such desperate situations that they can be expected reliably to "consent" to almost anything that might improve their condition. Consequently, for judgments of exploitation, coercion, and deception we need to inquire into more than whether a person is made better off by an offer from a researcher. In clinical trials we are asking subjects to participate in the trial for research purposes. Entering this relationship creates a duty of care on the part of the researcher—a fiduciary relationship. That duty will often be carried out by providing the control arm with what the researcher *knows* is the best standard of care, or otherwise by not taking advantage of their vulnerable position.

In many cases of coercion or undue influence, A, the coercer, is not responsible for the misery of B. A didn't create the unsavory conditions of B. In the case of the Nigerians, Pfizer can say that it is not its fault that the people lack medical resources and find themselves in miserable conditions. Nevertheless, the fact that A has not created the terrible situation of B does not mean that A can use that situation for his own profit. Central to the notion of vulnerable populations is that they are relatively bad off and thereby more open to exploitation, coercion, or advantage taking on the

[22] David Resnik, "Developing Drugs for the Developing World: An Economic, Legal, Moral, and Political Dilemma," *Developing World Bioethics*, v. 1, n. 1, 2001, pp. 11–32; Harold Varmus and David Satcher, "Ethical Complexities of Conducting Research in Developing Countries," *supra.*

part of the researcher. Obviously if we created (and sometimes allowed to go on) the misery or desperation of others, then we have moral responsibilities in that situation. Notice, however, how difficult it is to determine whether someone is responsible for the miserable baseline condition of another. In the African case, it is argued that the standard of care was no treatment, so the clinical trials with placebos made the subjects better off. But, Udo Schuklenk argues:

> [T]here is no such thing as a fixed local standard of care. Rather, the local standard of care in, for example, India, is a standard of care determined by the prices set by Western pharmaceutical multinationals. The only reason why the trials Lurie et al. criticized took place at all, is the pricing schedule set by the manufacturer of that drug. Glaxo-Wellcome therefore, more than anything else, determines what is described by some bioethicists and clinical researchers as the 'local standard of care'....It we take the local standard of care idea to logical conclusion, it would be in the interest of Western companies to keep the prices sufficiently high to prevent many people from access to drugs, because this would legitimize further research on other drugs that could not otherwise take place.[23]

The influence and effect of big multinational pharmaceutical companies on drug prices raises the question of their complicity in the low baselines of the people in the developing world. The excuse that the trials make people "better off" is convenient on a number of levels. Having the people in these nations so deprived provides an ample supply of "volunteers." And it provides a powerful incentive to maintain the *status quo*. But even if we reject the responsibility of the pharmaceutical companies for the terrible conditions of many in the developing world, it does not follow that it is morally acceptable to *take advantage* of their misery. Those clinical trials can still be exploitative and coercive. More globally, Western governments themselves are complicitious in the poverty and paucity of good leadership in many of these developing nations. Many dictatorships were supported by the West for their own interests, and the governments were permitted to enrich themselves and indebt the citizens, further depleting the funding for medical resources and leaving the populous in miserable conditions.

Because of the impact of globalization, clinical trials now function as a one-way street. Developed nations use the developing world to test drugs for the developed world's peoples and corporate profit. This arrangement is unjust. The developing world is bearing the burdens and the developed world is reaping the benefits. This injustice has been perpetrated by exploiting the vulnerabilities of the people in the developing world. In nations where there is a tremendous amount of disease and very little in the way of health care researchers run the risk of the most egregious form of exploitation, coercion and undue influence because of the desperate needs of the people. Certainly all these trials should be considered as ones with "vulnerable populations" or ones that need heightened levels of oversight. The designation of "vulnerable population" should mean that researchers, IRBs, and other oversight agencies must be particularly careful about the procedures for consent and other

---

[23] Sckuklenk, "Protecting the Vulnerable: Testing Times for Clinical Research Ethics," *Social Science and Medicine*, v. 51, 2000, pp. 969–977.

ingredients in research designs. There are reasons to believe that subjects drawn from vulnerable populations may not understand the information in the consent process, or that their ability to make fully voluntary choices is compromised in some way. People in developing nations who suffer crushing poverty and illness are not going to be in the best position to decide what an acceptable balance of risks to benefits is. Their rational abilities may be diminished due to poor nutrition and illness as well. And yet, due to their impoverished circumstances they may well see these experiments as a rational choice, as the best of bad alternatives. But, offering to make someone "better off" than his or her *status quo ante* does not preclude exploitation, coercion or moral censure.

Part II
Coercion and the State: Justification and Limits

Chapter 5
Coercion, Justice, and Democracy

Alistair M. Macleod*

1   Two Concepts of Coercion?

I begin with two quotations, one from Alan Wertheimer's booklength treatment of the concept of coercion, the second from G.A. Cohen's critique, in his Gifford Lectures, of the Rawlsian doctrine of the "basic structure as subject."
Wertheimer writes:

> At the most general level, there are two views about coercion. One view holds that coercion claims are essentially value-free, that whether one is coerced into doing something is an ordinary empirical question. Another view holds that coercion claims are moralized, that they involve moral judgments at their core. I argue that the second view is correct.[1]

These two views offer competing accounts of what Wertheimer calls "coercion claims." Paradigms of coercion claims are such claims as the following: "He made me do it," "I was forced into doing it," "I did it under duress," "He coerced me," and "I didn't act of my own free will."[2]
After noting that the "basic structure" of society is sometimes taken by Rawls to comprise a society's "(legally) coercive" institutions, G.A. Cohen writes:

> In this widespread interpretation of what Rawls intends by the 'basic structure' of a society, that structure is legible in the provisions of its constitution, in such specific legislation as may be required to implement those provisions, and in further legislation and policy which are of central importance but which resist formulation in the constitution itself.[3]

Critical though Cohen is of various features of the doctrine of the "basic structure as subject," it is clear that he finds absolutely no paradox in the Rawlsian view that (legally) coercive institutional rules can satisfy principles of justice.

---

*I am grateful to David Reidy and Walter Riker for their excellent editorial suggestions and to Colin Macleod and Margaret Moore for their invaluable help in the editing process.

[1] Alan Wertheimer, *Coercion*, (Princeton: Princeton University Press, 1987), Preface, p. xi.

[2] Wertheimer, *op cit*, p. 3.

[3] G.A.Cohen, *If You're an Egalitarian, How Come You're So Rich?* (New York: Oxford University Press, 2000), pp. 136–137.

These quotations are of interest for my purposes in this paper because they point to two very different contexts in which the notion of coercion has an application.[4]

In one of these—typical of the sorts of cases Wertheimer discusses—the coercing and coerced agents are identified, along with the action performed by the latter under coercion. In this sort of situation, interest focuses on such questions as (a) whether the action was voluntary, (b) whether it's an action for which responsibility is properly imputable to the agent, and (c) whether the agent should be relieved, wholly or partially, of the blame that would otherwise be appropriate, given the nature of the action. Blame would normally be appropriate because what has been done would typically be regarded as morally wrong were it not for the fact that the agent has been coerced into performing it. The fact of coercion—provided the coercion at issue is of the required sort and degree—normally serves to excuse the agent (wholly or partially) but the action may still have to be viewed as wrong in some important sense. It's because this sort of case is taken to be central to Wertheimer's discussion that he devotes so much attention to the status of coercion as an excusing or exculpatory consideration.

In the other sort of context, what is at issue is the coercive character of the institutional arrangements through which the state articulates, interprets, applies, and enforces the rules, substantive and procedural, that give content and structure to the institutional framework within which individuals have to live their lives. While the arrangements and the rules may be characterized as "coercive" in the sense at issue, it seems not to be the case that, whenever an individual member of society does what is required by these rules (or refrains from doing what these rules proscribe), he or she is normally either said or thought to be acting under "coercion." Acts of law-observance are not normally seen as coerced acts. Relatedly, the acts in question aren't presumed to be acts that would be wrong if the coercive rules requiring them didn't so much as exist. Nor do questions typically arise about whether the acts are voluntary, or about whether responsibility for their performance is properly imputable, or about whether (any degree of) blame attaches to their performance. On the contrary, it is entirely consistent with the recognition of a society's institutions as "coercive" in the sense here at issue to regard the acts of normal law-abiding individuals as (a) entirely voluntary actions, (b) actions for the performance of which full responsibility is normally imputable, and (c) actions that are fully justified rather than fully or partially excused. I say that (a), (b), and (c) are **consistent with** recognition of the coerciveness of institutional arrangements (in the sense of "coerciveness" under discussion) because it depends, of course, on whether the arrangements in question (and the coercive rules they embody) are themselves morally defensible arrangements (and rules). The point is that their coercive character in no way rules out the possibility that they may well be (found to be) morally defensible arrangements and rules.

---

[4] Whether these different contexts also point to the need to distinguish two **concepts** of coercion is a question I don't pursue here, despite the provocative heading I provide for this section of the paper.

When attention focuses on the second of these uses of the notion of coercion, a question that naturally arises is how coercive institutional rules are to be justified. This is the principal question I want to discuss in what follows.

2 Some Clarificatory Remarks

(i) It's important to distinguish between two very general types of answers to the question how coercive institutional arrangements are to be justified. On the one hand, the content of the rules, both substantive and procedural, embedded in coercive institutional arrangements may be held to be in conformity with the relevant justificatory norms, whether these are thought to be principles of morality of some sort or, more specifically, principles of justice. On the other hand, whether or not the (substantive and procedural) rules embedded in coercive institutional arrangements can be represented as morally defensible in virtue of their content, the processes by which they have come to be adopted may be held to be defensible processes—defensible, again, either in the sense that they are (in some general way) morally acceptable processes or, more specifically, in the sense that they are processes that satisfy principles of procedural justice.

(ii) Since what makes institutional rules coercive is the nature of the sanctions attached by the state to non-compliance with them, there are at least two questions to be asked. The first, while recognizing that the rules in question have sanctions attached to them, asks merely whether there is a moral justification for the requirements and prohibitions that give content to these rules when questions about the appropriateness of the penalty provisions linked to them are bracketed. The second asks expressly about the defensibility of the penalty provisions themselves. Thus, it's one thing to ask whether the state is justified in having on the books laws that prohibit murder or assault, and another to ask whether it would be morally defensible for the punishment for murder to be death and the punishment for assault life imprisonment. The first of these questions can be asked independently of the second. Indeed, the second question has to be faced only if the rules requiring or forbidding actions of certain sorts under threat of penalty are themselves morally defensible rules. Where there is no moral justification for these requirements and prohibitions, it will be a foregone conclusion that there cannot be any moral justification for the infliction of punishment on those who violate the rules. In what follows I will examine questions of the first sort. However, it should be noted that even if it could be shown, in the ways I explore, that given institutional rules enforced by the state are in principle morally defensible rules, the question whether the penalty provisions linked to these rules are themselves morally defensible would remain to be determined. It must consequently be conceded that even when the constraints on individual conduct imposed by a society's coercive institutional arrangements are thought to be morally defensible, the particular enforcement devices employed by the state (including the penal provisions of the criminal code) may be open to serious moral objections.

(iii) It is sometimes supposed that there is always a prima facie objection to coercive rules because they restrict the freedom of those who are subject to them. This argument rests on the assumption that freedom as such is a good thing, and that there is therefore a standing case for protecting it, other things being equal. The assumption, however, is false. For example, the freedom to kill people, or assault them, is not a good thing, even prima facie. Rules that prohibit such acts under threat of punishment—and such rules are, of course, veritable paradigms of the coercive rules that make up the criminal law—cannot be objected to on the ground that they restrict the freedom to act in these ways.

(iv) It might be thought that the obvious way to mount the required moral justification for a society's coercive institutional arrangements is to try to represent these as arrangements to which the members have consented, while also holding that in the absence of such consent, the arrangements would be simply indefensible. There are two objections to this strategy. The first is that there seems to be no plausible interpretation of "consent" in this sort of context under which the coercive institutional arrangements in any known society could be represented as arrangements that all the society's members have consented to. The second is, that even if, miraculously, there happened to be this sort of universal consent, the fact of consent to institutional arrangements does not guarantee their moral acceptability. **What** is being consented to must also satisfy certain (consent-independent) moral requirements. Consent to egregiously unjust arrangements, for example, doesn't show that the arrangements are morally defensible.

(v) A distinction is sometimes drawn between the moral defensibility of institutional arrangements and their "legitimacy." While I have no wish to deny that there may be contexts in which it is important to highlight issues concerning the "legitimacy", as distinct from the moral defensibility, of the authority exercised by states, the question I want to explore is whether it is possible for coercive institutional rules to be represented as justified by being shown to be **morally defensible**. If they can, I think my own view would be that their "legitimacy" would also be assured, but I recognize that this is still a controversial view, one for which I shall not be able to argue in this paper. However, I do not wish even to **claim** that the "legitimacy" issue collapses into the moral defensibility issue. Even if the moral defensibility of coercive institutional arrangements goes hand-in-hand with recognition of their "legitimacy", the converse need not be true. The moral defensibility of coercive arrangements may be a sufficient condition of their "legitimacy" without also being a necessary condition. Indeed, it seems likely that, once the distinction is drawn in some appropriate way between the moral defensibility and the (mere) "legitimacy" of coercive institutional arrangements, arrangements that fail to meet the (somewhat demanding) moral defensibility requirements, may nevertheless have to be seen as satisfying the (presumably less demanding) criteria for "legitimacy." However, these are complicated questions, and no answers to them are presupposed by the argument of the present paper.

While I want in what follows to leave room for the view that criteria of "legitimacy" provide a possible basis for the defense of coercive institutional rules, the focus of the discussion will be on the question whether such rules can be shown to be justified by direct appeal either to principles of justice or to the democratic ideal. I want to ask two questions. (1) Under what conditions are these successful ways of casting a society's "coercive" rules in a favorable light? (2) How far do these justifications diverge? Indeed, do they, in the end, converge—perhaps because the democratic ideal, in its most readily defensible version, is itself a justice-grounded ideal?

3   Coercive Institutional Arrangements and Principles of Justice

I want first to contrast two very general—ostensibly justice-based—approaches to the question whether the coercive institutional arrangements of a society can be regarded, appropriately, as morally defensible. One of these, which offers a rather "thin" view of what justice requires of institutional arrangements, seems to be rather plainly inadequate: if it were the best that could be offered from the standpoint of justice, a justice-based defense of coercive institutional rules couldn't succeed. The other approach provides a much richer account of what makes institutional arrangements just, and it is the sort of account that helps show how coercive institutional arrangements that satisfy the requirements of justice might thereby be represented as defensible arrangements.

3.1   *Justice as Equality (or Consistency, or Uniformity) of Treatment*

According to the first of these contrasting approaches, what justice crucially requires of the coercive rules that give content and structure to institutional arrangements is that they be applied and enforced impartially. All who are subject to the demands on them of the rules must be accorded equal treatment. All, and all equally, must be subject to these rules and the rules must be applied and enforced without fear or favor by those whose responsibility it is to determine whether or not there has, in particular cases, been compliance with them. This is a view of justice that has a number of familiar formulations. For example, there is the view that respect for "the rule of law"—interpreted narrowly to mean little more than that what the state requires of the members of a society must be mediated by consistently interpreted and applied general rules—is what is distinctive about just institutional arrangements. Again, there is the view that commitment to equality under the law—on a minimalist understanding of this ideal according to which it does not call for the content of the law itself to meet certain standards—is what is centrally important if a society's institutional arrangements are to be just. Yet again, there is the view that the hallmark of a just institutional order is its "equal treatment" of all who are subject to its rules. And so on.

It is no doubt true that when justice is conceived, narrowly, as consisting in the consistent application of institutional rules the individual members of a society can make decisions about how to live their lives on the basis of stable expectations about how they are going to be treated by the state as the guardian of society's coercive institutional arrangements. It can be objected, however, that stabilizing people's expectations through consistency in the application of institutional rules is only a good thing when the rules in question are reasonably benign rules. If all that justice, conceived as consisting in the uniform application of institutional rules, could deliver for the members of a community who are being skewered by these rules is the knowledge, well in advance, that they are going to be skewered, it is not at all clear that the proffered rationale for the establishment and maintenance of these rules would have much normative punch. Uniformity in the application of institutional rules is worth celebrating only when, in addition, the rules are just rules, or at any rate when they aren't grotesquely unjust.

The trouble with the narrowly drawn account of justice for which it consists in the uniform application of institutional rules and procedures is that, precisely because it leaves unsettled all questions about the content of these rules and procedures, it commits its sponsors to holding that a society's coercive institutional arrangements can be just even when the rules and procedures that set the parameters within which its members are permitted to lead their own lives are substantively objectionable. That this possibility is not ruled out provides the basis for a two-step critique of the "uniform treatment" account of justice. The first—as has just been noted—is that it yields strongly counter-intuitive results in a certain range of cases, viz., those in which a society's institutional rules and procedures are substantively objectionable, as was the case, e.g., in apartheid South Africa. In these cases, it is no saving grace that the authorities—and in particular, those whose task it is to interpret and enforce the law—apply the rules and avail themselves of the procedures in a meticulously consistent manner. The second step in the critique consists in showing that if the account offers an unacceptable interpretation of what justice requires in societies with "wicked legal systems"[5] consistency requires that it be recognized that, in other cases too, mere uniformity in the application of rules and procedures is not a sufficient condition of justice in judicial and administrative contexts. In all such contexts, uniform application of existing rules and strict adherence to existing procedures cannot on its own show that justice is being done.

---

[5] I here borrow the expression used by David Dyzenhaus in his characterization of pre-independence South Africa. David Dyzenhaus, *Hard Cases in Wicked Legal Systems* (New York: Oxford University Press, 1991).

Uniformity in the treatment of particular cases in judicial and administrative contexts is at best a necessary, not a sufficient, condition of justice. A further condition is that the rules must be just (or at any rate not unjust) and the procedures fair (or at any rate not unfair).

3.2 Justice as Equality of Opportunity to Make Satisfying Life-Shaping Choices

A "thicker" account of the principle that underpins judgments about the justice of coercive institutional arrangements in society identifies it with an expansive version of the principle of equality of opportunity. According to this view, a society has just coercive rules if these rules can be shown to be needed to ensure that all its members, and all equally, enjoy the institutionally-securable opportunities for the living of satisfying and fulfilling lives. By accenting the importance of making "opportunities" available, this account of the ideal of justice gives appropriate recognition to the role inevitably played by the individual members of a society in actually living satisfying and fulfilling lives through the decisions they make over time about whether, and how, to take advantage of the life-enhancing opportunities afforded them by a just society. This makes it possible to maintain that, even in a just society, not all individual lives will go well, let alone equally well. Nevertheless, a proper division needs of course to be effected between the sorts of things individuals must be prepared to do for themselves if their lives are to go well and the sorts of things it is beyond their power as individuals to do for themselves, these being (in at least many contexts) things that can be secured through the establishment and maintenance of the appropriate kinds of public institutions. These institutions will be just only if they provide, on a virtually guaranteed basis, the kinds of opportunities that are also indispensable to the living of a satisfying and fulfilling life. Once the distinction is in place between the personal responsibilities of individual members of society and the responsibilities the state must assume on their behalf, it is appropriate for the equal opportunity principle that forms the core of the ideal of justice to be articulated in a way that calls for the fulfillment of two conditions. First, the opportunities to be made available to the members of a society through its institutions must be understood comprehensively as opportunities for the living of a satisfying and fulfilling life. The opportunities that must be "equal" are too narrowly conceived, for example, if the focus is entirely on the opportunity to secure employment on the basis of merit. And the opportunities that a just society should make available in the economic domain are mistakenly (or at any rate, misleadingly) characterized if they are conceived (merely) as opportunities to "get ahead." Ensuring social mobility is only part of what is needed in an equal opportunity society. Secondly, the opportunities to be made available must be readily seizable opportunities. They must be opportunities the members of a society are in a position to take advantage of by the doing of things that are within their power.

Acceptance of a demanding version of the equal opportunity principle as the principle of justice that must be satisfied if a society's coercive institutional arrangements are to be represented as morally defensible is consistent, of course, with a good deal of disagreement about where precisely the line should be drawn between what the individual members of a society should be expected to do for themselves and the contribution the state should be expected to make by providing a sufficiently rich menu of opportunities to enable the most important goals in life of the individual members to be achieved. There are, for example, more and less demanding versions of the ideal of self-reliance. The ideal is sometimes thought to require individuals to assume personal responsibility, in all matters that affect their own well-being, for doing absolutely everything it is possible for them, as individuals, to do, no matter how stringent and taxing these requirements. On other versions of the ideal, it combines insistence on the importance of having individuals take responsibility for their own lives with a less exacting conception of the degree to which they should bend every effort to avoid the assistance or cooperation of others. These less exacting versions of the self-reliance ideal may be favored for one or more of a number of reasons: out of a recognition of ordinary human weakness, or in order to provide space for more compassionate attitudes towards even culpable failures on the self-help front, or perhaps simply because the stricter versions of the ideal unnecessarily add to the stresses and strains of everyday life. The equality of opportunity principle, on the expansive interpretation of its import I have been sketching, also provides ample scope for recognition of the importance (and for recognition of a variety of accounts of the significance) of individual autonomy. The fact that what justice calls for is providing the members of a society with seizable life-enhancing opportunities leaves it very much up to them to shape their lives in ways of their own devising, either by taking advantage of, or by passing up, the proffered opportunities.

But while disputes are only to be expected about the preferred version of the ideal of self-reliance or about how the ideal of individual autonomy can best be accommodated, a great many of the rules embodied in these institutional arrangements will be rules whose defensibility is beyond serious controversy. Thus, the rules (embedded in criminal law) that prohibit acts of murder or acts of assault are veritable paradigms of the sorts of "coercive" rules for which there is an unassailable justification: no matter how stringently we think the ideal of self-reliance ought to be interpreted and applied and no matter how wide-ranging we think the domain ought to be within which an individual should be encouraged or enabled to make "autonomous" decisions, rules forbidding acts of murder and assault under threat of severe punishment for violation are indispensable to any realistic effort on the part of the state to provide for all the members of a society opportunities for the living of a satisfying and fulfilling life. Again, given the manifest inability of individuals, no matter how energetic and resourceful, to secure by individual effort the kinds of opportunities—for example, for education in its many important forms, or for avoidance of debilitating sickness or disease—that are indispensable to the living of a satisfying and fulfilling life, a society's rules for the establishment of readily accessible educational and healthcare facilities are further examples of institutional rules that, despite their "coerciveness", seem entirely defensible from the standpoint of an account of justice for which equality of opportunity is the animating principle.

4 Coercive Institutional Arrangements and Democracy

Even if a sufficiently demanding account of what justice requires of coercive institutional arrangements makes it not unreasonable to represent arrangements that either conform to or come feasibly close to conforming to these requirements as morally defensible, a plausible alternative to this sort of justice-based rationale for a society's coercive rules might well be thought to be available. On this view, these rules are morally defensible if recognizably democratic procedures have been employed in their adoption. By contrast with the justice-based account of what makes coercive institutional rules morally defensible, this account abstracts, it would seem, from the content of the (substantive and procedural) rules that give determinate shape to a society's institutional arrangements, and gives prominence, instead, to questions about how these arrangements have come into being, how they are maintained, and how they are amended from time to time. In its most general form, it is the view that democratically endorsed institutional rules are morally defensible despite their inherently "coercive" character.

Unsurprisingly, however, the "democratic endorsement" condition can be more or less demanding. In its less demanding versions—which correspond to relatively "thin" accounts of the democratic ideal—"democratic endorsement" may mean little more than that the institutional arrangements have been established and are maintained by the elected representatives of the members of a society: little or no attention need be paid to the general conditions under which representatives have been elected or whether their views (and the legislative and policy decisions they make) adequately reflect the views and priorities of members of the general public.

In its more demanding versions a society's institutional arrangements can be said to have received "democratic endorsement" only if, in addition to having been put in place and maintained by the elected representatives of the public at large, the legislative and policy decisions to which these arrangements owe their existence adequately reflect the views and priorities of the members of the society. This additional condition requires for its fulfillment much more than that the shapers of institutional arrangements find themselves in office on the basis of an election in which all the members of the society have been permitted to cast a vote and in which there has been no resort either to fraud or to intimidation. Further requirements of thicker versions of the democratic ideal may include: the requirement that the electoral system be so structured as to give approximately equal weight to the votes cast by members of the public, or the requirement that the procedures for the selection of those who stand for election be such as to give a fair opportunity to potential candidates from all segments of society, or the requirement that campaign practices be such as to afford members of the public a reasonable opportunity to identify the legislative or policy predilections of candidates, or the requirement that the media provide balanced coverage of the platforms of the contending parties, and so on.

While the competing versions of the democratic ideal need to be set out in detail before a satisfying verdict can be rendered on the role the "democratic endorsement" account of the rationale for a society's coercive institutional arrangements should be allowed to play, it seems antecedently implausible to assign any normative weight to the thinnest of these versions. It is only when thicker versions of what "democratic endorsement" amounts to are in place that it is plausible to view the decisions about the shape of a society's institutional arrangements made by duly elected representatives as reflecting the views and priorities of the members, and it is only when these arrangements can be thought to have the backing of the members that the coercive rules embedded in the arrangements can perhaps be viewed as morally defensible.

An interesting feature of the democratic ideal in its more demanding versions is perhaps worth underlining to bring out part of the force of this observation. A crucial part of what gives the democratic ideal in its more demanding versions its normative appeal is that it can be represented, not as an ideal that is independent of (and thus perhaps also potentially at variance with) the justice ideal in the ambitious form in which it calls for equalization of the opportunity to live a satisfying and fulfilling life, but rather as itself a justice-grounded ideal. This is because the opportunities for the living of a satisfying and fulfilling life that are to be made available on the same basis to all the members of a just society include, importantly, the opportunity to participate on equal terms in the collective decision-making processes that serve to determine the shape of institutional arrangements. This is partly because providing the members of a society with this sort of opportunity is **an effective means** of trying to ensure that the institutions that are put in place underwrite adequately the various opportunities that individual members must enjoy if they are to be in a position to live a satisfying and fulfilling life. That effective participation in collective decision-making processes is likely to contribute, directly and indirectly, to the enactment of laws and policies, and to the establishment of institutions, that enable the members of a society to enjoy life-enhancing opportunities on an equal basis is, of course, an empirical claim, but it seems to be the sort of empirical claim it would be easy to substantiate. Again, giving all the members of a society the opportunity to participate, effectively and on terms of equality, in collective decision-making processes may well be **indispensable** to ensuring that the society's institutional arrangements are a reasonable approximation to those mandated by (the expansive version of) the equal opportunity principle. In a society in which political participation prerogatives are not guaranteed on the same basis for all members, there is every likelihood that institutional arrangements will not provide those who lack political clout with opportunities for the living of their lives as extensive or as assured as those enjoyed by members who have the opportunity to participate effectively in collective decision-making processes. This again, is fundamentally an empirical claim, but it seems to be the sort of claim for which supporting evidence could readily be adduced. There is, however, a third—and arguably more fundamental—reason why the kind of participatory prerogatives mandated by (thicker versions of) the democratic ideal should be viewed as required by considerations of justice. An important part of the rationale for the significance individuals attach to having opportunities for the living of satisfying and fulfilling lives is the value they assign to the freedom to control the direction of their lives. It is of course important to this end that there should be reasonably extensive areas in their lives as individuals within which, in face of the opportunities with which they are provided, they can freely determine the course of their lives. While it is of course impossible for them to expect to be able to exercise effective control, as individuals, over the boundaries of these areas or over the kinds of life-enhancing opportunities they enjoy within these areas, what they **can** do to increase the measure of control they have over the shape of their own lives is to **participate** in the collective decision-making processes that establish these boundaries and opportunities. And since all the members of a society have, for these sorts of autonomy-related reasons, a stake in being able to participate in these crucial processes, what they can reasonably hope to be in a position to enjoy, in a just society, is the opportunity to participate in collective decision-making processes on terms of equality with others. Thus, while the democratic ideal in its more demanding versions may rightly be endorsed for reasons that don't reduce to reasons of justice—a society that is democratically organized can be expected, for example, to be more stable, over time, than one that is not, and there seems to be impressive evidence that democratic societies are also less likely than non-democratic societies to go to war with one another—one of the most important arguments for the ideal is a justice-grounded argument. The institutional arrangements of a just society must provide its members not only with a rich menu of life-enhancing opportunities—opportunities for the living of satisfying and fulfilling lives—but they must also afford them all the opportunity to participate, effectively and on equal terms, in the society's collective decision-making processes, the processes through which coercive institutional arrangements are established and maintained.

5   Justice and Democracy: Convergent Ideals?

If a society's democratic arrangements are, in an important sense, themselves grounded in justice considerations, too sharp a distinction ought not to be drawn between attempts to defend coercive institutional arrangements by asking whether they satisfy principles of justice and attempts to defend them by asking whether they have received "democratic endorsement." It's worth asking, consequently, whether the justice and democratic arguments for the defensibility of a society's coercive rules (insofar as they can still be distinguished) are arguments that must be seen, in a sense, to converge.

The case for the convergence hypothesis is powerful when two conditions are fulfilled. First, the coercive institutional arrangements in question must be **clearly** (unproblematically, uncontroversially, etc.) arrangements that contribute in indispensable ways to equalization of the opportunities the members of a society enjoy to live satisfying and fulfilling lives. Second, a society's processes for the making of collective decisions concerning the content and structure of institutional arrangements must be fully in line with a rich version of the democratic ideal, one that is firmly rooted in the view that all members must, as a matter of justice, have readily seizable opportunities to participate on equal terms in these processes.

The first of these conditions is arguably fulfilled for at least a significant subclass of the coercive rules that are in place in an equal opportunity society even if difference of view is perhaps to be expected about the precise boundaries of this subclass. For example, the rules that give content and structure to central parts of a legal system—to criminal law, contract law, and the law of torts, for example—are for the most part rules that play an indispensable role in the institutional arrangements of an equal opportunity society, as also are the rules that regulate access to education and employment or to healthcare facilities.

It's the second condition that might seem more problematic, for two reasons. First, there is the difficulty in practice of arranging for a society's political participation processes to conform to the requirements of a demanding version of the democratic ideal. Second, the significance of the stipulation that this version must be rooted in the view that the members of a society should have, as a matter of justice, the opportunity to involve themselves in these processes on an equal basis, is perhaps in need of elucidation and support.

So far as the first of these difficulties is concerned, it must of course be conceded that the practical obstacles to full realization of the democratic ideal are formidable. Indeed, it should perhaps also be conceded that even in societies with secure and long-established democratic traditions some of these obstacles may still have to be overcome.

As for the second difficulty, it should be recalled that the most persuasive argument for requiring a society's political arrangements to be fully democratic is that such arrangements have an essential role to play in the establishment of a just institutional order. If this is so, then a society's collective decisions about the preferred shape of its institutional arrangements may have to be regarded as acceptably "democratic" only if these decisions are not egregiously at odds with the equal opportunity principle itself. While there is understandably a good deal of dispute about the detail of the constraints to which "democratic" decision-making must be subject, the view that there must indeed be such constraints and that these include justice-related constraints[6] is the hallmark of all attempts to defend "constitutional" forms of the democratic ideal.

---

[6] When legislation that is judged to be incompatible with constitutionally protected rights is declared to be unconstitutional—and the authority of the judiciary to hand down such judgments is arguably in no way at odds with defensible versions of the democratic ideal—the decisions that democratically elected members of a legislature have made are being overruled because they breach rights-related (or justice-grounded) constraints that circumscribe the authority of legislatures.

Now if the "democratic endorsement" argument for given parts of a society's coercive institutional framework must be deemed to fail if the coercive rules in question are at variance with any of the uncontroversial requirements of the equal opportunity principle, then of course the very possibility of divergence, in such cases, between justice-based and putatively "democratic" grounds for the moral defensibility of coercive institutional rules has to be ruled out. The convergence hypothesis will be true—though only, admittedly, for a limited range of cases—in virtue of the way the democratic ideal is itself understood.

What, though, of all those cases where, even if a justice-grounded version of the democratic ideal is still being adhered to, the first condition—the condition that requires defensible coercive institutional rules to be **clearly** required by the equal opportunity principle—is unfulfilled? These will be cases where it simply isn't true that coercive institutional rules can be identified which are **clearly** (unproblematically, uncontroversially, etc.) defensible on justice grounds—defensible, that is, because they make an indispensable contribution to the establishment or maintenance of equality of opportunity in society. There are at least three classes of such cases. First, there are cases where it is simply unclear—and where it is acknowledged on all sides that it is unclear—whether proposed institutional arrangements are or are not required by the principle of equality of opportunity. Second, there are cases where there is disagreement within a society about the need, on equal opportunity grounds, for proposed institutional arrangements. Third, there are cases where, despite widespread agreement about the kinds of institutional arrangements an equal opportunity society ought to **aim** at establishing and maintaining, there is difference of view about the defensibility of proposed **means** to their establishment or maintenance. No doubt these are not sharply contrastable kinds of cases, especially given the difficulty of distinguishing, in many decision-making contexts, between questions about ends and questions about means. Nevertheless, in cases of all three sorts, it may be morally defensible for institutional rules to be adopted— perhaps in some situations on a provisional, partly experimental, basis—if they receive "democratic endorsement" despite the fact that, ex hypothesi, they have no assured direct basis in considerations of justice. In these circumstances, although justice-based arguments for or against the coercive institutional rules in question may well have to be viewed as unavailable or inconclusive, the "democratic endorsement" argument has a useful role to play in determining their moral defensibility.

Chapter 6
Democratic Legitimacy and the Reasoned Will of the People

Walter J. Riker

1 Introduction

The modern democratic state is a coercive legal apparatus meant to order and regulate a number of important societal activities, for the purpose of securing or advancing some notion of the general will or good of the people. There are a number of competing justificatory accounts of the state's authority to coerce. Here I will discuss and defend a deliberative account. Deliberative accounts draw on the liberal tradition's emphasis on the natural freedom of individuals, and, in particular, on the idea that the state's ultimate authority derives only from the reasoned judgment of the people.

2 Legitimating Democratic State Coercion

In modern liberal democracies, citizens regard one another as the free and equal co-authors of the laws that bind them into and order the basic institutions of their polity. Ideally, then, a moral justification of the state's coercive power should be publicly acceptable (in some sense) to nearly all citizens.[1] This is an idealized notion, but my point is this: no society that is maintained over time through force or deception deserves to be called a "liberal democracy." Societies can be maintained over time in these ways, of course, but these societies are not stable for sound normative reasons, nor can they be regarded as liberal and democratic.[2] So, what could render the liberal democratic state's coercive action more than mere force for nearly all citizens, each of whom regards herself vis a vis others as a free equal? When does the liberal democratic state's coercive activity have prima facie moral

---

[1] The idea of "publicly acceptable" reasons or justifications is controversial. I will say more about what I mean by "publicly acceptable" in later sections of this paper.

[2] See, e.g., John Rawls, *Political Liberalism* (New York: Columbia University Press, 1996), pp. 140–144, and *Justice as Fairness: A Restatement* (Cambridge, MA: Harvard University Press, 2001), pp. 185–186.

D.A. Reidy and W.J. Riker (eds.), *Coercion and the State*.
© Springer Science + Business Media B.V. 2008

value, and thus merit at least some measure of moral respect from citizens generally?

One common answer is that the democratic state's authority to coerce is morally justified so long as it serves the ends of justice. However, we should not assume that every just use of the state's coercive power is within the scope of the state's genuine authority. The state's authority is always constituted authority, i.e., the state's genuine powers are nothing more than the set of powers that citizens collectively (as final co-sovereigns) authorize the state to exercise, and it is not difficult to imagine citizens putting some just acts beyond the scope of the state's constituted authority. One might respond that citizens who did this would be making a serious moral mistake; what else is the state for if not to secure justice for all? While there is something right about this claim, the issue is more complicated than it seems.

First, we cannot move directly from the claim that some moral requirement is important (or even required by justice) to the further claim that that important moral requirement can be coercively enforced against all by the state.[3] The mere fact that justice demands something does not itself show that that demand ought to be coercively enforced by anyone. The claim that the state has a right or the authority to coercively enforce all the demands of justice requires some moral defense.[4]

Second, justice-based accounts of the state's authority have trouble with the fact of reasonable disagreement.[5] Equally sincere and thoughtful people have deep disagreements about what justice ultimately requires. This is so, even though it seems to be the case that nearly all liberal democratic citizens believe that justice implies principles of freedom and equality for all. The problem is that this agreement does not get us very far in real democratic politics, because these same citizens disagree deeply about what their shared commitments to freedom and equality imply. For instance, do freedom and equality imply a right to abortion? Do they imply a right to gay marriage? What kind of taxation and redistribution scheme do they imply? What sort of social security is required? One might respond that these are the sorts of disagreements that ought to be resolved through democratic decision procedures, but this just pushes the problem back a step, because there are also reasonable disagreements over which democratic decision procedures are most consistent with

---

[3] Arthur Ripstein, "Authority and Coercion," *Philosophy and Public Affairs*, v. 32, 2004, pp. 2–35.

[4] Allen Buchanan argues that the state has a right to enforce at least some of the demands of justice. See, e.g., "Political Legitimacy and Democracy," *Ethics*, v. 112, 2002, pp. 689–719. However, Buchanan's argument is controversial, and, in any case, does not purport to show that all of the demands of justice can be coercively enforced, but just certain particularly vital ones.

[5] For discussion of the nature and implications of reasonable disagreement, see, e.g., Charles Larmore, *The Morals of Modernity* (New York: Cambridge University Press, 1996), John Rawls, *Political Liberalism*, and Jeremy Waldron, *Law and Disagreement* (Oxford: Oxford University Press, 1999).

freedom and equality.[6] And so on. Thus, while there are undoubtedly good reasons for thinking that appeals to justice should play a role in moral justifications of the democratic state's authority, considerations of justice alone are insufficient.

If justice-based accounts cannot morally vindicate the state's authority to coerce, then what can? We ought to focus instead on the legitimacy of state action.[7] Justice and legitimacy are distinct moral properties that a state might possess. Justice refers, in the broadest sense, to some appropriate distribution of benefits and burdens (however defined) among the morally significant entities (e.g., individuals, associations, peoples) in a society (domestic or global). Political legitimacy refers to a state's right or authority to use coercive force against its citizens to compel obedience to its laws.[8] Most believe justice and legitimacy vary somewhat independently of each other. For instance, Rawls insists that justice and legitimacy differ from one another, but also holds that any law "too gravely unjust" cannot be considered legitimate.[9] The upshot of the distinction between justice and legitimacy is that it may sometimes be legitimate to enforce unjust laws, and illegitimate to enforce just laws. For instance, one might argue that current laws against same-sex marriage are legitimate, insofar as they have been properly enacted, but unjust, as they fail to treat people equally, or to properly respect liberty rights. Or one might argue that justice requires a more equitable distribution of wealth in (for instance) the U.S., but that it would be illegitimate to enforce an executive or administrative order requiring this, or to enforce a just law ex post facto.

---

[6] For an introduction to the breadth and depth of reasonable disagreement regarding the relative merits and defects of different approaches to democracy, see Robert Dahl, *A Preface to Democratic Theory* (Chicago, IL: University of Chicago Press, 1956) and *Democracy and Its Critics* (New Haven, CT: Yale University Press, 1989). Compare also Ian Shapiro's *The State of Democratic Theory* (Princeton, NJ: Princeton University Press, 2003) with Amy Gutmann and Dennis Thompson's recent book, *Why Deliberative Democracy?* (Princeton, NJ: Princeton University Press, 2004).

[7] For useful discussion of different accounts of political legitimacy, and of its relationship to justice, see Allen Buchanan, "Political Legitimacy and Democracy," *Ethics*, v. 112, 2002, pp. 689–719, Richard Flathman, "Legitimacy," in R. Goodin and P. Pettit, eds., *A Companion to Contemporary Political Philosophy* (Malden, MA: Blackwell, 1993), pp. 527–533, and A. J. Simmons, "Justification and Legitimacy," *Ethics*, v. 109, 1999, pp. 739–771.

[8] Legitimacy is thus different as well from political obligation, which is traditionally understood as a citizen's moral duty to obey the law or the government. For a useful introduction to political obligation, see A. J. Simmons, *Moral Principles and Political Obligations* (Princeton, NJ: Princeton University Press, 1979). The nature of the relationship between legitimacy and political obligation is the subject of some controversy. For example, in "Political Legitimacy and Democracy," Allen Buchanan argues that legitimacy is a necessary but not sufficient condition for political obligation. He claims legitimacy exists but that, given what would be required, no one ever has a political obligation. Ronald Dworkin argues that political obligation and legitimacy are roughly the same thing (*Law's Empire*, Cambridge, MA: Harvard University Press, 1986, p. 191). On his view, if we have political obligations, the state may legitimately force us to satisfy at least the most important ones.

[9] Rawls, *Political Liberalism*, pp. 427–429. For instance, laws denying basic liberties to minorities could not be considered legitimate.

So what we need is some account of what could legitimate the liberal democratic state's use of coercive force. In general, coercive state action is legitimate when it falls within the scope of the state's constituted authority. This authority to coerce is constituted by both procedural and substantive norms. The problem we face here, then, is understanding what this means in the context of a liberal democracy, where citizens regard themselves as free and equal and engaged in fair social cooperation.[10] Three minimal components of democratic legitimacy seem apparent.

First, the state's constituted authority must respect certain minimal republican ideals. This is the republican component of democratic legitimacy. The state's authority must be aimed at and limited to securing the common good, within the constraints imposed by constitutionalism and the rule of law. Were this republican commitment to the common good to require consensus regarding the nature of that good, this ideal would be implausible. As I will show in Section 4, however, this republican ideal does not require consensus.

Second, the state's constituted authority must respect some canonical list of basic liberal rights. This list of rights begins with the protections guaranteed by constitutionalism and the rule of law, and includes freedom of conscience, religious freedom, freedom of speech, freedom of assembly, and similar liberal rights. This is the liberal component of democratic legitimacy. Coercive state action that violates these key liberal rights is always illegitimate.

Third, the state's constituted authority to coerce must be connected in some way to the will of the people, democratically expressed. This is the uniquely democratic component of democratic legitimacy.

3   The Democratic Component of Democratic Legitimacy

The democratic component of legitimacy requires that the state's authority to coerce must be tied in some way to the will of the people, democratically expressed. But there are a number of different and competing accounts of what this means. Here I will consider three: aggregative, competitive, and deliberative views. My purpose is not to refute the first two views, for the sake of the deliberative view, but rather to describe the kinds of problems with the first two views that ultimately make the deliberative view attractive.

On the aggregative view, the general will or good is constituted or revealed through an impartial "democratic" aggregation of individual preferences.[11] It is revealed or constituted through elections in which individuals vote according to their personal preferences. The state has the legitimate authority to coerce in the

---

[10] Ibid., pp. 15–22; idem, *Justice as Fairness*, pp. 5–8.
[11] See, e.g., Jack Knight and James Johnson, "Aggregation and Deliberation: On the Possibility of Democratic Legitimacy," *Political Theory*, v. 22, 1994, pp. 277–296.

name of this revealed or constituted general will or good. Thus, the impartial aggregation of individual preferences, expressed in democratic elections, links the state's authority to coerce to the will of the people or the common good.

Unfortunately, there are a number of well-known problems with aggregative views. First, many (including Kenneth Arrow, William Riker, and others) argue that there is no uniquely fair and rational democratic way to aggregate individual preferences, and hence no way to see any particular aggregation as a genuine expression of the general will or common good.[12] Second, it is not clear that the mere aggregation of individual interests is genuinely "public," especially since the individual interests aggregated democratically are just that, expressions of private individual, and not common or public, interests. Citizens thus have good reason to doubt that an impartial aggregation of individual interests reveals or constitutes their common good, and, further, to question whether this is the sort of democratic outcome that the state ought to be authorized to enforce. Third, the aggregative view does not require that the will of the people be "reasoned," because it does not require citizens to reason at all about what preferences they ought to have or express in democratic elections. It takes these preferences as given. This is a problem, because the state's authority to coerce ought to be tied to more than mere preferences. The state should be authorized to coerce only in the name of some reasoned understanding of the common good democratically expressed. But, insofar as an aggregation of individual preferences constitutes a general will or good at all, it does not constitute a reasoned will or good.[13]

Worries about our capacity to identify the general will or good in any robust sense have led some to develop accounts of the democratic component of legitimacy that appeal only to very thin notions of the general will or good. Competitive accounts of the democratic component of legitimacy do just this.[14] On competitive accounts, when public officials are chosen through general elections held on a regular basis, they are authorized to use the state's coercive power within the bounds imposed by the constitution, as long as they respect citizens' canonical liberal rights. The power wielded by citizens in democratic elections—the potential means to remove public officials from office—is thought to tame the behavior of public officials, who must compete for the votes of citizens. For instance, Ian Shapiro argues that since properly structured

---

[12] Kenneth Arrow, *Social Choice and Individual Values* (New Haven, CT: Yale University Press, 1951), William Riker, *Liberalism Against Populism* (Prospect Heights, IL: Waveland Press, 1982) and *The Art of Political Manipulation* (New Haven, CT: Yale University Press, 1986). See Donald Green and Ian Shapiro, *Pathologies of Rational Choice Theory* (New Haven, CT: Yale University Press, 1994), for a critique of these and related efforts to apply rational choice theory to political theory.

[13] This is one of the problems with the aggregative approach that Bruce Ackerman and James Fishkin try to fix in *Deliberation Day* (New Haven, CT: Yale University Press, 2004).

[14] See, e.g, Joseph Schumpeter, *Capitalism, Socialism, and Democracy* (New York: Harper, 1942), and Ian Shapiro, *The State of Democratic Theory* (Princeton, NJ: Princeton University Press, 2003).

democratic institutions are more likely to secure citizens' basic interests—the "obvious essentials that [people] need to develop into and survive as independent agents in the world"—than available alternative political institutions, democratic citizens always have good normative reason to accept (or at least defer to) democratic outcomes.[15] There is no general will or good, according to Shapiro, other than the very thin interest citizens share in protecting their capacity for agency. These thin basic interests, for Shapiro, form the normative bedrock of the democratic component of legitimacy.

Unfortunately, while competitive views have the virtue of practical realism, they are impoverished views of legitimacy at best. They fail to link the state's legitimate authority to the reasoned will of the people in any meaningful way. Citizens get to choose the candidate they think will best secure their basic interests, but they otherwise have little role to play in how the state's power is used. Further, citizens' preferences are taken as given, which means that competitive views also fail to link the state's authority to a reasoned will.

A third account of the democratic component of legitimacy is the deliberative view of democracy.[16] The deliberative alternative takes up the republican ideals and liberal rights, and adds to them the notion that the state's legitimate authority derives from the reasoned will of the people, democratically expressed. This view emphasizes the liberal tradition's respect for individual freedom, and for each individual's capacity for rational agency, by insisting that social and political institutions, and the state's capacity to exercise coercive power, ought to be acceptable, or at least be capable of being made acceptable, to every individual subject to them.[17] For instance, Gutmann and Thompson define "deliberative democracy"

> as a form of government in which free and equal citizens (and their representatives) justify decisions in a process in which they give one another reasons that are mutually acceptable and generally accessible, with the aim of reaching conclusions that are binding in the present on all citizens but open to challenge in the future.[18]

Unlike the aggregative and competitive views, the deliberative view does not take preferences as given, but instead requires that citizens be prepared to justify them to others in terms those others might accept. The insistence on justification links the state's exercise of power not simply to the will of the people, whether understood as an aggregation of individual preferences, or more simply as the shared interest all citizens have in securing their basic needs, but to a reasoned will.

---

[15] Shapiro, *State of Democratic Theory*, p. 45.

[16] See, e.g., James Bohman and William Rehg, eds., *Deliberative Democracy* (Cambridge, MA: Massachusetts Institute of Technology Press, 1997), Joshua Cohen, "Deliberation and Democratic Legitimacy," in A. Hamlin and P. Pettit, eds., *The Good Polity* (Malden, MA: Blackwell, 1989), pp. 17–34, John Elster, *Deliberative Democracy* (New York: Cambridge University Press, 1997), and Amy Gutmann and Dennis Thompson, *Democracy and Disagreement* (Cambridge, MA: Harvard University Press, 1996) and *Why Deliberative Democracy?*

[17] See, e.g., Jeremy Waldron, "Theoretical Foundations of Liberalism," *Philosophical Quarterly*, v. 37, 1987, pp. 127–150.

[18] Gutmann and Thompson, *Why Deliberative Democracy?*, p. 7.

The deliberative alternative's appeal to shared justifications or reasons does invite the objection that the deliberative view is too demanding to be realistic.[19] There is simply no reason to believe that citizens in modern liberal democracies can reach consensus regarding the proper nature of their common social and political institutions, or the scope of the state's legitimate authority to use coercive power. If this is what it is being asked for, then deliberative accounts must fail. Fortunately, deliberative accounts do not require consensus. This has been recognized by many liberal political theorists, going back as far as Kant.

Kant is not concerned in his political theory with exploring and resolving the political implications of the fact of reasonable disagreement. He aims instead to produce a non-voluntarist social contract theory of legitimate political authority.[20] What he develops is a view that we today would regard as a deliberative justification of the state's legitimate authority to coerce, and his justification does not depend on consensus. Kant argues that the law must be based on "the will of the entire people," because "the will of another person cannot decide anything for someone without injustice."[21] However, he continues,

> ... we need by no means assume that this contract ... based on a coalition of the wills of all private individuals in a nation to form a common, public will for the purposes of rightful legislation, actually exists as a *fact*, for it cannot possibly be so.... It is in fact merely an *idea* of reason, which nonetheless has undoubted practical reality; for it can oblige every legislator to frame his laws in such a way that they could have been produced by the united will of the whole nation.... This is the test of the rightfulness of every public law. For if the law is such that a whole people could not *possibly* agree to it (for example, if it stated that a certain class of *subjects* must be privileged as a hereditary *ruling class*), it is unjust; but if it is at least *possible* that a people could agree to it, it is our duty to consider the law as just, even if the people is at present in such a position or attitude of mind that it would probably refuse its consent if it were consulted.[22]

Kant provides an example:

> If a war tax were proportionately imposed on all subjects, they could not claim, simply because it is oppressive, that it is unjust because the war is in their opinion unnecessary. For they are not entitled to judge this issue, since it is at least *possible* that the war is inevitable and the tax indispensable.[23]

Kant recognizes that the exercise of power without any basis in public consensus is unavoidable in politics, but he does not give up on the liberal ideal of justification

[19] See, e.g., Jeffrey Stout, *Democracy and Tradition* (Princeton, NJ: Princeton University Press, 2004), pp. 65–67.

[20] For discussion of Kant's social contract theory see H. S. Reiss, ed., *Kant: Political Writings* (New York: Cambridge University Press, 1991), Allen D. Rosen, *Kant's Theory of Justice* (Ithaca, NY: Cornell University Press, 1993), chapters 3 and 4, and Waldron, "Theoretical Foundations," pp. 141–143.

[21] Kant, "On the Common Saying 'This may be True in Theory but it does not Apply in Practice'" in *Kant: Political Writings*, p. 77.

[22] Ibid., p. 79.

[23] Ibid. See Kant's footnote.

or shared reason that forms the normative core of the deliberative account. He does not insist that the law be something that all citizens do in fact agree to, or something that no reasonable citizen could reasonably reject; it is enough for the law to be something that all citizens *could* agree to, even if in fact they don't.

One might object that this deliberative view does not respect individual judgment and freedom, or respond to the general will or good, any more robustly than the aggregative or competitive views do. After all, in Kant's example the citizens do not agree that the war is necessary—some see no or insufficient reason for it. How, then, is the promise of a reasoned and general will fulfilled by Kant's deliberative view? Won't minority democrats (those on the losing side) simply regard the majority's actions as the sheer imposition of will? Though this worry is reasonable, I think it is ultimately mistaken. The demand for deliberation is a demand for a certain kind of reciprocity in politics.[24] The demand for reciprocity is, in turn, a demand for a certain kind of respect. It is a demand that persons be treated in ways that each could see as justified. By offering reasons at all for political activity, we show respect for each person's rational agency, for each person's capacity for judgment. When we offer reasons we think another person could accept, from a shared moral point of view, we show respect as well for that person's political freedom and equal political status as a fellow citizen. While Kant does not require shared reasons in the fullest sense (terms of association all persons do in fact converge on, or that could not reasonably be rejected by anyone), his view nevertheless requires reciprocity (laws that *could* have been produced by the united will of the nation) and thereby evinces a respect for the rational agency, liberty and equality of citizens (a law has genuine force only when it is the kind of thing that citizens *could* freely affirm).

Though it might be interesting to pursue Kant's view further, I will leave it here. My primary purpose in what follows is to develop an interpretation of John Rawls's conception of legitimacy. Properly understood, Rawls's account is both normatively compelling and practically realistic. The core of Rawls's view is a line of thought developed in the works of H. L. A. Hart and Philip Soper. In Section 4, I will develop this Hart/Soper line of thought. In Section 5, I will offer a plausible and realistic reading of Rawls's view.

4   Hart and Soper on Law and Obligation

In *A Theory of Law*, Philip Soper develops a generic account of the law's normative force ("legal obligation") and the citizen/subject's moral duty to obey it ("political obligation").[25] His account is rooted in republican commitments to the common

---

[24] See, e.g., Gutmann and Thompson, *Why Deliberative Democracy?*, pp. 98–102.

[25] Philip Soper, *A Theory of Law* (Cambridge, MA: Harvard University Press, 1984). The problems of legal and political obligation are old ones in the history of political philosophy. Plato discusses the problem in the *Crito*, where Socrates must decide whether or not to obey a legal but unjust decision. See Plato, *Five Dialogues*, trans. by G. M. A. Grube (Indianapolis, IN: Hackett, 1981), pp. 52–56. Perhaps the most influential contemporary works on the nature of law and legal obligation are H. L. A. Hart, *The Concept of Law*, 2nd ed. (New York: Oxford University Press, 1994) and Ronald Dworkin, *Law's Empire* (Cambridge, MA: Harvard University Press, 1986).

good, constitutionalism, and the rule of law.[26] However, Soper acknowledges reasonable disagreement about the common good, and so he adds a deliberative twist to his republican view. We might think of it as a deliberative republican account. Soper explicitly contrasts his work with H. L. A. Hart's *The Concept of Law*.[27] While Soper draws much from Hart, he ultimately rejects Hart's legal positivism. Since Soper offers his account as a kind of correction of Hart's, it is helpful to begin with Hart.

Hart argues that a society's laws have genuine normative force when three conditions are met: (a) the laws are generally obeyed by citizens and officials, (b) the laws are generated in accord with rules prescribing a law-making process ("secondary rules"), and (c) the law-making rules are internalized by officials.[28] When officials regard these rules as standards of criticism, including self-criticism, of deviations, the laws generated pursuant to them have normative force. Under these conditions the law does not express official will as such, but instead expresses commitments shared by officials. For Hart, this constraint on the official will distinguishes law from mere force. Officials may not simply do as they wish; they may only do as the rules require or allow. Their authority is constituted and rule-governed and thus not mere will. Under these conditions, the law generates genuine legal obligations.

Soper's theory responds mainly to two problems that he sees with Hart's account. First, to Hart it does not matter why citizens obey the law, as long as they do.[29] The fact that they may obey for prudential reasons, say, out of fear of punishment, does not change the law's normativity. Hart does not think that this is usually what happens. Still, the mere possibility troubles Soper, because the law is supposed to generate normative duties for citizens. But when citizens see the law as mere force, they do not see law as a genuine source of normative obligations. Soper holds that citizens have normative obligations to obey the law, only when they have normatively significant reasons to respect it.

Second, Hart does not place normative restrictions on why officials accept their secondary, law-making rules. Officials could accept the rules for self-interested reasons.[30] What matters to Hart is that officials accept the rules, not why they do so. Again, Hart does not think that this is what usually happens. Nevertheless, the possibility troubles Soper, because citizens in this situation can reasonably conclude that the law represents nothing more than official self-interest, even when officials are constrained by rules.[31] And if the law appears to serve only official self-interest,

---

[26] Soper no longer affirms the view he developed in *A Theory of Law*. His new view can be found in *The Ethics of Deference: Learning from Law's Morals* (New York: Cambridge University Press, 2002). Interestingly, Rawls took up themes introduced in Soper's original account, and continued to apply them in his work even after Soper moved away from them.

[27] Hart, *The Concept of Law*.

[28] Ibid., pp. 116–117. Hart's account of legal obligation is developed in chapters 5 and 6.

[29] Ibid., pp. 115–117.

[30] Ibid., p. 203.

[31] Think, for instance, of the Mafia. Members of the Mafia internalize certain shared rules that guide the way they interact with one another and those in the community subject to their power. Nevertheless, the fact that the Mafia's behavior is rule-governed does not imply that the power they exercise over others amounts to anything more than mere force. Instances like this suggest that Hart's theory really cannot distinguish law from force.

citizens have reason to see the law as mere force, and will see no genuine normative reason to respect it.

So, if the law is to merit the moral respect of citizens, and thereby factor into their moral calculations about how to live, it must give citizens some normative reason to respect it. When does the law do this? Soper answers that "legal systems are essentially characterized by the belief in value, the claim in good faith by those who rule that they do so in the interests of all."[32] The law deserves the respect of citizens when citizens have good reason to believe that officials sincerely regard the law as promoting justice or the common good. Soper uses the terms "the interests of all," "the common good," and "justice" interchangeably as placeholders, and they must be read loosely.[33] He makes no strong claims about what should count as a theory of justice, or a commitment to the common good, for two main reasons. First, he intends his theory to be generic, to account for the law's normativity in all societies with genuine legal systems, and not just in liberal democratic ones. He does not presume that only liberal democracies have legitimately enforceable law. Second, he recognizes that individuals in all societies disagree about what justice requires. If he were to say much at all about justice or the common good, he would run the risk of violating his own acknowledgement of the fact reasonable disagreement. Soper insists on only two things. First, a theory of justice must give some (but not necessarily equal) consideration to the interests of all citizens. Second, officials must appeal only to theories of justice that are publicly available to members of their society, that are part of a known discourse or tradition of political thought. This is the deliberative aspect of Soper's theory of law. The link to a publicly available discourse is necessary, Soper holds, because citizens will not see any normative reason to respect the law if they cannot see it as grounded in some notion of the common good. These two conditions form the core of Soper's approach to reciprocity and deliberation.

Soper's theory is a deliberative view because it requires two kinds of reciprocity. First, it requires something similar to what Reidy calls "reciprocity in advantage."[34] Soper requires that officials sincerely consider the interests of all citizens when proposing and enforcing law. Reciprocity in advantage is a central component of deliberation. We cannot justify the authority of law to citizens if they have reason to regard having a legal system as worse than not having one. If the law ignores a citizen's interests altogether, or, worse, if it threatens her interests, she has no reason to regard law as preferable to anarchy, to the state of nature or of no law. It is

---

[32] Soper, *A Theory of Law*, p. 55.

[33] Ibid. Soper does not mean that law must actually do the good that officials claim it does, or that officials correctly judge their law to be just or to otherwise promote the common good. He is trying to give an account of the law's normative force that respects reasonable disagreements about what justice requires.

[34] See David A. Reidy, "Reciprocity and Reasonable Disagreement: From Liberal to Democratic Legitimacy," *Philosophical Studies*, v. 132, 2007, pp. 243–291.

not reasonable to expect citizens to accept law under these conditions. Thus, a minimum condition of law being something citizens could affirm is that citizens can see the law as something that respects (in some way) their interests. While this requires the law to show some consistency (e.g., what Hart calls the law's "formal aspect of justice" and its "minimum necessary natural law content"), it does not imply that all citizens must be treated equally. The interests of citizens can be respected in many ways short of giving each full and equal status, and we might expect to find just this in societies that do not share modern, liberal democratic values.[35]

Second, Soper's theory requires something similar to what Reidy calls "reciprocity in justification."[36] Soper holds that if the law is to have genuine normative force, officials must make a sincere appeal to a theory of justice or the common good that is part of a publicly available or known discourse or tradition. Every society with a legal system also has a public discourse about things like law, justice, the common good, the good for human beings, citizenship/membership, and so on. In any given society, this public discourse is typically vast and contains many conflicting ideas. The exact nature of these ideas also varies from society to society. For example, in the U.S. today it is unreasonable to deny women the right to vote, but this was not so early in the 19th century. At that time this was a question over which reasonable people could disagree. Today, of course, this is no longer the case in the U.S., but in other societies it still may be deemed reasonable to deny women the vote. On Soper's view, the law's normativity does not depend on whether or not women get to vote. What matters instead is that officials draw the reasons they offer in support of such laws from their society's publicly available political discourse. Here is another example. Today in the U.S. we affirm the ideal of one person, one vote, but some societies may reject this ideal, perhaps because they think it is a mistake to regard individual persons as having an equal basic right to political participation.[37] Even in these non-liberal, non-democratic cases, law-makers go some distance toward reciprocity in justification simply by appealing to publicly available ideas. In effect, officials say to citizens the following: "people relevantly similar to you— some of your fellow citizens—actually do affirm these ideas, so it is reasonable to believe that these are ideas that you *could* affirm as well (even if you don't)."

Soper does not mean that officials must correctly judge their law to be just or otherwise to promote the common good. He is trying to give an account of the law's

---

[35] John Rawls's decent societies are one example of this kind of society. See *The Law of Peoples* (Cambridge, MA: Harvard University Press, 1999). Decent societies are non-liberal, non-democratic societies that nevertheless have genuine law, i.e., law that is legitimately enforceable. In fact, Rawls holds that decent societies deserve full and good standing in the international community, not because they are just (they are not just, on his view), but because they are genuine structures of political authority (i.e., political authority in decent societies is authorized by citizens insofar as it is consistent with reciprocity and shared reason in Soper's sense).

[36] See Reidy, "Reciprocity and Reasonable Disagreement."

[37] Rawls finds this view expressed by Hegel in *The Philosophy of Right*. See Rawls, *Law of Peoples*, p. 73.

normative force that connects it to significant shared commitments like justice and the common good, but that also respects reasonable disagreements about what justice and the common good require. In the case of particular laws that are obvious failures, of course, officials would be hard pressed to offer sincere defenses of them. But with most laws it is not so obvious. People reasonably disagree about the justice of many laws, and about the impact many laws have on the common good. Nor does Soper think it necessary for citizens to agree with officials about the justice of the law; it is sufficient that citizens can see that officials sincerely believe that the law takes everybody's interests into account in a morally significant way (at least as morality is understood in the culture/society in question).[38]

5 Rawls on Law and Legitimacy

John Rawls was influenced by both Hart and Soper.[39] In *The Law of Peoples*, Rawls argues that certain non-democratic, non-liberal constitutional republics ("decent" societies) deserve full and good standing in the international community.[40] Decent societies meet enough conditions of right and justice to merit the respect of liberal democracies and the right to self-determination, to be free from the interference of other societies.[41] One condition of decency is that a society's system of law imposes genuine moral duties and obligations on citizens/subjects.[42] An early version of this idea appears in *Political Liberalism*.[43] There Rawls says that in order to be viable, the legal system of a decent society must be guided by something like Soper's common good idea of justice, coupled with either Hart's minimum content of natural

---

[38] How can citizens know when officials are being sincere about their claims? For this reason, Soper says citizens always have a "right to discourse" in any society with genuine law (*A Theory of Law*, pp. 119–125). This is roughly a right to engage public officials in dialogue and debate about the law's relationship to justice and the common good. This is not a right to free speech. It is intended mainly to allow citizens to accurately judge the commitment of officials to the general welfare.

[39] While Rawls clearly draws inspiration from Hart and Soper, he does not offer a definition of law. He rejects Soper's claim that the sincerity condition and its implied natural rights define law proper, and says he does not want to argue that entities like the antebellum South did not have legal systems (*Law of Peoples*, p. 66, note 5). But Rawls does regard Soper's theory as an adequate account of the class of laws that do give rise to obligations, regardless of whether it adequately defines law as such. Rawls actually leaves open the question of whether some command that does not give rise to obligations might properly be called law.

[40] Rawls, *Law of Peoples*.

[41] For discussion of this point, see my paper "The Democratic Peace is Not Democratic: On Behalf of Rawls's Decent Peoples," *Political Studies*, forthcoming.

[42] Rawls, *Law of Peoples*, pp. 65–66, especially footnote 5.

[43] Rawls, *Political Liberalism*, pp. 109–110, especially footnote 15.

law or Soper's natural rights to security, formal justice, and discourse. Rawls develops this idea further in *The Law of Peoples*.[44]

Rawls's liberal principle of legitimacy can be understood as an application of Soper's generic account to the context of democratic political culture.[45] We are seeking a moral justification for the liberal democratic state's use of coercive force against citizens. One way to understand Rawls's liberal democratic project is to see it as an effort to provide the potential means for assessing the sincerity (in Soper's sense) of democratic government officials' claims to being justified in using the state's power to coercively regulate citizens' behavior in the name of the general will or common good. This project is complicated by unique features of democratic political culture. In democracies, all citizens are public officials too. In fact, "citizen" is the primary public office in a democracy. In the state of nature, there are individuals, but there are no citizens. The "citizen" is a political role that gets constituted just as the body politic gets constituted. To the extent that the constitution of a body politic is a political act, it must be effected by agents invested with some political power. In liberal democracies, this political power is initially created through the constitution of "citizens," public officials who then constitute for themselves the basic political terms of their democratic institutions (including the offices of other public officials, such as legislators and the president). And, insofar as citizens regard one another as the final co-authors of their law, as the co-sovereigns of their state, they regard one another as the ultimate or final source of their state's legitimate authority. Of course, what I am describing here is a logical progression, not an actual or historical one. But the point is important to understanding Rawls's theory of legitimacy.

Two other characteristics of modern liberal democracies have to be mentioned. First, citizens in modern democracies affirm a plurality of reasonable but irreconcilable religious, moral, and philosophical understandings of the good for human beings.[46] Second, most democratic citizens affirm comprehensive views that are not inconsistent with the essentials of democracy.[47] Thus, Rawls holds that liberal

---

[44] Rawls, *Law of Peoples*, pp. 65–67.

[45] Although Soper talks about political obligation, Rawls prefers to talk about political legitimacy. Rawls does this because he thinks obligations can only arise through consent, but that very few citizens ever consent to be governed in any politically meaningful sense (*A Theory of Justice*, rev. ed., Cambridge, MA: Harvard University Press, 1999, pp. 296–297). Given this, Rawls concludes that citizens in general have no political obligations to their states, though they do have a "natural duty" to support or at least not undermine reasonably just institutions. Legitimacy, however, does not depend on obligation. Rawls makes this distinction between legitimacy and obligation, and affirms their independence, in *Lectures on the History of Political Philosophy* (Cambridge, MA: Harvard University Press, 2007). For instance, he says that "Hume's critique of the social contract view is effective for Locke's account of political obligation, but it doesn't touch Locke's account of legitimacy" (p. 15).

[46] See, e.g., Rawls, *Political Liberalism*, p. xviii.

[47] Ibid.

democracies are constituted by citizens who cannot resolve their political differences, or even find mutual understanding, in terms of their various and irreconcilable understandings of the final human good, but who nevertheless do not reject the essentials of liberal democracy.[48] This situation—the condition of reasonable pluralism—raises three fundamental political problems: how can citizens so divided constitute themselves as a democratic body politic that is (a) just, (b) stable, and (c) legitimate? Over the course of his career, Rawls proposed solutions to all of these problems. In *A Theory of Justice*, his first sustained effort to answer (a), the justice question, he developed "justice as fairness."[49] Not long after he finished *A Theory of Justice*, he realized that it contained a serious flaw. Roughly put, in answering (b), the stability question, Rawls assumed that citizens raised under justice as fairness would eventually converge on a Kantian moral outlook, and that everyone would eventually come to see internalizing and acting from justice as fairness as a component of his or her own good, as a bit of self-realization as an autonomous being.[50] By the time he wrote *Political Liberalism*, Rawls had realized that this assumption conflicted with his own understanding of reasonable pluralism.[51] Under conditions of reasonable pluralism some citizens will affirm comprehensive doctrines that do not affirm as part of the human good Rawls's notion of self-realization as an autonomous being. Thus, for some reasonable citizens the human good is completely distinct from the realization of justice in society. At this point Rawls sought an answer to (c), the legitimacy question: under what conditions might a liberal democratic state coercively enforce something like justice as fairness, given that citizens might reasonably reject the comprehensive ideals with which Rawls associated it in *A Theory of Justice*, and might even reject other aspects of justice as fairness? This is the issue at the heart of *Political Liberalism*. His answer to (c) is his liberal principle of legitimacy.[52]

Rawls's liberal principle of legitimacy has caused a great deal of confusion. This is partly due to Rawls's own ambiguous statements of the principle[53], but also to his modifications of it through time. It first appears in *Political Liberalism* in his discussions of public reason and political stability.[54] However, Rawls later revised his understanding of public reason. His final view is expressed in "The Idea of Public Reason Revisited." It is here that we get his most mature, and least ambiguous, formulation of his principle of legitimacy:

---

[48] Ibid., pp. xviii–xix. Rawls recognizes that some individuals in every liberal democracy reject democracy. He calls these people unreasonable and says we need to "bracket" them, to keep them from disrupting society.

[49] Rawls, *A Theory of Justice*.

[50] This is the subject of Part III of *A Theory of Justice*.

[51] Rawls discusses this in his two Introductions to *Political Liberalism*. See, e.g., pp. xvii–xxx.

[52] Ibid., p. 137, and "The Idea of Public Reason Revisited," in *Law of Peoples*, p. 137.

[53] Reidy discusses the ambiguity of Rawls's statements of the principle in "Reciprocity and Reasonable Disagreement."

[54] Rawls, *Political Liberalism*, p. 136, 216.

> Our exercise of political power is proper only when we sincerely believe that the reasons we would offer for our political actions—were we to state them as government officials—are sufficient, and we also reasonably think that other citizens might also reasonably accept those reasons. This criterion applies on two levels: one is to the constitutional structure itself, the other is to particular statutes and laws enacted in accordance with that structure. To be reasonable, political conceptions must justify only constitutions that satisfy this principle.[55]

The principle does not apply to all political discourse, but is meant mainly as a constraint on discussion and action regarding constitutional essentials and matters of basic justice that occurs in what Rawls calls the public political forum.[56] This forum consists of the discourse and action of judges (especially supreme court justices), of government officials (especially legislators and the executive), and of candidates for public office (in particular when they make public political statements). The principle applies only indirectly to citizens, mainly in their selection of public officials.[57] Constitutional essentials have to do with, e.g., what political rights and liberties could reasonably be included in a written constitution, and matters of basic justice have to do with questions of basic economic and social justice not covered in the constitution.[58]

Rawls holds that legitimacy requires us (as public officials) to be prepared to justify the state's coercive power in terms of reasons that we think other citizens could reasonably accept. For Rawls this means that political activity (regarding constitutional essentials and matters of basic justice) must ultimately be based on a reasonable political conception of justice. A political conception of justice (simpliciter) is a normative conception of the basic political and social institutions of a society, what Rawls calls the basic social structure.[59] It is a more-or-less coherent set of rules and practices that define a society's constitution, basic legal procedures, laws regulating trials, property, markets, economic production and exchange, the family, and so on. In a liberal democracy, political conceptions should be worked out from and presented in terms of ideas drawn from the public political culture.

Rawls holds that liberal democratic citizens, though divided by their comprehensive doctrines and conceptions of the good, nevertheless have access to a common fund of (abstract) liberal democratic ideals. The ideals he has in mind include some that are explicit in public political culture, e.g., those mentioned in the preamble to the U.S. Constitution, such as a more perfect union, justice, domestic tranquility, the general welfare, the common defense, and others that are implicit, such as equal basic liberties, equality of opportunity, and the idea that society is a fair system of cooperation over time.[60] Political conceptions should not depend exclusively on

---

[55] Rawls, "The Idea of Public Reason Revisited," p. 137.

[56] Ibid., p. 133.

[57] For example, suppose the citizens of some county in the U.S. face a vote on whether or not to allow alcohol to be sold on Sunday's in their county. In cases like this, neither officials nor citizens need to seek or provide public reasons. No constitutional essentials or matters of basic justice are at issue in instances like this.

[58] Rawls, "The Idea of Public Reason Revisited," p. 133, note 7.

[59] Ibid., pp. 143–144.

[60] Ibid., p. 144.

ideas drawn from any person's controversial religious, moral, or philosophical commitments (i.e., comprehensive doctrines or conceptions of the good). This does not rule out the possibility of a close relationship between some person's comprehensive doctrine and her political conception. In fact, a political conception could be entailed by a comprehensive doctrine. What matters is that the political conception is presentable in political terms, without depending on controversial comprehensive commitments, and can be judged on its own merits in terms of political values publicly available in liberal democratic political culture. It does not matter how the political conception is ultimately derived.

But not all political conceptions are reasonable. The "limiting feature," for Rawls, "is the criterion of reciprocity, applied between free and equal citizens, themselves seen as reasonable and rational."[61] Reasonable citizens see one another as free and equal in a system of social cooperation, and are willing to offer one another fair terms of cooperation. To be reasonable, citizens must develop and act from political conceptions they think other citizens could accept from the common and shared moral point of view of "democratic citizen." Many possible political conceptions meet this requirement—Rawls refers to them collectively as "liberal political conceptions."[62] Minimally, these assign basic and familiar rights and opportunities to individuals, give them priority over the common good and perfectionist values, and secure their effectiveness with an adequate form of social security. Rawls's justice as fairness is one liberal political conception, but many others are possible. Rawls specifically mentions Habermas's discourse conception of legitimacy and Catholic views of the common good as possible competitors, provided that these views are expressed in terms of political values.[63] In order to be legitimate, law must be enacted and enforced in accord with and pursuant to a liberal political conception. The only political conceptions that fail Rawls's test are illiberal ones.

One common objection to Rawls's theory of legitimacy holds that when Rawls asks for a political conception all citizens could accept, he ignores the very diversity among citizens that raises the problem of legitimacy.[64] It is obvious, critics say, that if citizens agreed on the justice of a political conception, there would not be much of a legitimacy problem. But since citizens do not agree on the justice of any particular political conception, Rawls simply ignores the real issue. This objection misses the mark. Rawls explicitly acknowledges that democratic citizens have different ideas about how to specify their shared democratic values—e.g., about what counts as a

---

[61] Ibid., p. 141.

[62] Ibid., pp. 140–143.

[63] Ibid., p. 142.

[64] This objection has been made by many theorists, including notable figures such as Kent Greenawalt, *Private Consciences and Public Reasons* (New York: Oxford University Press, 1995), pp. 106–120, Stout, *Democracy and Tradition*, pp. 65–76, and Waldron, *Law and Disagreement*, pp. 1–2, and chapter 7.

more perfect union, or justice, or the general welfare—and thus that there are many possible liberal political conceptions consistent with public democratic values.[65] And since all liberal political conceptions are rooted in public democratic values, and all can be assessed independently of particular and controversial religious, moral, and philosophical commitments, all of them could be accepted by citizens from the shared moral point of view of democratic citizen. Thus, for Rawls, all liberal political conceptions meet the demands of the liberal principle of legitimacy. The principle does not single out one political conception as correct, but simply narrows the field of discourse to liberal ones. Rawls is explicit on this point:

> Political liberalism, then, does not try to fix public reason once and for all in the form of one favored political conception of justice. That would not be a sensible approach.... Even if relatively few conceptions come to dominate over time, and one conception appears to have a special central place, the forms of permissible public reason are always several. Moreover, new variations may be proposed from time to time and older ones may cease to be represented. It is important that this be so....[66]

Exactly which liberal conception should inform coercive enforcement of the law in any particular democratic society at any given time can only be determined by that society's citizens through actual political processes. In elections, candidates for office should offer their liberal political conceptions in public political debate, and then citizens should choose the one they think best captures shared and fundamental democratic political values. Though it is reasonable to reject any particular liberal political conception for another one, the one actually chosen by the majority is morally binding on citizens and ought to be accepted as such. For Rawls, majoritarianism is tied to the democratic self-understanding.

Thus, when public officials in a liberal democracy base their political activity on a liberal political conception, citizens have good reason to think their officials are sincerely committed to justice and the common good. Of course, some citizens will always see their laws as suboptimal in ways—as not the most just, or not the most reasonable—but the law's normative authority does not depend on such agreement. Laws deserve moral respect when they are reasonably seen as rooted in shared democratic ideals, that is, when they are linked to some liberal conception of democratic justice. When laws are grounded in this way, their coercive enforcement does not disrespect any citizen as a citizen. Further, laws so grounded at least approximate liberal justice. This is the most that we can expect of law under the conditions of reasonable disagreement and dissent that we face in modern liberal democracies.

On my reading, then, the view that Rawls develops in *Political Liberalism* and "The Idea of Public Reason Revisited" is a plausible deliberative account of democratic

---

[65] Rawls, "The Idea of Public Reason Revisited," pp. 140–144.
[66] Ibid., p. 142.

legitimacy. Rawls takes seriously the fact of reasonable disagreement over both comprehensive doctrines and public political conceptions of justice. Nevertheless, he seeks to vindicate the liberal tradition's commitment to individual freedom and political autonomy, by appealing to a reciprocal notion of reason-giving between citizens. He does not wrongly aim at some implausible consensus, so he avoids this standard objection to deliberative accounts. What is important to Rawls is that citizens regard one another as free and equal, and seek to resolve their political differences through some process involving reciprocal reason-giving. Still, the will of some will rule all. Rawls, like Kant, acknowledges that. But minority democrats will have good reason, even after losing, to see the will of the majority as reasoned and addressed to them as free and equal citizens. Minority democrats can thus see that they are not being subjected to force alone, or even force backed by nonpublic reasons. They are being subjected only to force backed by public reasons that satisfy the demand for public reciprocity between citizens.

6 Conclusion

In modern liberal democracies, the state's power almost always has to be exercised in the face of reasonable dissent and disagreement. Consensus regarding its use is simply not within our reach. This is the modern condition. But we need not let this reality force us into accepting some thin, impoverished notion of democracy or into abandoning liberal ideals of legitimate authority as rooted in shared reason-giving. Of course, democratic decision procedures do tend to protect our basic interests, and to keep our inevitable disagreements from degenerating into actual physical struggles for political dominance. But democracy can be more than this too. Deliberative accounts offer a vision of a democratic society in which individuals have the sort of political autonomy that makes them collectively into a self-determining body politic. This may be utopian, but it is realistic too.

Chapter 7
John Brown's Duties: Obligation, Violence, and 'Natural Duty'

Christian T. Sistare

On December 2, 1859, John Brown was hanged in Charles Town, Virginia, for the crimes of treason, murder, and inciting slaves to insurrection, following his seizure of the Harper's Ferry Federal Armory. Since that time Brown has been, variously: dismissed as a madman or religious zealot who stumbled onto a just cause, depicted as a violent fanatic and terrorist who pursued a just cause too far, or—the minority view—revered as a man who transcended the boundaries of racial division and sacrificed his own life to promote the freedom of his fellow human beings.

In this paper, I argue that Brown's willingness to employ violence to bring an end to slavery in the United States was justified for a citizen who believed his nation guilty of brutalizing and murdering innocent persons, in violation not simply of his religious convictions but also of that nation's legitimating political morality. My argument specifically addresses the problem of legal obligation and the standard liberal rejections of violent civil disobedience. These views typically define 'civil disobedience' so as to preclude violence, relegating violent means to the aims of revolution and militant resistance.[1] In contemporary popular language, such views must depict Brown as either a 'terrorist' or a 'freedom fighter,' thus disallowing his inclusion among the ranks of civilly disobedient citizens who wish to reform, rather than overthrow, existing political orders. I argue that Brown can be regarded as a civilly disobedient citizen whose recourse to violence was a reasonable response to the institutionalized oppression and daily torment of millions of innocent

---

[1] There are a number of definitional questions surrounding these terms. Some of these matters are taken up later in this paper, but I do not pursue the classificatory issues thoroughly. A useful exploration of these classificatory concerns is provided by Kimberley Brownlee, "Civil Disobedience", *The Stanford Encyclopedia of Philosophy (Spring 2007 Ed.)*, Edward N. Zalta (ed.), URL = <http://plato.stanford.edu/archives/spr2007/entries/civil-disobedience/>. Here, my point is that the use of violence, particularly against persons, is said to be incompatible with 'civil disobedience' as defined by the leading liberal conceptions. Given that claim, Brown's actions at Harper's Ferry must be classified as something other than civil disobedience: as revolutionary action, militant action, or some other form of violent resistance. One implication of this definitional move is to deprive Brown of the special presumption of moral right to disobey that typically attaches to 'civil disobedience,' even when particular acts of civil disobedience may appear unjustified in themselves.

D.A. Reidy and W.J. Riker (eds.), *Coercion and the State.*
© Springer Science + Business Media B.V. 2008

persons when persuasion and normal political recourse became futile[2]. Further, I suggest that Brown's conduct was not merely permissible but was, in fact, in accordance with basic natural duties to promote justice by combating gross injustice. The state's claim to legitimacy when it comes to coercion does not always preclude a valid claim on the part of citizens.

1   The Setting

To adequately assess John Brown's resort to violence in his fight against slavery, we require some understanding of the historical situation within which he made his choices. After the passage of the Missouri Compromise in 1820, the 'Slave Power'—the institutionalized mixture of economic and political forces that supported slavery and its expansion—dominated federal politics in the United States. Between 1829 and 1853, six pro-slavery Presidents occupied the White House; five of these Presidents were slave-holders.[3] The success of Slave Power politicians followed both from those constitutional compromises accepted as necessary to win approval of the *Constitution*[4] and from the 'fire-eating' tactics of the pro-slavery advocates, whose frequent threats of secession were heeded by all who sought to maintain the union.[5]

---

[2] I recognize that justification of Brown's use of violence against institutionalized slavery appears to open the door to justifications of violent resistance by anti-abortion activists, eco-saboteurs, and others. To fully distinguish the slavery case from these others would require significant discussion; however, one relevant distinction is that between the moral status of living human persons and the moral status of fetuses [or, 'unborn infants'] and non-humans. While we ought not to be too quick to dismiss claims about the moral status of fetuses and non-humans, the fact that these are highly contested claims imposes justificatory limits on the use of violence in defense of fetuses and non-humans. And, although some pro-slavery advocates spoke of blacks as less than fully human, the practices of slave owners, themselves, give the lie to such beliefs: *viz.*, the frequency with which white males had sexual relations with black women, the commonality of having white infants nursed by black women, the practice of giving white children slave playmates, and the general reliance on slaves to fulfill a variety of domestic and business responsibilities.

[3] The slave-holding Presidents included: Andrew Jackson of Tennessee; William Harrison of Indiana, by birth a Virginian; John Tyler of Virginia, later a member of the Confederate Congress; John Polk of South Carolina, whose war against Mexico was trumpeted as part of the plan to conquer South America 'for slavery;' Zachary Taylor of Louisiana. Millard Fillmore of New York succeeded Taylor; although not a slave-holder, Fillmore was a proponent of what became the Compromise of 1850.

[4] On July 4th, 1855, William Lloyd Garrison publicly burned a copy of the U.S. Constitution before an approving Boston crowd, proclaiming it to be a "covenant with Death." This view of the Constitution—as an ugly compromise which purchased national unity at the cost of human freedom—was common among abolitionists.

[5] John Calhoun was especially disposed to raise the specter of secession whenever pro-slavery interests were threatened, or when he felt pro-slavery advocates were being insulted.

In 1850, the infamous "Compromise of 1850" was passed as a series of bills providing for: (1) California's admission as a free state; (2) territorial organization without determinations as to slavery in New Mexico, Nevada, Arizona, and Utah; (3) and a new Fugitive Slave Act which denied captured persons any right to a hearing while placing on them the burden of proving that they were not escaped slaves. The Act instituted a system of individual 'commissioners' to approve claims for rendition, with the stipulation that they be paid double for decisions favorable to the slave-catchers, and imposed serious criminal penalties on any one who helped a black person evade capture or who refused to aid the slave-catchers in taking blacks captive[6]. In 1854, The Kansas-Nebraska Act was signed into law by President Franklin Pierce to achieve western expansion and to pacify Southern pro-slavery forces. The bill permitted slavery to be decided by "popular sovereignty" in the two future states—officially repealing the 1820 Missouri Compromise and its prohibition of slavery north of latitude 36o30' [with the exception of Missouri, itself][7].

The North and the South responded to the opening of the Kansas and Nebraska territories with a wave of emigration. Kansas was the particular object of concern on both sides of North-South sectionalist dispute, because Kansas—unlike Nebraska—was regarded as promising for a slave economy and because it bordered Missouri, a committed slave-state. Although there were multiple parties and groups, each with its self-proclaimed name and platform, our purposes permit a simpler categorial scheme of the opposing forces: on the Northern side, there were the Free-Soilers or Free-Staters; on the Southern side, there were pro-slavery forces and, specifically, the Border Ruffians. The latter group consisted primarily of Missourians who either squatted in Kansas temporarily or simply crossed the border into Kansas from Missouri as needed to wage guerrilla war against Free-Soilers and to thwart normal democratic processes.

Northerners and Southerners, alike, came well supplied with weapons; both sides were convinced that their opponents were dangerous—politically and physically. From the perspective of the Free-Soilers, in particular, the pro-slavery forces seemed ready to resort to violent means to bring slavery to Kansas. The redoubtable Senator Atchison played a special role in generating fear among the Free-Soilers by creating and leading his own band of highly armed Border Ruffians and by calling publicly for Missourians and other pro-slavery forces to "exterminate" Free-Staters and abolitionists. He did this both in speeches and in an eponymous publication

---

[6] The effect on Northerners, both abolitionists and non-abolitionists, was explosive. Formerly pacifist abolition leaders publicly endorsed abandoning 'moral suasion' for violent resistance, especially in defense of black residents threatened with seizure. In Boston, 300 federal deputies and 250 soldiers were called in by President Fillmore to enforce the rendition of Thomas Sims to Georgia. In Christiana, Pennsylvania, the townspeople united against Marylanders seeking escaped slaves and killed one of the southerners. President Fillmore responded to the 'Battle of Christiana' by sending in the Marines and arresting some 40 citizens for treason.

[7] Northerners responded to the Kansas-Nebraska Act with rage; the repeal of the Missouri Compromise was seen as evidence of the North's final submission to the 'Slave Power.'

created specifically for the Kansas slavery dispute. His close ties with the Pierce Administration and his role as President *pro tem* of the United States Senate completed, for the Free-Soilers, the picture of the Slave Power's hold over the federal government and its readiness to violate any law in order to achieve its ends. As the historian James McPherson observes, even before John Brown reached Kansas, "[p]artisans of both sides were walking arsenals."[8]

"Bleeding Kansas" framed John Brown's last attempts to do battle with slavery by normal political means. The Border Ruffians had invaded Kansas during territorial elections; by swelling the vote with their numbers, as well as by engaging in theft of ballots and intimidation of suspected Free-Soilers, they managed to install a pro-slavery legislature. The Lecompton Legislature, as it became known, passed laws imposing fines and imprisonment of not less than 5 years at hard labor for anti-slavery speech of any form, 10 years for helping fugitive slaves, and the death penalty for 'encouraging' slaves to escape or 'insurrection.'[9] The laws, borrowed from Missouri state laws, prohibited any anti-slavery man from sitting on a jury or holding public office. They also retroactively validated the votes of the non-resident Border Ruffians who had put the Lecompton Legislature in power. Social order in Kansas broke down completely. Pro-slavery forces, frequently assisted by federal troops, invaded Free-State towns, drove Free-Staters out of the territory, and beat or killed those who resisted.

2   Dred Scott, the Slave Power Conspiracy, and Harper's Ferry

Other national events of 1857–1858 had increased the wrath and desperation of anti-slavery parties in Kansas and across the nation. Among these, and preeminent in many minds, was the infamous *Dred Scott* decision handed down by the pro-slavery U.S. Supreme Court.[10] Justice Taney—a slave-holder already well known for previous pro-slavery and pro-South decisions—used *Scott* to make his stand on the entire slavery question. The majority opinion declared that (1) no black person, slave or free, could ever be a citizen of the United States; (2) that the federal Congress had no power to control slavery in the territories or the individual states; and (3) that the original Missouri Compromise, and its limitation on slavery expansion, was unconstitutional. The decision electrified opponents of slavery of all stripes; it radicalized a great many former moderates and horrified all who had hoped for the limitation of slavery by political means. Responding to *Scott* in his

---

[8] McPherson, *Battle Cry of Freedom: The Civil War Era* (New York: Oxford University Press, 1988), p. 148.

[9] Stephen B Oates. *To Purge This Land With Blood; A Biography of John Brown.* (Boston, MA: University of Massachusetts Press: 1984); p. 100.

[10] *Dred Scott v. San[d]ford.* 60 US 393 (1857).

'house divided' speech, Abraham Lincoln warned that "[slavery's] advocates will push it forward, till it shall become alike lawful in all the States, old as well as new—North as well as South;" if anyone doubted this, Lincoln suggested the doubter "carefully contemplate that now almost complete legal combination—piece of machinery, so to speak—compounded of the Nebraska doctrine, and the *Dred Scott* decision."[11]

The 'machinery' to which Lincoln referred in his speech was political conspiracy: the combined efforts of the Democratic party and the Slave Power to slowly move the nation to extend slavery and assert final control over the North. *Dred Scott* was the newest stage of the conspiracy's development, a belief widely shared by Northerners and anti-slavery activists. Lincoln's analysis of the conspiracy delineated what abolitionists such as John Brown saw revealed in the events of the mid-1840s, through Bleeding Kansas, and culminating in the *Scott* decision:

> The new year of 1854 found slavery excluded from more than half the States by State Constitutions, and from most of the national territory by Congressional prohibition. Four days later [with the Kansas-Nebraska Act], commenced the struggle which ended in repealing that Congressional prohibition. This opened all the national territory to slavery, and was the first point gained [by the Slave Power]....
>
> ...in the notable argument of "squatter sovereignty," otherwise called "sacred right of self-government," which latter phrase, though expressive of the only rightful basis of any government, was so perverted in this attempted use of it as to amount to just this: That if any one man choose to enslave another, no third man shall be allowed to object....
>
> [Under the Kansas-Nebraska Act] The people were to be left "perfectly free," "subject only to the Constitution." What the Constitution had to do with it outsiders could not then see. Plainly enough now, it was an exactly fitted niche, for the Dred Scott decision to afterward come in, and declare the perfect freedom of the people to be just no freedom at all....
>
> [The Court made clear] that what Dred Scott's master might lawfully do with Dred Scott, in the free State of Illinois, every other master may lawfully do with any other one, or one thousand slave, in Illinois, or in any other free State....
>
> We cannot absolutely know that all these exact adaptations are the result of preconcert. But when we see a lot of framed timers, different portions of which we know have been gotten out at different times and places and by different workmen—Stephen [Douglas], Franklin [Pierce], Roger [Taney] and James [Buchanan], for instance—and when we see these timbers joined together, and see they exactly make the frame of a house or a mill, all the tenons and mortices exactly fitting, and all the lengths and proportions of the different pieces exactly adapted to their respective places, and not a piece too many or too few—not omitting even scaffolding—or, if a single piece be lacking, we see the place in the frame exactly fitted and prepared yet to bring such a piece in—in such a case, we find it impossible not to believe that Stephen and Franklin and Roger and James all understood one another form the beginning, and all worked up a common plan or draft drawn up before the first blow was struck.[12]

Moreover, if Lincoln and other anti-slavery advocates were correct about the conspiracy, worse was yet to come. Justice Nelson, in his concurring opinion in *Dred*

---

[11] Lincoln, Abraham. Springfield, Illinois, June 16, 1858. http://www.bartleby.com/251/1001.html

[12] *Ibid.*

Scott, laid open the way for 'popular sovereignty' to decide all slavery questions within each state as well as within the territories: "except in cases where the power is restrained by the constitution of the United States, the law of the State is supreme over the subject of slavery within its jurisdiction."[13] In light of this, Lincoln argued, "Put this and that together, and we have another nice little niche, which we may, ere long, see filled with another Supreme Court decision, declaring that the Constitution of the United States *does not permit a State to exclude slavery from its limits.*" "Such a decision is all that slavery now lacks of being alike lawful in all the States," Lincoln predicted. "We shall lie down pleasantly dreaming that the people of Missouri are on the verge of making their State free, and we shall awake to the reality instead, that the Supreme Court has made Illinois a slave State."[14] The entire nation would submit to the Slave Power and to slavery.

Indeed, Lincoln continued, it was only a matter of time before the slave trade was resumed. How could the country regress to that? Lincoln and others saw it as a matter of legal logic: if the Congress and the Supreme Court regarded it as "a sacred right of white men to take negro slaves into the new Territories," how could anyone deny "that it is less a sacred right to buy them where they can be bought cheapest?" A political cabal of Presidents, congressmen, and the Supreme Court had sought "to reduce the whole question of slavery to one of a mere right of property." What court or Congress could now "refuse that *trade* in that 'property' shall be perfectly free," as well?[15]

Perhaps it is difficult, from the perspective of our own time, to fully appreciate the cogency of this line of argument. And, perhaps, Lincoln was engaging in political hyperbole. But, to John Brown, certainly, Lincoln's speech would have accurately described the state of affairs that existed in the United States in 1859. The Slave Power had neither receded nor given an inch in its struggle for domination. Rather, it had reached new heights of power across the nation. It had effectively controlled the Presidency and the Congress for all of Brown's 59 years of life. In the last 10 of them, at least, he had seen it not only achieve ascendancy over the political processes of the federal government but also increase its geographical reach to Mexico and beyond. Its interpretation of the *United States Constitution*—typically accompanied by ridicule of principles expressed in the *Declaration of Independence*—was pronounced the law of the land by the highest federal court. It was poised not simply to persist in its own 'peculiar institution' of enslavement of human beings, but to import that institution to those parts of the nation where slavery had been abandoned.

"*Will anything be done?*"[16] Brown had already decided that something must be done. He had vowed that there would be no peace until slavery was 'done for,' not

[13] Nelson, Samuel, J., *Dred Scott, supra*, note 10.
[14] Lincoln, Abraham, 1858; emphasis added.
[15] *Ibid*; emphasis added.
[16] John Brown in a letter to Congressman Joshua Giddings; cited in. Oates, *supra*, note 9, p. 115.

merely in Kansas, but in the United States. During 1856–1858, Brown traversed the Northeast, trying to raise money and materials for his war on slavery. He was met with enthusiasm by many abolitionists and did manage to obtain some of what he sought, although it seems he may have received more encouragement and sympathy than material support. Nonetheless, with the help of supporters, later known as 'The Secret Six,' Brown assembled a substantial store of weaponry and raised a group of men ready to do battle against slavery. More precisely, they set out to do battle against the Slave Power and its 'instrument,' the federal government. While the details of Brown's plans remain obscure—partly because he himself seems to have altered them as he proceeded—the raid on the Harper's Ferry Federal Armory in Virginia was its public consummation. Brown and approximately forty-five others seized the Armory on October 16, 1859.[17] They had some hopes that slaves in the area would escape to join them, ultimately leading to a general breakdown in the control of the whites over the black populace throughout the Southern slave states. The expected fugitive reinforcements never appeared, and Brown, possibly under the sway of a fatalist sense of destiny, remained with his men at the Armory as they were surrounded by local residents and, eventually, federal forces. Brown, and those of his men who had not already been killed or escaped, refused to surrender to Colonel Robert E. Lee and Lieutenant J. E. B. Stuart, then United States officers. On October 17, the federal troops attacked: ten of Brown's band, including two of his sons, were killed; Brown and six others were beaten and arrested. The rest escaped, though some were caught in later weeks. The entire affair was over by noon on October 18.

The Harper's Ferry Raid lasted less than 3 days. John Brown was tried and executed on December 2, 1859; his captured compatriots were all tried and executed by March of 1860. Yet, more than the interminable political contests and maneuvers that led to geographical sectionalism in the nation, more than the often vitriolic debates in the press and on the floors of Congress, more than the years of 'Bleeding Kansas,' John Brown's seizure of the armory at Harper's Ferry and his subsequent trial and execution aroused the nation. Frederick Douglass wrote, "The announcement [of the raid] came upon us with the startling effect of an earthquake. It was something to make the boldest hold his breath."[18] Southerners feared a widespread slave insurrection; James McPherson observes that "The news of Harper's Ferry sent an initial wave of shock and rage throughout the South, where wild rumors circulated of black uprisings and of armed abolitionists marching from the North to aid them."[19] The Northern reaction, at first echoing the shock and condemnation of

---

[17] Brown probably had up to 50 men with him; some were left to guard their safe house and others, including Owen Brown, were set to keep watch outside Harper's Ferry. W.E.B. Du Bois notes that the number in the Brown company is often given as 22; this number does not include all the free and escaped *blacks* with the Brown party. W.E.B Du Bois. *John Brown* (New York: Modern Library, 2001). p. 167. Originally published in 1909 by G.W. Jacobs (Philadelphia).

[18] Frederick Douglas; cited in Du Bois, *ibid.*, p. 211.

[19] McPherson, *supra*, note 8, p. 208.

southerners, shifted as Brown's responses to his interrogators and his trial testimony circulated:

> If it is deemed necessary that I should forfeit my life for the ends of justice, and mingle my blood further with the blood of my children and *with the blood of millions* in this slave country—whose *rights* are disregarded by *wicked, cruel, and unjust enactments*— I say, Let it be done.[20]
>
> I want you to understand that I respect the rights of the poorest and weakest of colored people, oppressed by the slave system, just as much as I do those of the most wealthy and powerful. That is the idea that has moved me, and that alone…*The cry of distress of the oppressed is my reason*…
>
> I claim to be here carrying out a measure I believe *perfectly justifiable*…to aid those suffering *a great wrong.*[21]

By the time of his hanging, John Brown had become a martyr to the cause of freedom in the North among abolitionists and non-abolitionists alike. Ralph Waldo Emerson proclaimed that Brown's execution in Virginia would make "the gallows as glorious as the Cross," and Henry David Thoreau, despite his reputed pacificism, penned a "Defense of Captain Brown" and of Brown's resort to violence.[22] Brown's failure at Harper's Ferry turned out to be a resounding success in his fight against slavery and the Slave Power in the United States. As Frederick Douglas put it, some 22 years later, "If John Brown did not end the war that ended slavery, he did, at least, begin the war that ended slavery."[23]

3   Disobedience, Violence, and Duty

Philosophers do not, as a rule, offer historical details of the kind presented in the preceding sections. We prefer to set principles and provide definitions with some degree of abstraction, since generality is at the heart of philosophical analysis. Ethicists, in particular, tend to invent hypothetical cases of their own to pursue specific issues and purposes. But, in the normative fields of philosophy, especially, it is wise to return to the lived facts of human experience to test and assess our abstractions. This is a practice with which most legal philosophers are acquainted, as ours is an area of theory in which human experience is always imminent.

The history of the ante-bellum United States and of the world of John Brown's experience gives us a context within which his choices and actions can be meaningfully evaluated. I do not propose to examine Brown's purported religious zeal, as such,

---

[20] John Brown at his trial; cited in McPherson, *ibid.*, p. 209.

[21] John Brown's responses to interrogators immediately following his capture; cited in Du Bois, *supra*, note 17, pp. 208–209.

[22] R.W. Emerson; cited in McPherson, *supra*, note 8, p. 209; Henry David Thoreau. *A Plea for Captain Brown* (Kila, MT: Kessinger Publishing, 2004).

[23] Frederick Douglass; cited in Du Bois, *supra*, note 17, p. 211.

or his sanity. He was, without question, a very religious man whose particular American Calvinism was central to his life.[24] However, the religious grounds of his antipathy to slavery need not be shared by those of us who wish to evaluate his actions in fighting slavery through the means he employed.[25] He was, also, an emotional man, highly agitated by what he experienced, but there is no evidence that he was unbalanced as a general matter. The question, for us, is whether his resort to violence can be justified in light of his real experiences.

How are John Brown's actions to be best understood, then?[26] A dominant tradition in contemporary liberal legal and political theory treats 'civil disobedience' as a highly specific form of disobedience to law. In particular, John Rawls, Hugo Adam Bedau, Martin Luther King, Jr., and others have argued for defining 'civil disobedience' so as to exclude any use of violence and to require willingness of the disobedient to accept punishment.[27] The standard argument is that violence is incompatible with the civilly disobedient purpose of reform through appeal to reason.[28] Thus, anyone who resorts to violence cannot be a civil disobedient. While some theorists have disputed these definitional prescriptions,[29] disobedients of Brown's sort are typically described either as terrorists or freedom-fighters, according to the disapprobation or approbation of those applying the terms. An alternative is to classify him as a revolutionary or radical—leaving the question of approval open.

But, Brown was neither a 'revolutionary' nor a 'radical,' if that nomenclature signifies the aim of complete overthrow of a political and legal *system*. It is true that Brown and other abolitionists frequently spoke of the pro-slavery and 'dough-faced' federal administrations of the ante-bellum period with great contempt. But, Brown's

---

[24] Louis De Caro, Jr. *Fire from the Midst of You: A Religious Life of John Brown.* (New York: New York University Press, 2002).

[25] Rawls made a similar point in assessing Dr. King's protest activities as effective appeals to public reason.

[26] I do not deal, in this paper, with Brown's activities in the Kansas 'wars,' which included the killing of several men taken from their homes at night. However, I believe that those killings, seen in the context of the territorial civil war in which Brown found himself, can be justified as pre-emptive acts of self-defense and defense of others. Steven Nathanson has suggested to me that Brown's situation in Kansas was akin to a State of Nature, wherein individuals do have the right to defend themselves and their families in the absence of effective social order.

[27] John Rawls, *A Theory of Justice.* (Cambridge, MA: Harvard University Press, 1971); Hugo Adam Bedau, "On Civil Disobedience" *The Journal of Philosophy*, v. 58, n. 21, 1961, pp. 653–661, and (ed.) *Civil Disobedience in Focus.* (London: Routledge, 1991); Carl Cohen, *Civil Disobedience: Conscience, Tactics, and the Law* (New York: Columbia University Press, 1971); Martin Luther King, Jr. "Letter from Birmingham Jail" in Bedau, ed., *Civil Disobedience in Focus.*

[28] Here, I do not explore Rawls' insistence that the appeal be further limited to one made to a "shared sense of justice." Peter Singer and others have adequately addressed the problems entailed by that limitation: Peter Singer, "Civil Disobedience as a Plea for Reconsideration," in Bedau, ed., *Civil Disobedience in Focus*, ibid.

[29] Notably: John Morreall, "The Justifiability of Violent Civil Disobedience," in *Canadian Journal of Philosophy*, v. 6, 1976, pp. 35–47.

intention[30] was not to replace the system of the United States with some other form of government; it was to bring the actual administration of that system into accord with what he believed to be its founding principles. Most Americans of Brown's generation recognized that the *U.S. Constitution* was a compromise document, a political *modus vivendi*, more than a pronouncement of political principles. Anti-slavery Americans viewed the *Declaration of Independence* as the statement of the founding principles of the American form of government, and they took quite seriously the apparent expectation of the signers of the *Constitution* that slavery would wither away over time.

What confronted Brown and other abolitionists in the mid-1800s was the increasing probability that slavery would not disappear from the United States but would, in fact, spread. Indeed, following the opening of the West, the number of slaves held in the United States and its territories had grown to an astonishing *four million*, and the espoused intention of the Slave Power to expand into the new territories required ever greater numbers of humans to be born or imported into that same bondage. Further, the well-evidenced political bondage of the federal government to the Slave Power meant that political efforts to stop slavery—at least, to stop its expansion—were futile. To the abolitionists, and even to the many northerners who had no interest in abolition or sympathy for non-whites, the conspiracy theory laid out by Lincoln was entirely believable; it articulated the true nature of American political events of the early to mid 19th century, and it revealed the course of events to come. That southern politicians had taken to openly deriding the principles of equality espoused in the *Declaration of Independence* was simply a public admission of the Slave Power's true political perspective.

Furthermore, the actions of the Slave Power parties and of pro-slavery forces—particularly in Kansas—demonstrated significant rejection of basic principles of democracy. Outright violence, intimidation, manipulation of the vote, and suppression of free speech were brazenly employed tools of pro-slavery and pro-South groups across the nation. Bleeding Kansas has captured the attention of historians as a particularly shocking and apt foreshadowing of the Civil War, but it was only one instance in a series of shocks felt by men like John Brown. The ruthlessness of the Slave Power was so fully evident to northerners that the abolition movement hardly needed to promote itself on its own terms. Many who had previously rejected abolitionism were converted, if not to genuine empathy for blacks, then simply to the movement as a seat of anti-southern resistance.

More significantly, for our concerns, the methods of the Slave Power moved many pacifist abolitionists to accept, if not undertake, violent means to end slavery. John Brown was not alone in abandoning the dictates of pacifism, although he may have come to that decision before some others in the abolitionist movement. Not surprisingly, blacks had been among the first to advocate violent resistance, as in David Walker's *Appeal*: "...they want us for their slaves, and think nothing of murdering

---

[30] Here, we might distinguish Brown's views from those of William Lloyd Garrison who was the more genuinely revolutionary of the two.

us… and believe this, that it is no more harm for you to kill a man who is trying to kill you, than it is for you to take a drink of water when thirsty."[31] And, although activists in the early Underground Railroad tried to avoid violent confrontations with slave-catchers, there had long been occasions of violent resistance by or on behalf of fugitives from slavery. Such methods were openly embraced after the Fugitive Slave Act of 1850, when not only individuals but also crowds of whites and blacks in the North attempted to prevent enforcement of the 'hated Acts.' By 1859, even a previously devoted pacifist such as Frederick Douglass would say, "I have little hope of the freedom of the slave by peaceful means. A long course of peaceful slaveholding has placed the slaveholder beyond the reach of moral and humane considerations….The only penetrable point of a tyrant is the *fear of death*."[32]

So, John Brown was not alone in coming to accept physical violence as an acceptable, even necessary, means in the struggle against slavery. But, was he justified in his own actions? We need not debate the meaning of 'violence,' here; John Brown did engage in physical violence at Harper's Ferry. I contend that Brown's use of violent methods can be justified on several grounds. These include the need to reform and resist a corrupt political order and to act in defense of others,[33] both as required by a conception of the Natural Duty to Justice similar to that presupposed by current liberal theories of political obligation and civil disobedience.

It should be clear that the raid on Harper's Ferry was in defense of others—the four million enslaved blacks of whom Brown frequently spoke and the uncounted millions more who would be born or dragged into bondage if slavery was not ended in the United States. Their suffering was not an historical abstraction to John Brown. Indeed, even among the 'ultra-abolitionists,' Brown was noted for a special gift: the gift of a 'black heart.'[34] By this term, the abolitionists meant genuine empathy of white people with black people. Such empathy was aspired to by some whites, but it seemed to all who met him that John Brown's very nature allowed him to transcend the racial divisions which encumbered everyone else. When Brown spoke of 'our' suffering under slavery, he spoke literally. He meant, in part, that white and black Americans suffered politically under the Slave Power. But, more than this, he meant that the misery, the abuse, the torture and maiming, the raping

---

[31] Walker, David. APPEAL to the COLOURED CITIZENS OF THE WORLD, but in particular and very expressly to those of THE UNITED STATES OF AMERICA. First published in 1829; passage quoted from http://www.iath.virginia.edu/utc/abolitn/walkerhp.html.

[32] Frederick Douglass; in a speech cited at http://www.educationanddemocracy.org/FSCfiles/C_CC7e_NonviolenceInAmHist.htm

[33] It should be noted that the political order confronting Brown was corrupted by persons who suppressed democratic processes, including those that otherwise survived the constitutional compromise which disproportionately enfranchised the pro-slavery states. In other words, I am not addressing, here, the legitimacy of the legal and political system in place in the ante-bellum U.S. As I argue further on, Brown accepted the system as legitimate, but regarded slavery as an aberration of justice in that system.

[34] John Stauffer. *The Black Hearts of Men: Radical Abolitionists and the Transformation of Race* (Cambridge, MA: Harvard University Press, 2002).

and killing endured by slaves, and the often violent discriminatory treatment suffered by free blacks, were real to him. He was especially moved by the plight of slave families, of slave women and their children. The sexual abuse of the women by white 'masters,' the cruel breaking apart of families whose members were sold away from one another, and the selling of mullatto children by their own white fathers—these evils repelled John Brown viscerally as well as morally. The 'peculiar institution' and all that followed from its workings were a horror, a horror that John Brown *knew*. He hoped to bring an end to this horror.

But what of violent actions taken against an established government? Although the natural rights of persons to revolution or, short of that, to violent resistance to oppressive laws and policies, are controversial in political theory, they are by no means unfamiliar. John Locke, disputing English Quakerism in his *Second Treatise on Government*, wrote,

> If the innocent honest man must quietly quit all he has for peace's sake to him who will lay violent hands upon it, I desire it may be considered what a kind of peace there will be in the world which consists only in violence and rapine, and which is not to be maintained only for the benefit of robbers and oppressors. Who would not think it an admirable peace betwixt the might and the mean, when the lamb, without resistance, yielded his throat to be torn by the imperious wolf?[35]

Of greater significance for John Brown, of course, were the *Declaration of Independence* and the principles that grounded the American Revolution. That fundamental American document and those principles were fully valid in Brown's view, as they had been for the founders of the United States. Should we conclude that the right to violent revolution against an oppressive government does not at least imply the right of violent resistance to oppressive acts of a system otherwise supported by a citizen? Must we choose, in other words, between outright revolution and pacific civil disobedience? If we frame the issue this way, rather than in terms of the proper definition of 'civil disobedience,' I think the answer is clear; more modestly, it is *not* clear that there is *no* such (at least implied) right to use violence, or the threat of violence, in the service of substantial reform rather than complete revolution.

John Brown believed, as did many northerners, that a just system—*his* national system—had been taken over by those not truly committed to its principles. The southern slave-owning states had arranged matters so that the Constitution gave them an electoral power far beyond the numbers of their voting population.[36] As a result, the Slave Power and its northern, "dough-faced henchmen" exercised control over the Presidency and the Congress for nearly a century. Southern politicians were increasingly inclined during the mid-1800s to ridicule the principles of equality

---

[35] John Locke. *A Second Treatise of Civil Government* (Cambridge: Cambridge University Press, 1960), p. 465.

[36] In 1849, the South accounted for 30% of the voting population; it controlled 42% of the electoral vote.

espoused in the *Declaration of Independence*, although it is worth noting that they embraced its warrant for revolution (or secession). And, as events such as the Kansas-Nebraska Act, the civil war in Bleeding Kansas, and the *Dred Scott* decision amply evidenced, the Slave Power had no intention of allowing mere democratic principles to stand in its way.

The repression of anti-slavery speech, which extended to making it a crime in most of the South for any white person to teach any black person—enslaved or free—to read, was especially galling to the North. Freedom of speech and press had been the hallmarks of the original American democratic movement. The abolitionists were denied so much as the opportunity to make the kind of 'appeal to reason' that contemporary theorists such as Rawls have insisted on as providing the only acceptable approach to civil reform. What hope had the abolitionists for undertaking "moral suasion" if they could not send their materials through the federal postal system or share those views with others—particularly with the people on whose behalf they wrote? John Brown, in fact, had more respect for the United States *system* of government than most pro-slavery advocates. What he hated and sought to overthrow was the Slave Power that, often undemocratically, and in violation of *all* principles of equality, had arrogated that system to its own purposes. Every violation of what we now term procedural justice was made in the service of what Brown—rightly, I assume—believed to be an appalling system of human oppression under which the grossest substantive injustices were daily realities.

Perhaps it will be argued that Brown and others were justified in taking violent action, but only because these failures of procedural and substantive justice were sufficient to render the political system of the United States prior to 1860 unjust, or not 'as just' as could 'reasonably be expected under the circumstances.' This could provide approaches to political obligation and civil disobedience of the received liberal type with a way to circumvent the problem of John Brown. I think this will not do. First, the standard liberal conception of 'reasonably just' is significantly procedural.[37] Thus, if the original constitutional provisions were properly observed, the United States, complete with slavery, might have been a reasonably just system.[38] Brown's only legitimate complaint, then, would be against subsequent violations of democratic procedures by the government itself. For the most part, these were not significant; the federal government did often fail to protect abolitionists and did not protect freedom of expression in all of the states. But the ascension of the Slave Power was, so to speak, according to the rules. And, responsibility for the violence in Kansas cannot be directly laid at the federal government's door, or not indisputably so; here, again, failure to exert effective power—in this case, to maintain the peace—was the government's clearest shortcoming, as distinguished from violation of constitutional procedures.

---

[37] See, e.g., Jeremy Waldron. "Special Ties and Natural Duties," *Philosophy & Public Affairs*, v. 22, no. 1, 1993, p. 9, note 5.

[38] We should note that there were a number of unjust features of our early political order, including significant limitations on the franchise by sex and economic criteria.

But, there is a second deficiency in the 'reasonably just regime' approach to legal obligation. Let us assume that we are primarily concerned with substantive justice, not merely with procedural issues. The Natural Duty approach to 'political obligation,' eloquently articulated by Rawls, holds that every person has a pre-political duty to 'support just systems and their institutions.' This grounds a *general obligation* to law, not merely a specific or particular obligation following from the rightness of individual laws; the general obligation is supplemented by specific moral duties and by the more narrowly defined legal obligations of those citizens who enjoy the benefits of the system. As peculiarities of terminology can be confusing, let us simply say that, on a certain type of liberal view, Natural Duty commits every human [without regard to actual benefits] to obedience to all the laws and policies of a reasonably just system. There may be other grounds for *specific* obedience, even *within* a system that is not reasonably just, but there is no *general* obligation grounded in Natural Duty *to* such an unjust system. Slavery was a very great substantive injustice, without question. Does this mean that the United States, from its creation through to the mid-1800s, was not a 'reasonably just system'? To the extent that the received liberal view of a just regime requires full adherence to substantive principles of justice, the United States probably was not a just system until long after the Civil War.[39] If so, are we to conclude that no one had any genuine *general* obligations of obedience to or under that system during that time? This conclusion seems theoretically implausible; the practical implications, particularly for all the ordinary political and legal business conducted during those years, would be stunning. That some citizens might have had specific obligations, despite the compromised legitimacy of the system, hardly improves the picture.

Yet, curiously and importantly, neither John Brown nor like-minded abolitionists seem to have thought the entire U.S. system was unreasonably unjust—despite the magnitude of the injustice of slavery. This is why he was not a genuine revolutionary, why he did not seek to overthrow the entire system but instead to reform it. Brown wanted to keep the system and any of its laws or policies that did not enable slavery. He seems to have regarded himself as fully bound to the real principles of the system and to all but the slavery aspects of its laws and policies. He violated other laws, not directly connected with slavery, in order to achieve the reforms he sought, as a necessity—neither in protest of those laws nor in the belief that they were anything but *valid laws*. The evil of slavery was great, the occupation of the political system by the Slave Power was thorough; nonetheless, Brown saw these as discrete aberrations that could be excised from a system which, in its conception, was fully legitimate. The now-familiar metaphor of cancer is apt: we excise the diseased tissue in order to save the body. The patient is not the enemy; the disease is the enemy and is fought against for the sake of the patient. However 'radical' a

---

[39] David Lyons argues that until the repeal of Jim Crow laws in the 1960s the United States was not a regime sufficiently just to create any presumption of obligation among its citizens. David Lyons, "Moral Judgment, Historical Reality, and Civil Disobedience," *Philosophy and Public Affairs*, v. 27, n. 1, 1998, pp. 31–49.

change the ending of slavery would be, Brown's aims were not as comprehensive as those of paradigmatic radicals and revolutionaries. That he resorted to violence cannot, itself, render his aims and his situation irrelevant to our classification of his actions or, more importantly, to our understanding of them.[40]

Something is amiss with the combined 'Natural Duty to obey and no right to violent civil disobedience' approach, something deeper than the farrago of definitional disputes which partly discloses the problem. The approach seems to either bind us too tightly or not at all. We must rely on the good sense of our fellow citizens, appealing only to their Reason, or take up arms in full-blown revolution.[41] But, as the case of John Brown and the ante-bellum abolitionists discloses, this is too simple to capture the realities of human political and social experience. Brown and others *did* attempt political resolution of the slavery debate; they *did* attempt "moral suasion." In fact, Brown never entirely abandoned the political struggle; even as he raised money and arms for the raid on Harper's Ferry, he continued to participate in Kansas Free-State legislative activities. Those efforts to reform the system through non-coercive moral and political processes were met with suppression of basic rights. They were met, in many cases, with violence. Meanwhile—all the meanwhile—black Americans were subjected to wretched lives of servitude and violence beyond anything Brown ever fomented. And, John Brown saw that *nothing was going to change.* Slavery would continue and grow; more millions would be enslaved, raped, maimed, and slaughtered. Is it theoretically plausible to claim that Brown had only two legitimate alternatives: civil submission or revolution? Is it practically desirable to suggest that a citizen has only these two choices? However we elect to apply terminology, we ought to theorize in ways which reflect and serve the interests of real human agents in their complex lived contexts.

We have considered John Brown's duty to obey the law and his 'right' to resist the government. Might he have had another duty: *a duty to resist*, to fight against slavery by whatever means proved necessary or most effective?[42] Brown stated on many

---

[40] A factor in the definitional disputes must be the relative importance of disparate features of the paradigm cases: intent of the disobedient, scope of her aims, motivation, and means employed. A subtle analysis of these features can be expected to reveal intersections, e.g., between aims and appropriateness of means.

[41] Michael Walzer similarly observes that a restrictive no-violence definition of civil disobedience "...virtually invites militants of various sorts to move beyond the bounds of civility altogether." M. Walzer. *Obligations: Essays on Disobedience, War and Citizenship* (Cambridge, MA: Harvard University Press, 1970), p.25.

[42] As a last nod to definitional concerns, I would note that the most effective means of ending slavery, by the mid-1800s, was the kind of 'direct action' undertaken by Brown at Harper's Ferry and by operatives in the Underground Railroad. Whether Brown believed that slaves would join him at Harper's Ferry, thus effecting their own liberation, remains a matter of speculation. However, it is clear that political means and moral appeals were utterly ineffective. Direct action, by its very nature, invites coercive response from authorities and, in this way, frequently necessitates violent resistance to that coercive response. The alternative to violent resistance is acquiescence to the authorities, which negates the original effort and, in some cases, may cost the resister her life.

occasions that he thought he had such a duty; he often expressed this in term of his duties to God and, through God, to humanity. Sometimes, he spoke of a direct duty to humanity, to his fellow human beings. Most abolitionists did speak in these terms. William H. Seward outraged southern Congressmen by giving a speech in which he proclaimed that there is a 'Higher Law' than the United States Constitution.[43] This was clearly an appeal to the ideas of Natural Law expressed in the *Declaration of Independence*. One need not accept the metaphysics of Natural Law theory to comprehend the basic notion: humans have both rights *and* duties that transcend those created by human institutions. This, of course, is precisely the intuition underlying the Natural Duty theory of obligation to law. Theorists may differ as to the origins and grounds of such natural rights and duties, but the fundamental notion is the same.

There is an interesting qualification to the theory of Natural Duty to just institutions as it is often presented: each of us has a natural duty to support existing [reasonably] just institutions, but we are not said to have a comparable natural duty to reform unjust institutions. At least, we have no *significant* duty to reform unjust institutions and, on Rawls' version, we have no duty to do so unless "this can be done with little cost to ourselves."[44] We needn't worry, here, about what constitutes a 'little' cost or risk. John Brown certainly incurred terrible costs and took terrible risks in his fight against slavery, and we might well wish to acknowledge Brown's willingness to incur such costs as morally supererogatory. I am concerned with the broader questions: Did John Brown have any *Natural Duty to struggle against the injustice* of slavery? Were John Brown and the less self-sacrificing abolitionists fulfilling a Natural Duty to end slavery? Did all those who did not join the struggle *fail to fulfill* a Natural Duty to protect others?[45] The Rawlsian Natural Duty approach demands much by way of obligation to just institutions but demands very little of individuals in a struggle to create justice.[46] This might reflect a pragmatic bias in favor of peaceful social relations. But, it is possible that this received view is too easy on citizens as moral beings. And, it is possible that what continues to worry us about John Brown is our realization that a man who could have lived a comfortable life risked it all—gave his own life, in fact—to fight for the lives and freedom of strangers, while we suspect (or know) that we would not have done the same.

---

[43] W. H. Seward, "Freedom in the New Territories," speech presented in the US Senate, March 11, 1851. Available online at http://www.senate.gov/artandhistory/history/resources/pdf/SewardNew Territories.pdf

[44] Rawls, John. *A Theory of Justice, supra*, p. 334, also p. 115.

[45] One feature of Rawls' analysis I find intriguing is that those who benefit most under a system have the strongest [specific] duty to obey the laws of the system but have no greater duty to reform the system than those who benefit least from it. This strikes me as an open invitation to dominant racial and ethnic groups to ignore the suffering of oppressed minorities in their midst and to do so under the cover of their own legal obligations.

[46] An interesting account of the move to narrowly define civil disobedience while emphasizing the strength of political obligation can be found in: J. Welchman, "Is Ecosabotage Civil Disobedience?," *Philosophy and Geography* v. 4, n.1, 2001, pp. 97–107. See, also, Lyons, "Moral Judgment, Historical Reality, and Civil Disobedience," *supra*, note 39, p. 48.

Let us grant that the extent of John Brown's self-sacrifice is aptly described as supererogatory. It is unreasonable to claim that each of us has an *absolute* Natural Duty to devote ourselves and our families to a just cause to the extent that Brown did. Such a duty would obligate every human being to complete self-sacrifice in the cause of justice, converting an agent-centered moral concern into a requirement to rival any agent-neutral obligation. Yet, is our Natural Duty limited to what can be done 'at little cost' to ourselves? Were all those free whites who simply ignored the evils of slavery adequately fulfilling their Natural Duties of justice? At what point does *indifference* become *complicity*? The received liberal theory of Natural Duties of justice cannot help us to answer this last question, and that may be the most telling indicator of its shortcomings. I will not argue at length, here, that Brown and other whites did have a Natural Duty to fight against slavery. I believe each human has a *prima facie* duty to contest gross injustice at something more than 'little cost' to herself; if this is correct, then John Brown should be acknowledged as a moral hero rather than condemned as a political villain or derided as a madman.

4   The Final Question

Leaving this argument for a later time, I wish to conclude by raising another possibility about John Brown's case and our understanding of it. That possibility is that, in addition to our amazement at Brown's own sense of his Natural Duties to combat the horrors of slavery, we are baffled by something specific to his case: John Brown was a white man, and the people on whose behalf he gave his life were black. Many of the northern abolitionists were white, of course. But John Brown had a 'black heart' to a degree unmatched by any other white abolitionist. John Brown thought that the fight against slavery was his fight; he felt the suffering of black slaves as though it were the suffering of his nearest friends or members of his own family. Is this why we find it easier to dismiss him as a religious fanatic or a madman than to carefully explore his duties to his fellow humans? If John Brown had been, for example, a Christian German who engaged in violent resistance to the slaughter of Jews, would we call him a terrorist, a lunatic, a religious zealot? Perhaps we would not name such a man a 'civil disobedient,' because we could take cover under the liberal judgment that the Nazi regime was not 'reasonably just' and, so, was owed no *prima facie* duty of obedience. Perhaps we would classify such a person a 'freedom fighter.' Yet, these theoretical maneuvers—particularly the definitional move—are not fully faithful to our natural intuition that what really matters is that such a person acts *rightly* in defense of others against grossly unjust practices and laws. The comparative justness or unjustness of the systems within which such defensive resistance is taken seems largely irrelevant to that intuition.[47] Such

---

[47] Nor, I think, do disparate assessments of likely success alter our intuition that it is right to defend others.

comparisons might inform our judgment as to justification of specific choices or a preferred sequence of reformative efforts; we might think John Brown was obligated to begin his struggle with non-coercive political means while admitting there was no obligation to turn first to comparable means under the Nazi regime. But, the rightness of the impulse, indeed, the *sense of obligation*, to defend others against gross injustice is not altered by disparate assessments of systemic legitimacy. We must confront the final question: if a white man who engages in violent resistance against other whites on behalf of horribly oppressed whites in Nazi Germany does no wrong, acts rightly, then did not John Brown do no wrong, act rightly, by adopting all necessary means to help free the millions of black slaves in 19th century America from their horrible oppression?

Part III
Coercion and the State: Legal Powers and Status

Chapter 8
Coercion, Neutrality, and Same-Sex Marriage

Emily R. Gill

1 Must Nonneutral Policies be Coercive?

Many modern liberal theorists hold that a hallmark of liberalism is the state's neutrality among rival ideas of the good. According to William Galston, on the other hand,

> "Every polity ... establishes at least a partial rank-order among individual ways of life and competing principles of right conduct" (Galston 1991, 96–97). Therefore, it cannot be neutral. Unlike nonliberal states, however, "The liberal state rests solely on those beliefs about the good shared by all its citizens, whereas every other state must coercively espouse some controversial assumptions about the good life" (93).

If Galston's account is correct, the distinction between liberal and nonliberal states rests not upon the presence or absence of neutrality, but on the presence or absence of coercion in the way that the state adopts or espouses its unavoidable assumptions about the good. Genuinely shared assumptions, those realized in a liberal polity, cannot by definition have been coercively espoused or imposed. In nonliberal states, assumptions not genuinely shared, typically those ingredient in the viewpoint of a dominant consensus, are coercively espoused or imposed by the state over and against dissenting viewpoints.

In a recent article, Daniel Brudney suggests that leaving the question of religious establishment to the majoritarian process, rather than making establishment or nonestablishment a constitutional principle, need not contravene liberal principles. What he terms modest noncoercive establishment protects the free exercise of religious liberty and does not use force. It makes only limited use of the public voice and the public purse—that is, of speech and spending. Any use of these tools that dampened the free exercise of religion because of fears of social ostracism would no longer be modest or noncoercive and would therefore not be compatible with liberal principles. Brudney's overall point is that strict constitutional separation of church and state assumes that all citizens need to have a strong psychological connection to the overall political community. Emphasis on the desirability of this connection, and thus the rejection of modest establishment, he concludes, is grounded on a substantive and disputable conception of the good, and is therefore potentially not in accordance with liberal principles (Brudney 2005).

Where Galston suggests that a lack of general consensus necessarily renders nonneutral public policies coercive, Brudney argues that the operation of majoritarian processes *may* prevent nonneutral public policies from being coercive. Although coercion is an elusive concept, F. A. Hayek's definition is a serviceable one: "Coercion implies both the threat of inflicting harm and the intention thereby to bring about certain conduct" (Hayek 1960, 134). Prohibitions against murder threaten to impose punishment and thereby intend to discourage such actions. Coercion is not always a straightforward objective matter of fact independent of the perceptions or feelings of the agent coerced, however. Sometimes the subjective perceptions or feelings of the agent coerced are central. Part of my concern in this essay is with the subjective perceptions or feelings of coercion experienced by those who find the range of opportunities extended to them, relative to the range extended to others in the community, limited by democratically enacted legislation.

I first argue that *every* religious arrangement in political life rests upon a partial and controversial view of the good. There is always some dominant consensus, not genuinely shared by all, that distinguishes between those who are favored and those who are not. This is true even where religious belief and practice are not coerced or made objects of direct compulsion. The existence of this dominant consensus often leads those not favored to perceive their opportunities as circumscribed relative to those of others, to feel limited in their choices by those more favored than they.

I then argue that both opponents and proponents in the debate over same-sex marriage agree that civil marriage is a great good. Given this agreement, it makes more sense to extend civil marriage to same-sex couples than to disestablish it as a civil institution altogether. The civil institution of marriage establishes a view of the good. To some, the exclusion of same-sex couples from this institution parallels an establishment of religion that excludes and hampers the free exercise of those whose understandings draw them to another religion. Therefore, civil marriage as currently defined represents a partial and controversial view of the good. Those excluded from it may feel coerced if they are compelled to choose between traditional marriage, which they cannot affirm, and the foregoing of the benefits, both material and nonmaterial, of marriage altogether. Although some may not care whether public policy is neutral or inclusive, attention should be paid, I believe, to those whose relative deprivation renders them second-class citizens in their own eyes.

2   Nonneutrality and the Dominant Consensus

If government makes use of the public voice and public purse to persuade citizens concerning the advisability of secular propositions and policies, wonders Brudney, why should these activities be impermissible when religious values are the object of persuasion? The key potential difficulty posed by religious establishment, he suggests, is the possibility that those not of the established religion will feel themselves demeaned, excluded, and not full members of the political community, and might therefore become alienated from its institutions. But although even modest noncoercive

establishment will affirm the superiority of the established religion(s) over nonestab-
lished religion(s), "such disrespect is a significant harm only if citizens find it important to be treated with equal respect *by the state* ... The state's failure to treat me
with equal respect can seem a significant harm only if I have a certain conception of
my proper relation to the state" (Brudney 2005, 820). This would be the case "only
if one values a sense of connectedness to the political community" (821).

On Rawls's view, our self-respect is partly dependent upon securing the respect
of others. But this, Brudney maintains, "does not entail that it depends on respect
from the state" (823). That alienation from the polity harms self-respect is a controversial and disputed premise upon which not all will agree. Why then, Brudney
asks, should a comprehensive doctrine that affirms this strong-connection-to-the-
polity thesis take precedence at the constitutional stage? Why should a complete
constitutional separation of church and state trump the democratic choice by a
majority for a modest noncoercive establishment in the light of the particular
empirical context of its society? If, following Rawls, we assume this is a matter of
basic justice and/or constitutional design to be settled by original position reasoning, then a strong constitutional separation of church and state would seem to
depend on agents in the original position reasoning from a controversial view of
at least part of the good (832), a failure of neutrality.

I want to suggest that *any* public stance regarding religion means espousal of at
least a partial view of the good. If, as Galston suggests, every polity at least partially
ranks ways of life and principles of right conduct, this must be true even of liberal
polities that valorize diversity. Even classic arguments for religious toleration such
as John Locke's, for example, recognize that civil authority must establish a civil
criterion of worldly injury to life, liberty, and property that then determines the
appropriate scope and limits of religious liberty. That is, to avoid harm to the
worldly rights or interests of citizens, the line between the civil and the religious
must be determined by civil government, not by religious believers who may differ
in their assessments both from secularists and also among themselves. Moreover,
this line may change along with the demands of the public interest, which is itself
civilly determined (Creppell 1996, 224; see also McClure 1990, 373–381). As
Kirstie McClure suggests, civil law that is neutral with regard to the religious truth
of particular practices is necessarily *not* neutral or politically indifferent toward the
practical embodiments of some religious visions of the good society.

The difficulty, however, is that "the civil discourse of facticity itself has become
a site riddled with conflicting interpretations of which particular sets of social
'facts' are to be considered indicative of the sort of 'harm' appropriately subject to
political jurisdiction" (McClure 1990, 383; see 382–383). Her examples include
Marx on property and Catherine MacKinnon on pornography. Both characterize
seemingly isolated practices as embedded within systems "which operate to recon-
stitute as injurious, and hence political, 'facts' which were previously understood
as civilly benign" (384). Assessments of harmlessness and injury, then, will depend
upon the context in which social facts are placed by their interpreters. The liberal
state therefore cannot rest on its neutrality or hospitality to diversity across the
board, but must instead be grounded on the particular range of values or preferences

that a given interpretation of liberalism puts forward. What is problematic is that those whose values or preferences are outside that range risk feeling alienated or excluded. Thus, although I believe that Galston is correct about the nonneutrality of even the liberal state, it is far from clear that the liberal state, as he suggests, rests only upon beliefs about the good shared by all its citizens.

In *Thornton v. Calder* (105 S.Ct. 2914, 1985), for example, the Supreme Court struck down a Connecticut statute that guaranteed to Sabbath observers the right to their weekly entitlement of 1 day off on their Sabbath. The Court believed that the law unfairly advantaged Sabbath observers over nonobservers, as only the former could select a coveted weekend day for their guaranteed day off. In *Sherbert v. Verner* (374 U.S. 398, 1963), however, the Court overruled the denial of unemployment compensation to a Seventh-Day Adventist fired for refusing to work on her Sabbath of Saturday. A state attending to Sabbath observance is on this view not violating neutrality but enforcing it in the light of religious differences. To force workers to choose between their religious convictions and their means of support would advantage those without religious duties over those with duties the exercise of which may conflict with secular expectations (Sandel 1987, 88–90).

Even in a polity whose Constitution has an establishment clause, these two cases exemplify alternative meanings of freedom of conscience. In McClure's terms, the set of social facts grounding *Thornton* classifies Sabbath observance as a choice; therefore, according more freedom to observant than to nonobservant workers in selecting a day off is not a civilly benign practice but is civilly injurious to people with less choice—that is, to those who cannot claim religious observance as a justification for choice. The set of social facts grounding *Sherbert*, however, classifies Sabbath observance as a duty; thus according freedom to observant workers who refuse to work on their Sabbath without forfeiting unemployment benefits is civilly benign across the board. Although applicants must accept available work to be eligible for benefits, Sabbath work is not "available" in the sense that observant workers may choose to perform it. In view of these social facts, it is civilly injurious to penalize Sabbath-observant workers, who have less choice than do the nonobservant, who can choose to accept available work at any time.

For our purposes, what is important here is that under either interpretation of how to avoid an establishment of religion, somebody loses out. With *Thornton*, Sabbath observers may be alienated: they must choose between failing to observe their Sabbaths, on the one hand, or risk unemployment by observing their Sabbaths even without the permission of their employers, on the other. With *Sherbert*, Sabbath nonobservers are those who may be alienated: Sabbath observers are accorded the privilege of "choosing" their day off without consequence, while nonobservers must take whatever day their employers assign. Why, they might wonder, should sabbatarian beliefs be privileged through exemptions granted for practices flowing from them, when other types of deeply held beliefs are not?

Even in a polity with an establishment clause mandating separationism, then, there is an "establishment" of a dominant consensus that guides particular policies. Any decision regarding the place of religious belief in the polity constitutes a partial view of the good, and subsequent decisions that flow from this "establishment" may alienate some portion of the political community. But does this matter? First, Brudney may be correct in stating that citizens' self-respect does not depend upon respect from the state. Second, if under every possible arrangement someone loses out and may feel excluded and become alienated, it appears there is no solution even if Brudney is incorrect. That is, even if citizens do value a strong psychological connection to the political community, no possible church-state arrangement will prevent the risk of feelings of exclusion and alienation in at least some citizens. The only question will be that of which group(s). This question does not seem to trouble Michael McConnell. In his view, "no citizen is demeaned by laws that he disagrees with, so long as he has an equal right both to advocate for laws he deems just and to disagree with arguments he does not find persuasive" (McConnell 2000, 105; see 100–105).

Brudney's modest noncoercive establishment is noncoercive in the sense it does not require adherence to the tenets of a particular faith tradition as a condition of full citizenship. But there is a dominant consensus that reminds those who dissent from it that they are outsiders. Even with church-state separation, varied interpretations will give rise to varied policies, some of which may alienate some individuals. With either arrangement, individuals and communities of varying faith traditions may be welcome to exert influence on public policy without constraint. But if majoritarian reasoning maintains over time that proposed policies are not in fact limiting or coercive, even if they might appear so to an outside observer, dissenters have no recourse. Although McConnell maintains that dissenters are not demeaned by laws they oppose as long as they can argue against them in favor of laws that suit them better, this appears to me like touting the right to whistle into the wind!

In her concurring opinion in *Lynch v. Donnelly*, Justice Sandra Day O'Connor argued that the First Amendment's establishment clause may be violated not only by the excessive entanglement of government with religious institutions, but also and more directly by "government endorsement or disapproval of religion. Endorsement sends a message to nonadherents that they are outsiders, not full members of the political community, and an accompanying message to adherents that they are insiders, favored members of the political community" (*Lynch v. Donnelly*, 465 U.S. 668 (1984), at 688). Any sort of establishment, I believe, conveys the message that those who adhere to the dominant consensus are insiders and favored members of the political community, while those who dissent from this consensus are outsiders and not full members of the political community.

Some citizens may not care. That is, as Brudney suggests, their self-respect may not in fact depend upon respect from the state. Additionally, if they may freely exercise their own beliefs and there is no religious test for any direct public benefit (Brudney 2005, 817), might we not argue that the state does in fact respect them? Why, in fact, should *we* value citizens' strong identification with the polity? First, a polity is healthier if citizens feel they have a stake in a common project. If there are some who do feel like outsiders, they are less likely to perceive the existence of this stake. Second, when some feel demeaned by the continued force of laws that seem to recognize others at their own expense(s), they may feel both alienated, if they repeatedly try unsuccessfully to alter laws that they find demeaning, and coerced, if even indirect public benefits that are accessible to others are inaccessible to them. If, as I have argued, any church-state arrangement constitutes a partial view of the good and sets up a distinction between insiders and outsiders, why not try to maximize the chances that citizens who do value it can experience a strong psychological connection to the broad political community? I believe that the controversy over same-sex marriage highlights the issue of respect from the state, particularly some of the ways in which citizens may feel not only alienated, but also coerced. It is to this issue that I now turn.

3   Same-sex Marriage: Insiders, Outsiders, and Disestablishment

Despite Brudney's conviction that our self-respect does not necessarily require respect from the state, he admits that emphasis on a strong connection to the political community seems widespread. "It is worth reflecting on the fact that people who otherwise seem hostile to state institutions, who deem them corrupt, wicked, or at best a necessary evil, nevertheless deeply want the state to endorse their point of view" as representative of "the people." He suggests specifically that this desire underlies the arguments of both opponents and proponents of same-sex marriage. "That dispute is increasingly not about the provision of concrete legal rights and benefits ... but about whether the term 'marriage' is to be applied to a relationship—and applied not by a minister, priest, rabbi, or imam but by an agent of the state" (Brudney 2005, 832).

Current debate reinforces Brudney's point. Uniting the various and often conflicting viewpoints is the implied conviction that the definition of civil marriage makes a statement about who is and who is not fully a citizen of the liberal democratic polity. As Jyl Josephson puts it, marriage is viewed as "the holy grail of gay politics by opponents and proponents alike," because "Advocates on both sides of the issue agree that there is a deep connection between access to the institution of marriage and full citizenship" (Josephson 2005, 269–270). Participation in this institution offers certain rights and material benefits, to be sure, but this is not all. "Marriage posits a specific desirable form for intimacy and family life—despite contemporary reality—and reinforces that form through legal, economic, political, and social privileges" (271). That is, the contours of the institution of marriage represent an endorsement of a particular and preferred view of how citizens should ideally conduct their lives.

Beyond this agreement, however, a range of conflicting views exists. Moreover, neither traditionalists nor nontraditionalists necessarily agree among themselves about what marriage should signify. For traditionalist opponent of same-sex marriage Maggie Gallagher, for example, the traditional marriage communicates a shared ideal of exemplary relationship that encourages ties and obligations crucial to the successful reproduction of society (Gallagher 2003, 17–19). To traditionalist proponent Andrew Sullivan, however, it is the very absence of social incentives and institutions that render opponents' expectations of same-sex behavior a self-fulfilling prophecy. Same-sex marriage would thus promote both individual welfare and social stability (Sullivan 1996, 7; see also 99–100, 106–116). For Jonathan Rauch, rather than simply "a lifestyle option," marriage should be expected of committed couples and privileged as "better than other ways of living" (Rauch 2005, 91). "Marriage is for everyone—no exclusions, no exceptions" (6). Where traditionalist opponents endorse a particular model of family relationship and exclude as outsiders those who do not conform, traditionalist proponents endorse the institution of marriage itself as an aspiration inclusive of all committed couples. For both types of traditionalist, marriage represents a preferred way of living and the state should endorse it as such; their differences are simply over who should be included.

Nontraditionalists also differ among themselves about the significance of marriage. Skeptics about traditional marriage extend their skepticism to same-sex marriage. Marriage implies a freely chosen contract, but in reality represents consent to a preordained status whose contours are defined by public policy. For Valerie Lehr, the recognition of same-sex marriage would extend a benefit to some, making insiders of former outsiders, but it would extend a forced choice between the rigidity of marriage and exclusion from a valuable status to many others who might not wish to participate, thus reinforcing their status as outsiders. Liberal advocates of same-sex marriage, however, regard the ability to marry the partner of one's choice as a basic human right. For David A. J. Richards, for example, discrimination grounded in sexual orientation, like other ascriptive characteristics, morally enslaves individuals: the dominant culture devalues some human beings as rights bearers, and then justifies this devaluation on the basis of history that itself bears the marks of the original dehumanization (Richards 1999, 6). Such intolerance violates the inalienable right to conscience (18). Moreover, insistence on a close link between sex and procreation is for Richards "a sectarian ideal" (98) which does not command universal allegiance and therefore should not be enforced at the expense of those who do not define their lives in this manner. Thus, the dominant culture defines some as insiders and others as outsiders by disabling the latter's ability to choose. Although some might choose to remain outsiders even if same-sex marriage were available, those who wish to make this commitment should be able to do so.

First, whatever their differences, all of these viewpoints suggest some line of demarcation between insiders and outsiders. For traditionalist opponents of same-sex marriage, it is between those participating in traditional marriage and everyone else. For traditionalist proponents, it is between committed couples, whether same sex or opposite sex, and everyone else. For skeptics, it is between those included and those still excluded, either by choice or circumstance, and perhaps marginalized, even if same-sex marriage were a reality. Finally, for liberal advocates of same-sex marriage, because inclusion is a matter of conscience, exclusion is alienating in ways similar to conventional assertions of religious orthodoxy and represents, in Richards's terms, a sectarian ideal.

Second and more important, for partisans of all of these viewpoints, respect from the state matters a great deal. Traditionalist opponents of same-sex marriage, for example, do *not* take comfort from the fact that that their own religious tradition(s) presumably will never pronounce a same-sex couple to be married. They want to ensure that the state does not do so either, and this desire is attested to by the widespread passage of state constitutional amendments to prohibit a legislative majority from ever recognizing same-sex marriage. Only traditional couples, we may infer, deserve the strong connection to the polity that marriage as a bedrock institution confers. Traditionalist proponents, on the other hand, want the *"Good Housekeeping"* seal of approval that the term "married" represents. Proponents such as Rauch, for example, suggest that couples should want the approval—and by implication, the psychological connection to the polity—that only "marriage" confers (Rauch 2005, 92).

Although skeptics about marriage recognize the centrality of marriage in cementing a strong connection to the polity, this very recognition is what makes them wary. Those who cannot or do not participate will experience a comparatively weaker connection than those who do. Finally, liberal advocates of same-sex marriage suggest that exclusion places nonparticipants in the same relation to the polity as that experienced by dissenters in the face of an established religion. Although the "religious" liberty of same-sex couples is protected in that they may live as if married, and although civil unions and/or domestic partner benefits, where available, may mean that there is "no religious test" for state benefits, without state endorsement of their status they are still second-class citizens (Richards 1999, 90–93). Moreover, individual state-instituted marriage-like arrangements do not entitle participants to federal benefits such as joint filing of income tax returns or the transfer of Social Security benefits to partners.

Thus in Hayek's terms, same-sex couples are subject to coercion in two ways. First, they suffer the tangible harm of being deprived of benefits available to traditional couples, plus the intangible harm of being deprived of the recognition afforded to traditional couples. Any individual may of course marry a partner of the opposite sex. But this "solution" would be akin to converting to an established religion which one cannot conscientiously endorse to avoid the harms of belonging to a religion that is not recognized. Second, if the threat of inflicting harm is meant to bring about some kinds of conduct to the exclusion of others, current public policy would seem to discourage the formation of stable same-sex unions, though this is unintended, a point recognized by traditionalist proponents of same-sex marriage. Because the state holds a monopoly on the benefits of civil marriage, both tangible and intangible, it would seem, as Hayek suggests, that to prevent the exercise of coercive power such a monopolist should be required "to treat all customers alike, i.e., … insist that his prices be the same for all and to prohibit all discrimination on his part" (Hayek 1960, 136). In any case, choices are available to traditional couples that are unavailable to same-sex couples.

If, as we have seen, any church-state arrangement can in some contexts give rise to distinctions between insiders and outsiders, what is to be done? One alternative would be to "disestablish" marriage altogether as a civil institution. Gordon Babst, for example, argues that the continuing ban on same-sex marriage in the United States can be attributed to a *de facto* "shadow establishment," defined as "an impermissible expression of sectarian preference in the law that is unreasonable in the light of the nation's constitutional commitments to all its citizens" (Babst 2002, 2, italics omitted). More specifically, "Nonpreferentialism ... is also establishment, whereby preference is given to religion, broadly conceived yet narrowly understood as Christian and as opposed to irreligion. Expression of this preference in the law is not a legitimate, publicly justified secular purpose" (57–58). Among other examples of nonpreferentialism, writes Babst, are Sunday closing laws, defended as having the secular purpose of providing a uniform day of rest, despite the fact that the reason most Americans, religious or not, regard Sunday as a family day of rest goes back to earlier religion-based laws that restricted Sunday activities (72–76). Both closing laws and the same-sex marriage ban "have successfully hidden the sectarian rationale for their existence behind a putatively legitimate governmental purpose" (78). Although there could be valid empirical reasons for disallowing same-sex marriage, such reasons are rarely proffered. The existence of this shadow establishment could be remedied simply by allowing same-sex couples to marry, but also by letting "individual couples decide for themselves within their communities of faith, or otherwise, what marriage signifies for them and their communities, rather than have a definition imposed on them by the State" (83).

McConnell observes that recognition of same-sex marriage "would not solve the 'establishment' problem, but would only broaden the 'establishment' to give favored status to two 'churches'" (McConnell 1998, 250). That is, marriage would still be a legally defined status that conditions participation on adherence to its terms. True disestablishment would require that unions be privately formed and celebrated, just as like-minded individuals exercise freedom of association by forming religious groups and institutionalizing them. McConnell notes that in *Reynolds v. United States* (98 U.S. 145, 1879), in which the Supreme Court banned polygamy, Reynolds was seeking neither benefits nor the recognition of polygamous marriage, but only to be left alone. "In other words, Reynolds unsuccessfully sought what homosexuals already have: the right to live with the person(s) of their choice, as if married, without hindrance from the state." Because "most combinations of human beings are ineligible for matrimony," the case for same-sex marriage as a free exercise or equal access claim is weak. Free exercise considerations already protect the rights of religious communities to celebrate same-sex unions. "It is one thing to say that the government may not interfere with a religious (or sexual) practice in the privacy of the home, and quite a different thing to say that the government must adjust the definition of a public institution to conform with the doctrines or desires of a minority" (249).

It may in fact be argued, from both a Rawlsian and a libertarian perspective, that "disestablishment" of the institution of marriage would best instantiate neutrality and could end the tug of war among competing viewpoints about who should define it. From a Rawlsian perspective, Edmund Abegg suggests that we should allow the state itself to perform only civil unions, but let it recognize as civil unions marriages, within limits, that are solemnized by religious communities. This suggestion harmonizes with the eschewing of comprehensive ethical and moral views characteristic of political liberalism (Abegg 2006). From a libertarian perspective, Richard Stith argues that "The argument for legal recognition of same-sex unions does not seek liberty. It seeks state involvement in what would otherwise be free personal relationships" (Stith 2004, 263), and is, as skeptics argue, not in the best interests of many who now seek such unions. Stith would grant legal recognition to unions only if or when children are being parented, to protect family members and to reward those whose burdens eventually benefit the entire community (266–269).

As we have seen, on Brudney's view, which would leave the matter to democratic legislation potentially based in religious reasons, rests on the assumption that citizens will not feel demeaned, excluded, or alienated because they are outsiders, or not full members of the political community. Insofar as the present institution of marriage constitutes a "partial establishment," however, it appears that many people of varying opinions about marriage care very much about who are insiders, who are outsiders, and overall, about experiencing a strong connection to the political community. That is, they want to be treated with equal respect not only by their fellow citizens, but also by the state. They want their favored form of marriage recognized by the state. Any church-state arrangement, as we have seen, may give rise in certain contexts to a distinction between insiders and outsiders, although, in my opinion, this is less likely with church-state separation than with some sort of establishment. With regard to same-sex marriage, on the other hand, disestablishing marriage entirely as a public institution, except perhaps where children are involved, would pull the rug out, so to speak, from under those who not only want to unite civilly, but want to *marry* civilly. It would be akin to the actions of some southern municipalities that, with the end of segregation, chose to close their swimming pools rather than allow African Americans to swim there. If, McClure suggests, seemingly isolated practices may be embedded within systems that render injurious "facts" that previously seemed civilly benign, we must take notice of the entire context. The context here is that of a "partial establishment." The question is whether this partial establishment, like Brudney's modest noncoercive establishment, protects religious liberty by allowing free exercise of religion and does not use force–that is, imposes no religious test for any direct public benefit (Brudney 2005, 817).

Because the state of matrimony confers benefits, both material and psychological, the exclusion of same-sex couples from the institution of marriage because they are same-sex couples in my view imposes a "religious" test on those who seek such benefits. Despite McConnell's view that the case for same-sex marriage as a free exercise or equal access claim is weak, civil marriage is held out by many as a goal to which to aspire. The inability publicly to make this commitment, not only "in the eyes of God and this congregation," but also in the eyes of the state, or the hypothetical assemblage of one's fellow citizens, can thwart individuals, in Richards's terms, in "the free exercise of the moral powers of rationality and reasonableness in terms of which persons define personal and ethical meaning in living" (Richards 1999, 18). If the ability to live out the implications of one's deepest commitments is a form of conscience, this should be protected, Richards argues, as our tradition of religious liberty has typically protected all forms of conscience, both theistic and nontheistic (Richards 1999, 88, 94).

Although free exercise protects the right of religious communities and their members to solemnize whatever unions they choose, my focus is on the individual, or on same-sex couples who, as two individuals, wish to participate in the institution of marriage. Couples denied religious solemnization of their unions in one religious community can generally find other religious communities that will accede to their wishes. What same-sex couples often want, however, is the solemnization of their unions in *civil* terms, in the eyes of the state. Their religious or their moral and ethical beliefs may impel them to participate in the institution of marriage not—or not only—to attain conventionally religious legitimacy, but also to attain civil legitimacy, or the full "*Good Housekeeping* seal of approval."

Therefore, although the free exercise of religious communities as such is not impeded, the free exercise of individuals *is* blocked. In *Thomas v. Review Board*, in a case finding that a Jehovah's Witness should not be denied unemployment compensation after leaving a job that compelled him to manufacture tank turrets despite the fact that not all Jehovah's Witnesses agreed with his scruples, Chief Justice Warren Burger stated for the Supreme Court, "Where the state conditions receipt of an important benefit upon conduct proscribed by a religious faith, or where it denies such a benefit because of conduct mandated by religious belief, … a burden upon religion exists. While the compulsion may be indirect, the infringement upon free exercise is nonetheless substantial" (450 U.S. 707, 1981, at 717–718). Members of same-sex couples cannot in good faith marry individuals of the opposite sex, as they cannot and do not experience the deep connection that they do to members of the same sex. But the material and psychological benefits of marriage are conditioned by the state on "conduct" in which they cannot in good conscience engage. Similarly, their deep connections to same-sex partners "mandate" that marriage, if available, be to these partners. But the state denies the benefits of marriage because of "conduct" that their consciences compel.

What this suggests is that those who oppose same-sex marriage may be viewed as trying to maintain a "modest establishment" that does in fact interfere with "religious liberty" or the right of conscience broadly defined. Moreover, those who want to constitutionalize either their opposition to same-sex marriage, as many states have done, or antidiscrimination laws protecting sexual orientation, as Colorado tried to do with Amendment 2 until this was overturned by *Romer v. Evans* (517 U.S. 620, 1996), are in effect posing a "religious test" for state benefits. I realize that the cultural or religious traditionalist will perhaps feel coerced or alienated, or like an outsider, in the face of same-sex marriage. On the other hand, as Karen Struening suggests, "We do not take from him what he needs to live *his life*" (Struening 1996, 512), as we would be taking from the dissident by failing to recognize that which he believes central to his own life. That is, if the possible alienation of some cannot be altogether avoided, we would do well to heed John Stuart Mill: "There is no parity between the feeling of a person for his own opinion, and the feeling of another who is offended by his holding it; no more than between the desire of a thief to take a purse, and the desire of the right owner to keep it" (Mill 1989 [1859], 84). The welfare of those directly affected should trump that of those indirectly affected.

Because there will always be some citizens who feel coerced by the dominant consensus, I favor working toward the consensus that allows the greatest degree of

individual "free exercise." Overall, nonrecognition of same-sex marriage may not
ostracize same-sex couples, and it does not constitute a ban on publicly acknowledged same-sex relationships. But it suggests the moral supremacy of an establishment that favors traditional couples, and thus implicitly betokens second-class
citizenship.

References

Abegg, Edmund. 2006. "The Magic of Marriage: Comments on Gill." Paper delivered at the bien-
    nial meeting of Amintaphil, St. Louis, MO (Nov. 2–5).
Babst, Gordon Albert. 2002. *Liberal Constitutionalism, Marriage, and Sexual Orientation: A
    Contemporary Case for Dis-Establishment.* New York: Peter Lang.
Brudney, Daniel. 2005. "On Noncoercive Establishment." *Political Theory* 33 (December),
    812–839.
Creppell, Ingrid. 1996. "Locke on Toleration: The Transformation of Constraint." *Political
    Theory* 24 (May), 200–240.
Gallagher, Maggie. 2003. "Normal Marriage: Two Views." *Marriage and Same-Sex Unions: A
    Debate,* ed. by Lynn D. Wardle, Mark Strasser, William C. Duncan, and David Orgon
    Coolidge. Westport, CT: Praeger, 13–24.
Galston, William A. 1991. *Liberal Purposes: Goods, Virtues, and Diversity in the Liberal State.*
    New York: Cambridge University Press.
Hayek, F. A. 1960. *The Constitution of Liberty.* Chicago, IL: University of Chicago Press.
Josephson, Jyl. 2005. "Citizenship, Same-Sex Marriage, and Feminist Critiques of Marriage."
    Perspectives on Politics 3 (January), 269–284.
Lehr, Valerie. 1999. *Queer Family Values: Debunking the Myth of the Nuclear Family.* Philadelphia,
    PA: Temple University Press.
Lynch v. Donnelly, 465 U.S. 668 (1984).
McClure, Kirstie. 1990. "Difference, Diversity, and the Limits of Toleration." *Political Theory* 18
    (August), 361–391.
McConnell, Michael W. 1998. "What Would It Mean to Have a 'First Amendment' for Sexual
    Orientation?" *Sexual Orientation and Human Rights in American Religious Discourse,* ed. by
    Saul M. Olyan and Martha C. Nussbaum. New York: Oxford University Press, 234–260.
McConnell, Michael W. 2000. "Believers as Equal Citizens." *Obligations of Citizenship and
    Demands of Faith: Religious Accommodation in Pluralist Democracies,* ed. by Nancy L.
    Rosenblum. Princeton, NJ: Princeton University Press, 90–110.
Mill, John Stuart. 1989 (1859). "On Liberty," *On Liberty and Other Writings,* ed. by Stefan
    Collini. New York: Cambridge University Press, 1–115.
Rauch, Jonathan. 2005. *Gay Marriage: Why It Is Good for Gays, Good for Straights, and Good
    for America.* New York: Owl Books of Henry Holt.
Richards, David A. J. 1999. *Identity and the Case for Gay Rights: Race, Gender, and Religion as
    Analogies.* Chicago, IL: University of Chicago Press.
Romer v. Evans, 517 U.S. 620 (1996).
Sandel, Michael J. 1987. "Freedom of Conscience or Freedom of Choice?" *Articles of Faith,
    Articles of Peace: The Religious Liberty Clauses and the American Public Philosophy,* ed.
    James Davison Hunter and Os Guiness. Washington, DC: Brookings Institution Press,
    74–92.
Sherbert v. Verner, 374 U.S. 398 (1963).

Stith, Richard. 2004. "Keep Friendship Unregulated." *Notre Dame Journal of Law, Ethics, & Public Policy* 18 (1), 263–271.

Struening, Karen. 1996. "Privacy and Sexuality in a Society divided over Moral Culture." *Political Research Quarterly* 49 (September), 505–523.

Sullivan, Andrew. 1996. *Virtually Normal: An Argument about Homosexuality.* New York: Vintage Books of Random House.

Thornton v. Calder, 105 S. Ct. 2914 (1985).

Chapter 9
The Cheshire Cat: Same-Sex Marriage, Religion, and Coercion by Exclusion

Kenneth Henley

The paradigm case of state coercion is a criminal sanction: the threat of loss of life, liberty, or property for disobedience to the state's commands. A prudent person will consider forgoing the pleasure of his favorite drug out of fear of punishment, even if he believes the prohibition unjust. But, as H.L.A. Hart emphasized, much law consists not of such primary, conduct-controlling rules, but rather of secondary, power-conferring rules that establish structures of interaction.[1] Private power-conferring rules include those governing contracts, covenants, conveyances, wills, trusts, and marriage. Since *Lawrence v. Texas*,[2] homosexuals in the United States no longer suffer the coercion of the criminal law for adult, consensual, private sexual conduct. And homosexuals, of course, have always had the legal power to make contracts and wills, to convey real property, and create trusts. Marriage is the last bastion of discrimination through exclusion. But is such exclusion an exercise of state coercion, and, if so, is it illegitimate, or (in the alternative) unjust? I will argue that the exclusion of same-sex couples from exercising the power-conferring rules of marriage now constitutes state coercion in the sphere of conscience and religious belief, for only religious barriers continue to make sense. There is both an establishment of religion issue and a free exercise issue. As Emily Gill argues, the liberal polity should maximize free exercise by minimizing establishment.[3] Because of changes in society, family law, and criminal law, this coercive exclusion from civil marriage totally fails to accomplish its secular goal. Once secular purposes are no longer served, the exclusion also, in addition to invading religious liberty, fails to respect the principle of equality of all persons before the law. Although I refer to U.S. Constitutional cases in passing, my argument should have purchase in any polity recognizing religious liberty and equality of persons.

---

[1] H.L.A. Hart, *The Concept of Law* (Oxford: Clarendon Press, 1961), pp. 27–28.

[2] 539 U.S. 558, 2003.

[3] Emily R. Gill, "Coercion, Religious Neutrality, and the Case of Same-Sex Marriage," in this volume, pp. 125–6.

D.A. Reidy and W.J. Riker (eds.), *Coercion and the State.*
© Springer Science+Business Media B.V. 2008

1   Religious Liberty and Religious Entanglement with Secular Law

The political and legal principle of religious liberty requires that reasoning deter-mining how to use the state's coercive power omit appeals that are specific and limited to any particular religious tradition, or appeals that presuppose the rejection of religious traditions. Rejection of this liberal principle is consistent only with theocratic conceptions of the state. As Kent Greenawalt argues, given "the underly-ing principles of our legal system....we need to limit ourselves to arguments and reasons that do not rest directly on unshared theological claims."[4] In *A Letter Concerning Toleration*, John Locke provided the fundamental liberal argument that the state's coercive authority is limited to secular, this-worldly purposes.[5] Of course, individuals are free to express their particular religious beliefs, but they have no right to impose such beliefs through coercion, private or state. Expressions of uncontroversial normative views using religious language are acceptable even in support of coercion, for everyone understands that the religious background is optional: "God wills that children be protected" or "Those who harm or neglect children acquire bad karma and a lower reincarnation" have the same normative content in this world as "Harming or neglecting children is wrong." Of course in discourse within a particular group, the shared views of the group may legitimately play a role—as long as the group's actions do not affect those outside in a signifi-cantly adverse way; minor inconveniences and irritations, however, are to be accepted for the sake of the broadest possible freedom of religious practice. The line-drawing will at times be difficult, and reasonable persons may disagree about what constitutes a significant adverse impact. (Consider the debate over whether to allow partly or wholly veiled photographs of women for driver's licenses, or the difficulty of accommodating rare religious practices within a workplace, including government workplaces.) Here is the well-trod but wavering path of interpreting and applying the Free Exercise Clause of the First Amendment of the U.S. Constitution.

There are a few issues where public reasoning must first directly treat the question of separating specific religious beliefs from the publicly shared princi-ples of basic social morality all are expected to recognize (though there may be disagreement about application in difficult cases). These issues of entanglement

---

[4] Kent Greenawalt, *Law and Objectivity* (New York: Oxford University Press, 1992), p. 222, and see John Rawls, "The Idea of Public Reason," in *Political Liberalism* (New York: Columbia University Press, 1996), pp. 212–254, especially pp. 240–247; Thomas Pogge, *John Rawls: His Life and Theory of Justice* (New York: Oxford University Press, 2007), pp. 139–144; and Ronald Dworkin, *Sovereign Virtue: The Theory and Practice of Equality* (Cambridge, MA: Harvard University Press, 2000), pp. 152–155.
[5] John Locke, *A Letter Concerning Toleration*, in *Political Writings* (Indianapolis, IN: Hackett, 2003), p. 393. First published in 1689.

(as I call them) have arisen because of the historical background of Western pluralistic free societies in a once unfragmented Christianity, where Church courts adjudicated various issues and both the authority and doctrine of the Church was not generally questioned. Religious toleration and the broader principle of freedom of conscience came out of the horror of religious wars and turmoil as that shared acceptance collapsed. For the sake of peace, we agreed to disagree about religious matters, and religion was consigned to the private sphere (a private sphere that of course typically includes groups of co-religionists). But there were some practices with a religious background that marked all of the succeeding polities, though with some significant differences, especially between Catholics and Protestants. Issues of entanglement cluster around the structuring points of birth, coming of age, sex, marriage, and death. This entanglement is inevitable, for there are rather often (but not always) public, secular interests at stake in these matters—unlike, for instance the question of whether there should be infant baptism or only believer's baptism, or whether to engage in worship of a divinity (and if so, how).

Historically marriage is an issue extremely entangled with religion. "God ordained marriage as the life-long union of one man and one woman for the rearing of children" would once have seemed in the West comparable and connected to "God wills that children be protected," the expression in religious language of an uncontroversial truth. But marriage varies across societies and religions. Divorce with the right to remarry was found in many traditional societies (and considered consistent with responsible child-rearing), but not in traditional Christendom. Monogamy combined with the formal prohibition of concubinage reflects the Christian emphasis on companionate marriage, as defined by Richard Posner: "marriage between at least approximate equals, based on mutual respect and affection, and involving close and continuous association in child rearing, household management and other activities...."[6] Not all religions and societies have emphasized companionate marriage or required monogamy. Surely the increasing diversity of Western societies must lead us to reflect upon this religious entanglement, as more people from polygamist religions and cultures live in traditionally monogamist legal regimes. Currently there is debate about validating gay marriage, and that debate has a clear religious background for many of those in opposition (though not all). But marriage has always been an issue entangled with religion in Western polities, and this debate is merely the newest chapter. Whether to allow divorce with a right to re-marry (and on what grounds or at will) has riven many polities, and still does. If marriage is viewed as simply a contract, then there can be no barrier to termination if both parties so wish, or if one party has broken the terms of the contract. And if marriage is seen as simply a contract, it will seem discriminatory to deny the right to contract to homosexuals.

---

[6] Richard A. Posner, *Sex and Reason* (Cambridge, MA: Harvard University Press, 1992), p. 45.

2   What Christian Marriage Once Was

However, although marriage was entered into "contractually" (i.e., by consent or agreement) and could be surrounded by contracts, marriage itself was not a contract. As Harold J. Berman explained, marriage, like clerical ordination and feudal lord-vassal contracts, was the exercise of "the power by contract to create a status" and "by a sacred vow, to enter into an indissoluble, lifelong relationship whose terms were fixed by law."[7] In both the lord-vassal relationship and the man-wife relationship the "contractual aspect was the consent to the relationship; the legal content of the relationship, however, was ascribed."[8] A wife who murdered her husband committed petty treason—worse than mere murder—just as did a vassal who murdered his lord. A husband who murdered his wife was not treasonous. Although it is unclear whether ever formally a part of English Common Law, the right of the husband to chastise his wife (including mild corporal punishment) was widely endorsed and frequently practiced. Marital status had immense legal implications for property and inheritance.[9] Originally only the Church courts had jurisdiction over the question whether there was a valid marriage. If legal questions arose, the status was religiously determined, though marriage did not originally require solemnization by the presence of a priest.[10] But that religious determination had secular consequences. The rift with Rome did not end this extreme entanglement; England merely substituted Church of England courts.[11] This historical inheritance of the conception of Christian marriage is very perplexing once there are no Church courts recognized as legal authorities in the state.

Although a contract to marry in the future was originally an important matter (precontract was a common ground for denying the validity of a subsequent marriage to a different person), this contract to be married in the future was never conflated with marriage itself, which required an indication of present consent to enter the married status immediately. Present consent of both parties established the marriage.[12] The act of marrying could be said to be contractual only in the sense that it was a matter of the agreement of both parties, but the result of the agreement was not the creation of a contract. Actual marriage (as opposed to a contract to marry in the future) created a status (really two clearly distinct statuses, for husband

---

[7] Harold J. Berman, *Law and Revolution: The Formation of the Western Legal Tradition* (Cambridge, MA: Harvard University Press, 1983), p. 230.

[8] Berman, *Law and Revolution*, p. 306.

[9] J.H. Baker, *An Introduction to English Legal History* (London: Butterworths, 1979), p. 391.

[10] Mary Ann Glendon, *The Transformation of Family Law: State, Law, and Family in the United States and Western Europe* (Chicago, IL: University of Chicago Press, 1989), pp. 23–30.

[11] Baker, *An Introduction to English Legal History*, pp. 112, 391, 394; Glendon, *The Transformation of Family Law*, p. 33.

[12] Baker, *An Introduction to English Legal History*, pp. 391–92; Glendon, *The Transformation of Family Law*, p. 25.

and wife respectively), rather than a contractual relationship between two contracting parties. The two parties were "approximately equal," but much more so before
the marriage than during it. There is clearly a wide spectrum within the category of
"companionate marriage," from barely companionate to radically companionate.
Here I would distinguish between companionate marriage as defined by Posner and
(legally) role-less marriage (which could be considered radically companionate).
The legal roles of husband and wife were distinct in traditional Christian marriage,
with the husband the head of the union. They were, however, approximately equal
when compared to non-companionate marriage, especially of the polygynous kind.
In respect to the contract to marry in the future, the man and woman were indeed
equal contracting parties, for she was and remained after the contract (until actual
marriage) an unmarried woman. Once married, her civil legal personhood for most
purposes was subsumed into her husband's (she went into coverture). Her status
significantly altered into that of a married woman, under the authority of her husband.[13] His status changed into that of a head of household, bearing the civil legal
person of both of them, and he acquired the obligation to support his wife. Both of
them lost the legal power to marry, until death of the spouse. Originally the husband
had control of her real property, though she retained title and could as a widow seek
to regain the property, since she was unable to gainsay her husband if he conveyed
it contrary to her interests.[14] The statuses of each spouse could not be ended by
agreement or on breach of some contractual provision, but only by death. The
annulment of a marriage did not, strictly speaking, end a status, for it declared that
neither party had ever had the respective status of being a married man or woman.

To an attenuated degree, marriage thus originally had many of the characteristics
that led John Stuart Mill to prohibit enforceable contracts of slavery: "The principle
of freedom cannot require that he should be free not to be free. It is not freedom to
be allowed to alienate his freedom."[15] Indeed, Mill's experience of the legal disabilities created by Harriet Taylor's first marriage seems likely to have influenced the
argument against contracts of slavery, and Mill himself makes the connection with
marriage, arguing that even the impact on third parties, crucially on children,
should not make the marriage bond legally indissoluble "at all costs to the happi-
ness of the reluctant party." Mill sees a conflict between a thoroughly companionate
conception of marriage and the indissolubility of marriage.[16]

The comparison with slavery is instructive, for being a slave was a status, and
the slave and slave-owner could not be conceived as equal contracting parties once
the slave lost his liberty. Most American slave states eventually either prohibited
manumission or made it very difficult,[17] so even the owner could not at will change

---

[13] Baker, *An Introduction to English Legal History*, pp. 395–99.

[14] Baker, *An Introduction to English Legal History*, p. 396.

[15] John Stuart Mill, *On Liberty* (Indianapolis, IN: Hackett, 1978), p. 101. First published 1859.

[16] Mill, *On Liberty*, pp. 102–03.

[17] Paul Finkelman, "Slavery, Law Of," in Kermit L. Hall (ed.), *The Oxford Companion to American Law* (New York: Oxford University Press, 2002), p.746.

the slave's status, just as the husband could not relieve his wife of the status of married woman. Of course, unlike the slave-owner, the husband could not transfer his mastership to another man by gift or sale; in this important respect traditional marriage was unlike slavery.

The evolution of marriage as originally found in the Christian West to the present institution was very slow. In Protestant nations generally, civil authority was established, but with the assumption that almost all of the substance of Christian marriage would remain.[18] Life-long marriage was enforced except in evidenced cases of adultery and a few other serious breaches. The American colonies did not use Church of England courts regarding marital matters, but much of the substance of the religious institution was retained as a matter of civil law. The woman was under her husband's authority, and it required reforming statutes in the mid-nineteenth century to allow married women to have control over their own property. Divorce with the right to remarry was severely restricted. The husband was legally the head of the household.

3   The Cheshire Cat: From Status to (Nearly) Contract

In the last forty years of the Twentieth Century, the legal institution of marriage in the U.S. and most of Western Europe has imitated the Cheshire Cat—only the smile remains. The two separate statuses are abolished, and man and woman become full legal equals, not only before but after the actual marriage. In France, prior to 1938, the mandatory civil ceremony included the requirement that the wife obey her husband; prior to 1970, the ceremony declared that the husband was head of the family; since 1970, the ceremony declares that the spouses have only mutual, equal duties and statuses.[19] Equal status of the spouses comes to be the norm in all of the United States. No fault divorce with the right to remarry gradually replaces or supplements the various fault divorce regimes.[20] This final development releases the two individuals from all but the most technical status-disability: each has the equal status-disability of being unable to marry as long as they choose to continue to have that disability; however, state action is required (a divorce) to regain the marriageable status. There are, of course, legal consequences of being married while that status remains; indeed, those consequences are the benefits sought by same-sex couples. Among these benefits are next-of-kin status, intestate inheritance, inheritance regardless of the provisions of a will, various private or employee insurance and pension rights and benefits, Social Security survivor benefits, automatic medical

[18] Glendon, *The Transformation of Family Law*, p. 31.
[19] Glendon, *The Transformation of Family Law*, pp. 71–2.
[20] Lawrence M. Friedman, *American Law in the 20th Century* (New Haven: Yale University Press, 2002), pp. 434–42; Glendon, *The Transformation of Family Law*, pp. 148–96.

surrogacy, the spousal testimonial privilege, various property rights upon dissolution of the marriage, and the right to bring wrongful death civil actions. As Emily Gill so persuasively argues, same-sex couples also seek something both intangible and yet deeply important: respectful recognition by the polity as a couple.[21] There are also obligations attaching to the married state, but now those are all reciprocal and equal, and so at least initially tolerable to both parties, unlike the asymmetrical obligations of earlier, traditional marriage. Only the Cheshire cat smile remains. But the smile is only bestowed upon heterosexual couples.

Once the quasi-slavery aspects of marriage ended, it seemed inevitable that same-sex couples would seek the benefits of the institution. The quasi-slavery aspects consisted of the inability easily to end the relationship and the husband's privilege as head of household. Before the headship was ended in law, in marriage one partner in a same-sex couple would have needed to promise to obey the other; this is only likely in a certain kind of domination-submission relationship. Before no-fault divorce, few same-sex couples would have considered entering into such legal bondage as marriage was then. Marriage has finally come near to being merely contract, though with special state involvement.[22] In 1861, long before significant changes in marriage, Henry Maine claimed that "the Individual is steadily substituted for the Family, as the unit of which civil laws take account," that, in progressive societies, contract displaces status: "Thus the status of the Slave has disappeared—it has been superseded by the contractual relation of the servant to his master. The status of the Female under Tutelage, if the tutelage be understood of persons other than her husband, has ceased to exist."[23] Now even the tutelage of the husband is ended. Since these troublesome, slave-like features have vanished, same-sex couples want to be smiled upon by the state with its Cheshire cat grin.

4 Same-Sex Unions, Polygamy, and Christian Marriage

The exclusion of same-sex couples certainly was a part of traditional marriage as originally found in Christian church law, Catholic and then Protestant. The exclusion was part and parcel of seeing woman as provided by God for man as helpmate and mother of his children. The original dependence on Church courts for marital matters left its mark on the civil institution of marriage, with the man as head of household and wife as obedient homemaker and mother. But marriage has now lost nearly all of that conception of the relationship of the two spouses: the obligations between the two are reciprocal and equal, so that the word "spouse" or "partner"

---

[21] Gill, "Coercion, Religious Neutrality, and the Case of Same-Sex Marriage," pp. 122, 124.

[22] Posner, *Sex and Reason*, p. 264.

[23] Henry Maine, *Ancient Law* (London: Dent, Everyman's Library, 1917), p. 99. First published 1861.

now captures the role of both, without need of "husband and wife" (and even less "man and wife"). So what can now be the secular rationale for continuing the exclusion of same-sex couples that depends upon that religious background, when all else of the religious background is gone?

It could be argued that the very idea that marriage can only be between one man and one woman is, as Patrick Devlin argued, "built into the house in which we live and could not be removed without bringing it down"[24] Devlin was considering only the restriction to monogamy, for when he wrote there was no thought of same-sex marriage, but there were polygamist unions in Moslem societies. The Christian background of the West undergirded both the monogamy component and the heterosexual component. (The Christian background also included the idea of life-long marriage, and removing that component does not seem to have brought down the house.) It is an empirical question whether removing one or both of these elements would destroy the edifice.[25] Perhaps an element that was once structural no longer bears weight, and perhaps another element bears even more weight than previously. No resolution of the disputes follows from this understanding—only an understanding of the entanglement. Perhaps there are non-religious reasons for prohibiting plural marriages, or for prohibiting homosexual marriages.

An assessment of marriage without Christian baggage was precisely the purpose of David Hume's essay "Of Polygamy and Divorces." Hume wrote: "...it is mere superstition to imagine, that marriage can be entirely uniform, and will admit only of one mode or form. Did not human laws restrain the natural liberty of men, every particular marriage would be as different as contracts or bargains of any other kind or species."[26] He then canvasses various legal restraints, considering the advantages and disadvantages, without reference to Christian teaching. The nature of companionate marriage precludes polygamy, but can be used to argue both for and against divorce. Polygamy, Hume argues, "destroys that nearness of rank, not to say equality, which nature has established between the sexes. We are, by nature, their lovers, their friends, their patrons: Would we willingly exchange such endearing appellations, for the barbarous title of master and tyrant?"[27] In favor of divorce is that "nothing can be more cruel than to preserve, by violence, an union, which, at first, was made by mutual love, and is now, in effect, dissolved by mutual hatred," and, secondly, "the heart of man delights in liberty."[28] A century later, Mill's view is remarkably similar. Hume contends that, on the contrary side of the argument, divorce

---

[24] Patrick Devlin, "The Enforcement of Morals" in David M. Adams (ed.), *Philosophical Problems in the Law* (Belmont, CA: Wadsworth, 2005), p. 204. First published 1959.

[25] H.L.A. Hart, *Law, Liberty, and Morality* (New York: Vintage Books, 1966), pp. 48–52 and "Social Solidarity and the Enforcement of Morality," in *Essays in Jurisprudence and Philosophy* (Oxford: Clarendon Press, 1983), pp. 248–62.

[26] David Hume, "Of Polygamy and Divorces," in *Essays Moral, Political, and Literary* (Indianapolis, IN: Liberty Fund, 1987), pp. 181–82. First published 1742.

[27] Hume, "Of Polygamy and Divorces," p. 184.

[28] Hume, "Of Polygamy and Divorces," p. 187.

causes great misery to the children, and, though the heart loves liberty, it also "submits to necessity, and soon loses an inclination, when there appears an absolute
impossibility of gratifying it."[29] And in contrast to the passion of love, the "calm and
sedate affection" of friendship actually "thrives under constraint" when the friends
must pursue a common goal: "We need not, therefore, be afraid of drawing the mar-
riage-knot, which chiefly subsists by friendship, the closest possible."[30] Hume concludes that European practice of excluding divorce and polygamy is preferable to
other forms of marriage. But his argument treats the two issues very differently, with
the rejection of divorce very shaky, and the rejection of polygamy solidly based on
the companionate ideal. The trajectory of subsequent Western development also
shakily embraced life-long marriage, until it fully embraced free termination on the
very grounds expressed by Hume in the first stage of his divorce dialectic.

The difference in firm grounding between the hesitant rejection of divorce and the
firm rejection of polygamy echoes the historical origins of the two rules. From the
viewpoint of Roman law and Jewish law, the Christian rejection of divorce was an
innovation, based upon Jesus's criticism of divorce in the Sermon on the Mount.[31] In
contrast, Roman law allowed only monogamous marriage. The Christian insistence
on monogamy was not only consistent with Roman law, it was developed from long
and slowly emerging Jewish custom: although not formally prohibited for
(Ashkenazic) Jews until the early 11th century of the Common Era, polygamy had
long been discouraged (to some degree even before the time of Jesus) and had grown
increasingly rare (found only among a few of the wealthy) long before its prohibition. By the time Western Christian conceptions of marriage were fully formalized
in Canon Law, (Ashkenazic) Jewish law prohibited polygamy. The gradual abandonment of polygamy was based on the ground that plural marriage inevitably degraded
women to a servile status. This is the same argument used by St. Thomas Aquinas,[32]
Hume (as recounted above), and also made recently by Mary Ann Glendon[33] and
Richard Posner.[34] Companionate marriage thus made polygamy seem unacceptable.
This argument has no application to the question of gay marriage, though it is
another question whether some other argument might offer a basis for the prohibition apart from a revelation that can have no role in public reasoning, since all are
free regarding such assertions of revealed truth. The non-revealed reason for prohibiting homosexual conduct offered by Catholic teaching would also lead to condemnation of contraception—a condemnation inconsistent with the principles accepted
by a large majority of the public, Catholic and non-Catholic. If Protestant thought

---

[29] Hume, "Of Polygamy and Divorces," p. 188.
[30] Hume, "Of Polygamy and Divorces," p. 189.
[31] Matthew 5.31–32.
[32] St. Thomas Aquinas, *Summa contra Gentiles*, III, 124 (4), quoted in Alan Donagan, *The Theory
of Morality* (Chicago: University of Chicago Press, 1977), p. 102.
[33] Glendon, *The Transformation of Family Law*, p. 54.
[34] Posner, *Sex and Reason*, pp. 253–260.

regarding this issue offers only reasons based on revelation (as for instance in the Calvinist tradition), it can give no public ground for the prohibition.

The entanglement of marriage with religion poses a difficulty for public reasoning determining the use of state coercion: no one can reasonably demand that all others accept a specific religious perspective (including as a religious perspective the rejection of religion), so if reasons that hold regardless of religious perspective are not available, and yet there must be a public resolution of the issue, we find ourselves perplexed.

The solution might seem to be a complete severing of religious marriage and civil marriage. France, with its insistent secularization of the state, more formal and absolute than in the U.S., requires a civil ceremony which cannot be varied from the Civil Code and must be performed prior to any subsequent religious ceremony.[35] But even if such a clear separation is helpful (as I believe), it is illusory that the entanglement issue can be so easily resolved. For the legal elements and consequences of marriage must still involve state action, even if there is complete clarity about the distinctness of religious and civil marriage. If priests, pastors, rabbis, and other religious officials were no longer authorized to perform marriages even once a license has been issued, the dispute regarding same-sex marriage would be unaffected, except perhaps through a long-term psychological impact that lessened the sense of dissonance due to conflating religious and civil marriage.

5 Marriage as Coercive Regime

Is marriage so different from contracts, covenants, wills, and conveyances? To what extent does the private law of contracts and covenants involve state coercion? To what extent does marriage law involve state coercion? These areas of law, after all, are not commands of the state, but power-conferring rules to facilitate private interactions. But even state enforcement of private covenants and contracts can be construed as state coercion. In *Shelley v. Kramer*[36] the Supreme Court held that the power of the state could not be used by the courts to enforce private, voluntary, racially restrictive covenants regarding real property. The enforcement of such restrictions constituted state action in violation of the Equal Protection Clause of the 14th Amendment, for state power was used to limit on the grounds of race, religion, or ethnicity those to whom real property could be subsequently conveyed. Would restrictive covenants concerning sexual orientation withstand Constitutional scrutiny given *Romer v. Evans*,[37] *Lawrence v. Texas*, and the background analysis of

[35] Glendon, *The Transformation of Family Law*, pp. 71–72.
[36] 334 U.S. 1, 1948.
[37] 517 U.S. 620, 1996.

Shelley v. Kramer? Even though sexual orientation is not a Constitutionally suspect classification like race, requiring strict scrutiny, for the classification to be acceptable there still must be a rational basis for the discrimination, and *Romer v. Evans* found that there is no rational basis in state interests for drawing a discriminatory line on the basis of sexual orientation.

Marriage is much more clearly a matter of state action than enforcing private contracts or covenants, for state authority is required to enter a marriage or end it, and the state itself attaches obligations and benefits to the status. Marriage also remains distinct in its level of state involvement because the rules are still formally rules for acquiring a legal status rather than rules for doing something, such as contracting, that leaves one's legal personal status untouched. As Richard Posner has explained, the imposition of the Christian requirement that sex be confined to companionate marriage could not be accomplished through a purely contractual model: "for the idea of marriage as the only legitimate channel for sexual activity to have substance, marriage must be a legally defined relationship having certain invariant properties, rather than just the name of an infinitely variable contractual relationship."[38] The similarity to Hume's account should be noted.

Thus *Loving v. Virginia*[39] nullified state prohibition of interracial marriage as a violation of the Equal Protection Clause of the 14th Amendment. As with restrictive covenants, the strict scrutiny of *Loving v. Virginia* would have to give way to a rational basis test when treating sexual orientation. If the analysis of same-sex marriage proceeds in terms not of sexual orientation, but simply the classification by sex as such, then the level of scrutiny would be raised above mere rational basis to the intermediate, heightened standard used, for instance, in *U.S. v. Virginia*.[40] Since *Romer v. Evans* ruled that there is no rational basis for legislative discrimination based on sexual orientation (even if a matter of a state constitutional provision), *a fortiori* such discrimination would not withstand the higher scrutiny accorded classification by sex.

Yet it may seem unclear that through its marriage law the state coerces anyone other than the married couple, who must seek state action (however easily obtained) to end the union. Is the state coercing same-sex couples by excluding them from marriage? After all, gay couples do not come under the restrictive regime of marriage precisely because of the exclusion. And what would constitute the coercive intent; that is, what would the state be using its coercive authority to require? As Friedrich Hayek so clearly argued, for there to be coercion there must be both a threat and a purpose: "Coercion implies both the threat of inflicting harm and the intention thereby to bring about certain conduct."[41] The harm is clear: same-sex

---

[38] Posner, *Sex and Reason*, p. 244.

[39] 388 U.S. 1, 1967.

[40] 518 U.S. 515, 1996.

[41] Friedrich A. Hayek, *The Constitution of Liberty* (Chicago, IL: University of Chicago Press, 1960), p. 134.

couples are deprived of the benefits of marriage and excluded from the full equality before the law that heterosexual couples enjoy if they so choose. In matters between private individuals, there is a distinction between withholding benefits and imposition of harm. This distinction is inapplicable to the state's role in regulating marriage, for the entire marriage regime is backed by the framework of state coercion. So the first half of Hayek's test for coercion is met. But what is the conduct that the marriage regime seeks to effect? This coercive intent would be a key to understanding the possible secular point of the exclusion of same-sex couples. For earlier, traditional forms of marriage, it is clear that the church and then the state sought to impose a closed choice on everyone: either enter into an authorized union of man and wife, in contemplation of child-rearing, or remain sexually abstinent. Alistair Macleod distinguishes between coercive institutional arrangements and interpersonal coercion.[42] The rules of the traditional marriage regime were part of a larger set of coercive institutional arrangements, including rules of criminal law concerning sex. The purpose of the exclusion of same-sex couples from marriage can only be to enforce sexual abstinence upon each of them unless they each enter a heterosexual union. The coercive intent toward homosexuals is simply an application to them of the original coercive intent of the whole traditional Christian marriage regime. This coercive intent toward homosexuals now seems odd and unrealistic, but in earlier social and legal circumstances the coercion frequently worked, at least in terms of what was publicly observed and admitted. Just as now a prudent person might forgo his favorite drug because of state coercion, in an earlier social and legal context a prudent homosexual seeking a companionate relationship might forgo homosexual companionship (though perhaps not sex) for heterosexual companionship. At least publicly, the goal of sexual regimentation was accomplished.

6   The Decline of the Coercive Regime

Various vestiges of this regime of sexual prohibition or restriction survived in the laws of various states until recently. Thus marriage law once cohered well with the legal disabilities attaching to illegitimacy, and laws prohibiting not only (obviously) adultery and bigamy, but also (and necessarily) fornication, cohabitation, contraception, and sodomy. All of these served the purpose of imposing a way of life through state coercion. The internal relationship between marriage and (legally and socially accepted) rearing of children ended with statutes allowing adoption (in derogation of the Common Law), the elimination of the legal status of illegitimacy, cohabitation as common and accepted, legal and effective contraception with intentionally childless marriages, and no-fault divorce even for spouses with children.

---

[42] Alistair M. Macleod, "Coercion, Justice, and Democracy," this volume, p. 64.

Adoption was unknown to the old Common Law, and the need for legitimate heirs could originally only be met through marriage and legitimate heirs of the body. The introduction of adoption in Common Law nations long predated the abolition of the legal status of illegitimacy, and adoption can be seen as itself diminishing the importance of marriage, by allowing both heterosexuals (married or not) and (eventually in most states) homosexuals to have their own children without procreative sex. (It is notable that adoption by gays is still prohibited in some states.) Furthermore, advances in technology have provided for various forms of child-bearing (for married and unmarried, heterosexual and homosexual) unimagined in the past.

The legal status of illegitimacy is particularly salient. In the past, bastards faced serious disabilities, both legally and socially.[43] The status of illegitimacy was internally connected to the status of marriage. Perhaps even more than severe impediments to divorce, the disabilities of illegitimacy made marriage the institution it once was. Many marriages resulted from the combined purposes of protecting the woman from dishonor and the yet-to-be-born child from bastardy. Although Canon Law held that subsequent marriage of the parents legitimated the child, English Common Law required marriage prior to the child's birth.[44] Until very recent times, the social stigma of bastardy attached regardless of the legal technicalities. But illegitimacy is no longer a legal status and society seems utterly permissive.[45] Both legally and socially, children born outside of marriage suffer from no significant stigma.

Increasing economic independence and employment opportunities for women lessens the need for marriage both for childless women and single mothers, and decreases the dependence of married women on their husbands, thus increasing divorce.[46] The Cheshire cat phenomenon again arises: except for the exclusion of same-sex couples from marriage, the elements needed to give the coercive institutional arrangements even a chance of some success at maintaining a certain way of life have disappeared (either formally or in practice) except as religious prohibitions and statuses. Now all that remains in the secular law of marriage is a Cheshire cat smile for heterosexual couples, but a frown for same-sex couples.

State coercive institutional arrangements once promoted and protected a certain way of life, including Christian sexual ethics and a particular mode of child rearing. That way of life had originally a religious origin and justification. But setting that justification aside, might not the monogamous, sexually restrictive way of life now serve this-worldly human interests: providing for better child-rearing, promoting social stability, and moderating the force of sexual desire and jealousy? This was Patrick Devlin's claim, as noted above: that though the origin of our view of marriage was Christian, legal enforcement of that view has the independent, secular

---

[43] Jenny Teichman, *Illegitimacy: An Examination of Bastardy* (Ithaca, NY: Cornell University Press, 1982), pp. 103–121.

[44] Baker, *An Introduction to English Legal History*, pp. 400–401.

[45] Glendon, *The Transformation of Family Law*, pp. 282–290.

[46] Posner, *Sex and Reason*, p. 252.

ground that "the house in which we live" will collapse without that enforcement. Whether or not that structure was optimal (for sometimes the best is the enemy of the good), this argument had some force in earlier legal regimes, but the Cheshire cat phenomenon has left so little of the traditional elements of marriage itself, and hardly anything of the surrounding criminal law (at least as enforced), that it is irrational to continue the one remaining coercive element. Allowing same-sex marriages in the present legal and social context will not decrease the coercive regime's effectiveness in promoting and protecting the traditional family structure and repressing non-marital sex (heterosexual or homosexual), for effectiveness in that regard has already hit zero. But the vestigial coercive marriage regime does still have an impact: same-sex couples are denied an opportunity (the legal power to marry) accorded to heterosexual couples. And that opportunity falls solidly within the category Alistair Macleod describes as "institutionally-securable opportunities for the living of satisfying and fulfilling lives."[47] The vestigial coercive marriage regime does not directly coerce same-sex couples, but the coercive institutional arrangements deprive same-sex couples of an opportunity that is directly provided by the state. (In contrast, for instance, to the indirect state action found in enforcement of racially restrictive real property covenants. Despite the fact that *Shelley v. Kramer* predates *Loving v. Virginia* by nineteen years, state action is much more obvious in policing a marriage regime than in enforcing private restrictive covenants.) Absent a secular reason for denial of such a deeply important opportunity, the denial is both unjust and, in a polity recognizing religious liberty, illegitimate.

7   No Secular Purpose Remains for Exclusion

Once effectiveness for its secular purpose reaches zero, only the original religious basis for exclusion of same-sex marriage remains. These ghosts of reasons haunt even many of those without the original religious beliefs. Once the state has deconstructed marriage itself and eliminated all of the surrounding coercive measures that once made the whole coercive regime at least arguably reasonable in secular intent, there is no rational basis for the state to pursue any legitimate state interest by retaining the exclusion of same-sex couples from marriage. The only remaining imaginable coercive intent is to enforce a particular religious conception of marriage, even though extremely attenuated. That intent is illegitimate in a state recognizing religious liberty. There is no remaining rational basis in civil interests for exclusion of same-sex couples from civil marriage. And so parties seeking a same-sex marriage should be respected as equals in civil society, regardless of whether they conform to a particular religious sexual ethic and the conception of marriage that coheres with it. The law no longer holds heterosexuals to such a sexual and

---

[47] Macleod, "Coercion, Justice, and Democracy," p. 69.

marriage regime, so equality of persons requires that homosexuals also be free of restrictive state coercion in this sphere of conduct.

If same-sex marriage were validated, the entanglement of civil marriage with Christian belief would seem then to leave only the bare idea of companionate marriage, itself radicalized by ending the headship of the husband. Indeed, the trajectory of development of marriage in the West has been from weakly companionate to radically companionate marriage—not just approximate equality retaining separate roles for husband and wife, but full equality with no legal differentiation of roles. Radically companionate marriage, however, can easily be given a non-religious, contemporary rationale, for it re-enforces political and legal conceptions of equality of the sexes, while offering a framework for stability and mutual support, both emotional and financial. Civil marriage seals the exclusive, mutual, equal commitment of care between the two persons. As Jonathan Rauch wrote, "Decent opinion has understood for centuries that, whatever else marriage may be, it is a commitment to be there."[48] It is a legitimate state interest to promote such mutual supportive unions. Worries that gay marriage will lead to incestuous marriage and marriages with a variety of animals can be put to rest, for companionship with sheep seems doomed to inadequacy, and the adult need for companionship pulls away from close family and toward peers (surely including cousins sometimes). But companionate marriage, as explained by Hume, Mill, Glendon, and Posner, is arguably inconsistent with polygamy (polygynous in form) and its tendency to elevate the man far above his wives.[49] Perhaps some nuanced accommodation (guarding the equality of women) could be made for those with religious beliefs allowing (even favoring) polygamy: this is just another example of free exercise of religion accommodation issues. Same-sex marriage needs no such accommodation in order to cohere with a regime of radically companionate marriage.

---

[48] Jonathan Rauch, *Gay Marriage: Why It Is Good for Gays, Good for Straights, and Good for America* (New York: Times Books, Henry Holt and Company, 2004), p. 26.
[49] Posner, *Sex and Reason*, pp. 253–260.

Part IV
Coercion and the State: National Security

Chapter 10
Indefinite Detention for Mega-Terrorists?

Don E. Scheid

> *If the practical circumstances of a given conflict are entirely unlike those of the conflicts that informed the development of the law of war, that understanding may unravel.*
> *—Justice Sandra Day O'Connor[1]*

> *The preventive detention of suspected future terrorists is likely to continue wherever terrorism is perceived as a serious threat. It is essential that democratic nations committed to the rule of law begin to develop a jurisprudence regulating this increasingly important preventive mechanism.*
> *—Prof. Alan M. Dershowitz[2]*

1 Introduction

How we should fight terrorism is a question that has consumed the United States since the attacks of September 2001 (9/11). One important part of that question is another: What rules should apply?

Before 9/11, the prevailing view was that terrorism should be dealt with primarily through the criminal-justice system, much like drug trafficking and other international crimes.[3] After 9/11, it was war—Pres. George W. Bush immediately announcing a "war

---

[1] *Hamdi v. Rumsfeld*, 504 U.S. 547 (2004).

[2] *Preemption: A Knife That Cuts Both Ways* (New York: W.W. Norton, 2006), p. 121.

[3] To be sure, there were occasional military strikes:

October 1983, Pres. Reagan ordered retaliatory strikes for the bombing of U.S. Marine barracks in Beirut;

April 14, 1986, the U.S. bombed military bases in Tripoli, Libya, for its alleged connection to terrorist bombing of discotheque in West Berlin frequented by U.S. servicemen;

President Clinton ordered missile attack against Iraq's intelligence facilities in 1993 in retaliation for alleged plot to assassinate former President George H. W. Bush;

In 1998, U.S. launched cruise-missile attacks on a pharmaceutical plant in Sudan and on terrorist training camps in Afghanistan following terrorist attacks on U.S. embassies in Nairobi, Kenya, and Dar es Salaam, Tanzania.

With these few exceptions, virtually all instances of terrorism in the 1980s and 1990s were handled as criminal cases.

D.A. Reidy and W.J. Riker (eds.), *Coercion and the State.*
© Springer Science+Business Media B.V. 2008

against terrorism" in his address to the nation the evening of September 11.[4] Again, on September 20, in his address to a joint session of Congress, Bush stated: "Our *war on terror* begins with al-Qaeda, but it does not end there. It will not end until every terrorist group of global reach has been found, stopped and defeated."[5] The plausibility of treating terrorism as a crime became untenable partly because of the sheer magnitude of the 9/11 attacks and partly because of the nature of the enemy, al-Qaeda. These were no ordinary crimes, and the perpetrators were no ordinary criminals. In accordance with the declaration of a "war on terrorism," it seemed that the law of war should apply.

This was a new and different kind of war, however. War may be the ultimate coercion: "an act of force to compel our enemy to do our will," as Clausewitz stated. But, while there are many forms of coercion, there are also many forms of warfare. Besides traditional or conventional warfare, as in World Wars I and II, there are also varieties of non-conventional forms, such as guerrilla warfare.[6]

If conventional warfare consists of an armed conflict between states conducted by regular armies, then the al-Qaeda attacks against the United States clearly constitute non-conventional warfare.[7] The enemy does not employ regular armies. Using terrorist tactics, as it does, the enemy ignores traditional rules of war, most especially those concerning the treatment of prisoners (e.g., torture, beheadings) and the rights of non-combatant civilians (e.g., non-combatants as direct targets). Moreover, the enemy is not a state, nor is it associated with a specific state, nor indeed, with any specific geographical location. Nevertheless, it is more than a criminal cartel, for while its proclamations rarely express a coherent grievance, it implicitly challenges the political legitimacy of the United States.

---

[4] In afternoon of September 11, President Bush met with his principle advisers by means of video teleconference and began the meeting with the words, "We're at war." *The 9/11 Commission Report*, authorized ed. (New York: W.W. Norton), p. 326.

[5] Pres. George W. Bush, *Address to a Joint Session of Congress and the American People* (September 20, 2001), emphasis added.

It has been pointed out *ad nauseam* that terrorism is only a tactic and that one cannot make war on a tactic. For example, in December 1941, President Franklin Roosevelt did not ask Congress to declare war on air power; instead, he asked for a declaration of war against Japan because of its aerial attack on Pearl Harbor. Nevertheless, it is clear enough that the phrase "war on terrorism" is intended to denote a war against those individuals and groups throughout the world who are intent on engaging in terrorist attacks against the United States, its friends and allies.

[6] Any number of distinctions have been made among various possible forms of warfare. While conventional warfare is between states employing regular, uniformed armed forces, 'irregular warfare' has been used to denote warfare between states and non-state actors, while *unconventional warfare* has been used to refer to guerrilla and covert operations, operations conducted with irregular forces. "Unrestricted warfare" refers to the title of a monograph by Qiao Liang and Wang Xiangsui, two army colonels from People's Republic of China, who envision warfare by both military and non-military means, including hacking into web sites of financial institutions, terrorism, the use of media for propaganda, etc.

[7] Attacks attributed to al-Qaeda include at least: The simultaneous bombings of U.S. embassies in Nairobi, Kenya, and Dar al Salaam, Tanzania, in 1998, and the bombing of the American destroyer U.S.S. Cole as it was refueling in Aden Harbor, Yemen, in 2000, as well as the attacks of September 11, 2001.

More than this, al-Qaeda represents a new kind of terrorism. Given its amorphous organization, there is no one with whom to negotiate—no one, apparently, who could effectively declare a ceasefire, no one with authority to conclude an armistice or peace treaty. Like a pandemic, this is a form of terrorism that is not confined to a single locale. We are told that al-Qaeda may have terrorist cells in 50 to 60 countries throughout the world. By contrast, most terrorist groups have been, and still are, national or regional in their operations, having local objectives and operating mainly within a single country—for example, the Revolutionary Armed Forces of Columbia (FARC), Tamil Tigers in Sri Lanka, and Hezbollah and Hamas in Lebanon and Palestine.

A second, and far more significant, feature of the new kind of terrorism al-Qaeda represents is the magnitude of the destruction sought. The new terrorism seeks catastrophic destruction with massive casualties. Technological developments have created the possibility of small terrorist cells wielding deadly force on a scale once the exclusive province of states. The possibilities of acquiring weapons of mass destruction, especially nuclear weapons, make al-Qaeda-type terrorism tremendously dangerous.[8] Indeed, it seems only a matter of time before a "suitcase" nuclear device obliterates a major city somewhere in the world. My focus of concern in this paper is this warfare of sustained campaigns of catastrophic terrorism—the kind of terrorism Richard Falk, quite appropriately, has dubbed "mega-terrorism."[9]

As new forms of warfare have evolved throughout history, new laws of war developed. Being a form of non-conventional warfare and a new form of terrorism, mega-terrorism presents conceptual challenges that require a reconsideration of the kind of rules that should guide us in this new struggle. In my view, the struggle is something of a "quasi-war"; and neither the criminal law nor the present law of war applies in any simple, straightforward manner. David Luban has criticized the Bush Administration for not consistently following either standard criminal law or the law of war but, instead, picking and choosing rules from both legal regimes as seems most convenient.[10] This is true enough, but I believe it is precisely this somewhat schizophrenic behavior by the Administration that is a symptom of the problem.

Many issues are involved and, no doubt, a number of approaches are possible. Here, I explore one possible approach to one issue, namely, the detention of

---

[8] In 2003, Osama bin Laden sought and received a *fatwa* from a radical Saudi cleric that the use of a nuclear bomb against U.S. civilians would be permissible under Islamic Law: "If a bomb that killed 10 million of them and burned as much of their land as they have burned Muslims' land were dropped on them, it would be permissible." See: Matthew Bunn and Anthony Wier, "The Seven Myths of Nuclear Terrorism," *Current History* (April 2005), p. 153.

[9] See: Richard Falk, *The Great Terror War* (New York: Olive Branch Press, 2003), especially chapters 1 and 2.

[10] David Luban, "The War on Terrorism and the End of Human Rights," *Philosophy & Public Policy Quarterly*, v. 22, n. 3 (Summer 2002), p. 10.

mega-terrorists. My subject is the moral case for indefinite detention. Although I refer to domestic and international law, I do not pretend to offer an analysis of what the legal status of mega-terrorist detainees would be under current U.S. or international law. The legal picture is confused—unsettled, at best.[11] Instead, my purpose is to offer a certain perspective and the underlying moral considerations that could support a practice of indefinite detention of mega-terrorists. The issue to be addressed may be put this way: *May mega-terrorists be subject to indefinite detention; and if so, on what moral grounds?* Punishment for past crimes is, of course, one justification for incarceration. But another justification is preventive detention, the incapacitation of persons because they are dangerous. In this article, I consider the possibility of this preventive-detention justification.

2 Preventive Detention

U.S. government officials have often stated that the main purpose in detaining "enemy combatants" is not to punish but, instead, to interrogate them for their intelligence value and to prevent them from rejoining terrorist efforts against the United States.[12] While I believe the interest in interrogation is a legitimate one, it alone could not justify indefinite, long-term detention. Admittedly, the prospect of indefinite detention might well demoralize prisoners and, conceivably, incline them to "break down" under interrogation. Nevertheless, the information given up would be useful only for a relatively short time. After a year or two, whatever the detainee knew about his terrorist organization, its methods and plans would be stale and out of date. Thus, based on the need for good intelligence alone, detention could be justified for only a few years, say three to five, at the very most. I believe we are left, then, with the interest in preventing detainees from committing future terrorist attacks.

---

[11] The issue of indefinite detention of terrorist detainees has not been addressed by the U.S. Supreme Court and was not addressed in the Supreme Court case of *Hamdan v. Rumsfeld* (June 2006).

[12] "We're detaining these captured combatants not to punish them and not to keep them in detention pending criminal charges, but to prevent them from continuing the fight against the United States and its allies, and to obtain intelligence necessary in the on-going global war on terrorism." [Stated by Navy Rear Adm. James M. McGarrah, director of Office of Administrative Review for Detained Enemy Combatants., as reported in Kathleen T. Rhem, "Review Boards Assessing Status of Guantanamo Detainees," American Forces Information Service/News Article (July 8, 2005)]. Referring to the detention of Jose Padilla as an "unlawful enemy combatant," Defense Secretary Donald Rumsfeld stated, "Our interest is not trying him and punishing him. Our interest is in finding out what he knows." CNN, June 11, 2002.

If American law is any indication, we certainly do think that detaining persons in order to prevent future harms or wrongs is sometimes justified. Preventive detention is a pervasive feature of American law, and its predominant justification is the individual's continuing dangerousness.[13]

3 Two Bad Arguments for Preventive Detention

Not all arguments put forward for the indefinite detention of terrorist suspects are good ones. Two common lines of argument, in particular, should be dismissed.

One such line of argument is based on the notion of "assumption of risk."

The form of the argument is: they assumed the risk, so they should take the consequences. Individuals who chose to fight for al-Qaeda, for example, knew they risked capture; and they knew, or should have known, that if they fell into the hands of their enemy, anything might be their fate, from short-term detention to execution. Therefore, they can have no complaint about their indefinite detention.

The rejoinder, however, is that even if the detainees themselves can have no complaint, this does not mean their treatment is morally acceptable or just on independent grounds. I know when I walk down the street in New York City, that I might be mugged; it is a risk I assume walking in the city. Nevertheless, getting mugged is an injustice. A woman knows she may be raped while jogging through Central Park; yet the risk she has assumed is the *risk of an injustice* being done to her. Assumption of risk is not the only factor to be considered in moral assessment. One assumes risks and must take consequences, but the consequences may yet be unjust on independent grounds. So assumption of risk alone in not enough to morally justify indefinite detention.

---

[13] A traditional example of indefinite, preventive detention is civil commitment of a person who is a danger to him/herself or to others as the result of mental disorder. The length of the commitment is indefinite, depending on the person's recovery to mental health. When the mental disorder indicates a lack of responsibility, or at least diminished responsibility, the mentally disabled person is not considered deserving of punishment. Like the person with a highly infectious disease who is put in quarantine to protect other members of the community, the mentally ill person is put in confinement for somewhat similar reasons.

In criminal law, sexual-predator statutes provide for continued commitment *after* the sexual offender has completed his sentence in prison. In *Kansas v. Hendricks* (1997), the U.S. Supreme Court permitted indeterminate confinement of dangerous individuals who have completed their sentences and have committed no new crime. Unlike persons civilly committed because of severe mental impairment, sexual offenders are regarded as responsible individuals; thus, they are deserving of punishment. Nevertheless, they are liable for further commitment after they have served their prison term when they are believed to pose a continuing danger to society.

The dangerousness rationale for preventive detention plays a role in many other places as well. Judges often consider an offender's dangerousness in determining the length of criminal sentences. Parole boards consider dangerousness when deciding whether or not to grant parole. There are also "habitual-offender" or "repeat-offender" laws that typically require state courts to hand down greatly extended sentences to persons convicted of serious crimes on three or more occasions.

Another argument purporting to justify the indefinite detention of terrorist suspects is this. Whether combatants are lawful or unlawful, when the battle is raging, it is morally permissible to shoot and kill enemy combatants. If this is so, then it must also be permissible to do any lesser harm to them. Assuming capture and indefinite detention is less harm to a person than his being killed, it is morally permissible to detain enemy combatants indefinitely. This is, perhaps, more appealing than the first argument; but it is still not right.

When you come at me with a gun, I have a right to kill you as a matter of self-defense. If, instead, I should manage to overpower you without killing you, I do not then have a right to make you my slave, even assuming my brand of enslavement is clearly a lesser harm than killing you. This may seem anomalous, but the same judgment is embodied in the law of war. It is permissible to kill the regular enemy soldier during battle; but if he is captured as a POW, you may not kill him, nor do anything at all harmful to him, even though enslaving him could be considered a lesser harm than being killed. While it is permissible to kill the enemy on the battlefield, the objective is to incapacitate, to render the enemy harmless. It is forbidden to kill wounded soldiers or soldiers who have surrendered, because they have become "*hors de combat*" and no longer threaten one's military purposes. Once the enemy is rendered harmless, no valid military purpose is served by imposing any kind of harm upon him, even if it is a harm less than death.

While the foregoing arguments are flawed, another remains. I believe we are lead to the simple consideration that the indefinite detention of certain terrorists is justified because of their continued dangerousness.

4   The Utilitarian Calculation

The general rationale for preventive detention is that the person to be detained is dangerous in that he presents a great risk of engaging in future harmful conduct. For example, the argument for sexual-predator laws is that certain convicted sexual predators are simply too dangerous to release even after they have served their criminal sentence. Similarly, some terrorist suspects (i.e., mega-terrorists) are far too dangerous to release once captured.

But how dangerous is dangerous enough to warrant preventive detention? It has been argued that the danger sexual predators pose is no greater than that of other kinds of violent offenders and that, if there is no justification for the preventive detention of other kinds of violent offenders, then there can be no justification for the preventive detention of sexual predators. I shall not join that debate here. It must be acknowledged, however, that the danger the mega-terrorist posses is orders of magnitude greater than that of a sexual predator. The argument from dangerousness is essentially utilitarian. Dangerousness is a function of the degree of harm or destruction and the likelihood of its occurrence; and as the degree of harm and/or the likelihood of occurrence increases, more and more drastic precautions become justified. If the danger to society ever warranted preventive detention, certainly that of the mega-terrorist must.

In saying a person is too dangerous to release, one implication is that, if released, he will not be deterred from further violence by the threat of criminal punishment. This may be because of mental disability, uncontrollable urges, or impetuous risk-taking desires. In the case of mega-terrorists, the individual is undeterrable by the criminal sanction, presumably, because he is committed to carrying out terrorist activities as a matter of firm, ideological conviction or religious belief. The possibility of being captured and punished or killed does not deter him. In fact, the prospect of becoming a martyr for his cause may actually be a positive incentive for him.

Since the person is undeterrable, his conduct cannot be significantly influenced by the criminal-justice system. Preventive detention is therefore justified as the state's only realistic option. Zacarias Moussaoui may provide an example. Imagine (contrary to fact) that he had not committed any significant crimes. Taking flying lessons is not a crime, for instance, even if he was uninterested in learning how to take off or land an airplane. Nevertheless, he was certainly dangerous and undeterrable. Imagine that Moussaoui had been acquitted of all charges at his federal trial. Should the Government have simply released him? Here was an avowed terrorist who repeatedly expressed approval of al-Qaeda's "jihad" against the United States and announced his own desire to kill as many Americans as possible.[14] To release such a person would be extremely hazardous. Indeed, had Moussaoui actually been acquitted, the Administration undoubtedly would have designated him an "enemy combatant" and held him in military custody.

5 Procedural Safeguards

In the context of domestic criminal law, a standard objection to a pure utilitarian rationale for punishment is that it would justify the punishment of the innocent in cases where that served the greater good of society—as, possibly, the case of punishing a person (known only by authorities to be innocent) as a scapegoat in order to "send a message" to the populace and thereby increase general deterrence.

While I believe the utilitarian approach is essentially correct with regard to preventive detention, the intent is to detain only very dangerous persons, that is, mega-terrorists. I am certainly not suggesting that we detain persons who are not terrorists—even if, in some peculiar circumstance, it might seem to be advantageous to do so.[15] First, it could be grossly unjust to those people. Second, if it became an established practice, the fact that innocent persons were being indefinitely

---

[14] Moussaoui stated, for example, "I will be delighted to come back one day to blow myself into your new W.T.C. if ever you rebuild it." Philip Shenon, "Man Charged in Sept. 11 Attacks Demands that Qaeda Leaders Testify," *New York Times* (March 22, 2003) at B-12.

[15] I consider myself a "moral pluralist" in the sense that I believe utilitarianism must be augmented with other, non-utilitarian principles.

detained would leak out and the state's moral authority would be undermined. Hence, we must do our best to determine that the people put into detention are, indeed, terrorists. This means we must have procedures for determining who is and is not a terrorist and who among them is a committed mega-terrorist. We must also have periodic reviews for determining whether, over time, an individual continues to pose a serious threat.

During the war in Afghanistan (Operation Enduring Freedom), the Department of Defense (DoD) issued the outline of a multi-step screening process for determining enemy-combatant status.[16] Unfortunately, what looked good on paper, did not always work out in practice. During the fighting in Afghanistan, most of the prisoners were initially captured by the Northern Alliance or local warlords and then turned over to U.S. forces later. Thus, U.S. military officers did not have firsthand knowledge of the circumstances of the detainees' initial capture. There were cases in which individuals were denounced to Northern Alliance forces by their neighbors because of local animosities or blood feuds having nothing to do with al-Qaeda or the Taliban. In some instances, one person would denounce another in order to get that person's house or land. In other cases, individuals were captured by bounty hunters and sold to the Americans, sometimes for $5,000 per person. In still other cases, innocent people were simply scooped up in the massive confusion of the war.

To the sort of objection these facts raise, one can only urge a more intense effort at accuracy in determining the status of captives. This undoubtedly means much more specialized training and a great many more personnel for handling the intake of prisoners. During Operation Enduring Freedom, there was a lack of adequately trained and experienced interrogators, and there were far too few personnel who knew the local language. Furthermore, the assessments made at many stages became routine and superficial. Obviously, the job was far more demanding than rounding up uniformed enemy soldiers in a traditional war.

A second objection to the DoD's multi-step process is that the assessment was one-sided. Although the detainee was interviewed, he had no opportunity to develop evidence or bring witnesses on his behalf, nor did he have a chance to dispute or correct the putative evidence against him.[17] Naturally, this would be entirely impractical at the initial capture or even in any of the field assessments. But once the detainee is safely situated in a permanent detention facility, every effort should be made to gain whatever evidence the detainee believes can corroborate his story that he is not a terrorist (assuming that is his claim). Again, this will require extra expense and well-trained personnel to assist detainees in gathering such evidence.

---

[16] See "Guantanamo Detainees," at: http//usinfo.state.gov/dhr.Archive/2004/Mar/17-718401.html.

[17] Referring to military "screening" processes, the *Hamdi* Court remarked: "An interrogation by one's captor, however effective an intelligence-gathering tool, hardly constitutes a constitutionally adequate factfinding before a neutral decisionmaker." 542 U.S. 507, 537.

6 Determining a Detainee's Continuing Threat and False Positives

One standard objection to preventive detentions of any kind is the difficulty in predicting a person's future behavior. It is notoriously difficult to predict who will commit a violent crime, for example. Using current methods of criminology, it is said there would be at least one "false positive" for every "true positive"; that is, at least one person who would never commit a future crime would be detained for every person correctly detained. In the context of domestic law, that would be unacceptably high, i.e., a 50/50 chance that the person detained would be a false positive.

In defense of preventive detention, it may be pointed out that no system is perfect. Our system of criminal justice is certainly imperfect, with many innocent persons mistakenly convicted and incarcerated each year. Nevertheless, the objection will be pressed that the ratio of false convictions to true ones in the criminal-justice system is surely much better than 50/50. Although there do not seem to be any reliable statistics on this, one can reasonably hope that the ratio of false to true convictions would be 10/90 or better. It is often said it is better that ten guilty persons go free than that one innocent person be punished. An implication one might draw from this maxim is that no one should be punished for a crime unless there is better than a 90 percent chance that he actually committed the crime.

Mistakenly punishing an innocent person is certainly a great harm to that individual (and, indirectly to family, friends, associates). It seems to outweigh the harm of a guilty person getting off without punishment. The thought is that while the innocent person suffers the harm of punishment, no one suffers any harm when the system fails to punish a guilty person, though retributive justice is not served. Surely, it is argued, it is far worse for John to be falsely convicted and hanged for a murder, when he justifiably killed a person in self-defense than for Bill to be set free (based on a bogus self-defense) when he truly did commit a murder.

But should the moral priorities always be this way? The preceding example does not take into account whether Bill will commit further murders when he is mistakenly released. Perhaps there are situations in which the priorities should be the other way around. Michael Corrado offers the following hypothetical. Imagine a group of ten people, six of whom will commit murder if allowed to go free; but we do not know which of the ten they are. If we let them all go free, six people will be murdered. If our concern is the risk of false positives, then the prospect that four innocent persons will lose their freedom must be weighed against the prospect that six other innocent persons will lose their lives.[18] What has been brought into the calculation is what the bad guys will do once they are mistakenly released.

---

[18] Michael J. Corrado, "Punishment and the Wild Beast of Prey: The Problem of Preventive Detention," 86 *Journal of Criminal Law & Criminology* 778, 793 (1996).

This example is also discussed in Christopher Slobogin, "A Jurisprudence of Dangerousness," 98 *Northwestern University Law Review* 1, 7 (2003).

In any case, the calculations about preventive detention shift radically when we move from the domestic context to that of mega-terrorism. This is simply because the dangers threatened are vastly greater. One mega-terrorist might easily cause the deaths of hundreds or even thousands of people. In these circumstances, mistakenly releasing a mega-terrorist would seem to be much more serious than mistakenly detaining an innocent non-terrorist. Under the threat of mega-terrorism, it appears that the dictum should go the other way: Better that ten innocents are detained than that one mega-terrorist go free.

If one accepts deterrence and incapacitation as legitimate justifying elements in a theory of punishment, as I do, then the system of domestic punishment may be seen as one mechanism for society's defense—defense against "the enemy within."[19] It is important to have some such defense mechanism; and we accept its necessity even with all its imperfections. When it comes to defense of the country in war, many other costly imperfections and mistakes are accepted as unfortunate necessities. Chief among these, of course, is the "collateral damage" of innocent people unintentionally killed in a war for the defense of the state. If detaining mega-terrorists (including the cost to those mistakenly detained, the false positives) increases the general welfare more than any alternative, then that is what we should do.

The "use" of innocent individuals (intentional killing of noncombatants) is prohibited in the Just War tradition, just as the "use" of innocent persons in punishment (i.e., intentionally punishing an innocent person when it is useful), is prohibited in the domestic context. So a similar kind of constraint on simple utilitarian calculations applies in both contexts. But the risks to the state are far, far greater in the case of war than in the case of domestic crime. And where the risks are greater, we should be willing to accept higher rates of mistake. It would be one thing to mistakenly release from detention a person who will murder one or two people; it is quite another thing to mistakenly release a mega-terrorist who will detonate a bomb that kills hundreds or thousands. However many false positives we think acceptable in the first case, the acceptable number of false positives must be far greater in the second case.[20]

---

[19] For a theory of punishment along these lines, see: Don E. Scheid, "Constructing a Theory of Punishment, Desert, and the Distribution of Punishments," *The Canadian Journal of Law & Jurisprudence*, v. X, n. 2 (July 1997), pp. 441–506.

See also: Phillip Montague, *Punishment as Societal Defense* (New York: Rowman & Littlefield, 1995).

[20] It may give one pause to consider that some anticipatory crimes create a very high percentage of false positives. For instance, drunk driving is presumably treated as a crime in order to prevent the future harm of automobile accidents. In fact, the vast majority of those drivers stopped and convicted of DUI (driving under the influence) would not have caused an accident if they had not been stopped. Thus, most people convicted of DUI are false positives. The justification for making drunken driving a crime is that, even if only a small percentage of drunk drivers ever cause accidents, the harm that is risked can be very great, namely, the maiming or death of one or more persons.

Our conclusion, I think, must be that problems about predicting detainees' future behavior and the inevitability of detaining false positives cannot not be a conclusive objection to the preventive detention of mega-terrorists.

7 Adjusting Due-Process Requirements, Implementing Thorough Status Review

In an ideal criminal-justice system, all and only criminals would be convicted and punished; innocent defendants would always be acquitted. In our less-than-ideal world, of course, this is not the case. We know that our justice system inevitably produces both *false convictions* (convictions of innocent persons) and *false acquittals* (acquittals of guilty persons). It would be nice if we could reduce both types of miscarriages of justice. Unfortunately, there is a trade-off. An attempt to reduce the number of false convictions by raising the standards of proof will also tend to increase the number of false acquittals. By the same token, relaxing the standards of proof would reduce the number of false acquittals but increase the number of false convictions. Between these two miscarriages of justice, false convictions seem worse in the case of ordinary crimes. Thus, the burden of proof is placed on the prosecution, and we insist on a high standard of proof for conviction (i.e., "beyond a reasonable doubt"). On the other hand, in the context of a quasi-war on terrorism, false acquittals (of mega-terrorists) would seem worse; so, perhaps, the burden of proof should be on the terrorist detainees and standards of proof for holding detainees should be relaxed.

Although arrest for common crimes normally requires "probable cause," the state should be able to pick up terrorist suspects on less evidence, since the stakes are so much higher. Given the extreme danger mega-terrorists pose, we should apprehend first and ask questions later. But once a suspected mega-terrorist is safely in custody, we really should ask questions in earnest; we should do everything possible to determine his true status. Even if one is picked up on only the merest suspicion of terrorism and held on thin evidence, the crucial concern for the individual is that he be cleared and released if, in fact, he is innocent.

The Combatant Status Review Tribunals (CSRT) and the Administrative Review Boards (ARB) that were instituted at Guantanamo might provide a start for the kind of careful review of detainees that is called for.[21] Published reports, however,

---

[21] Initially, the United States held prisoners at Guantanamo without access to any court to challenge their detention. Combatant Status Review Tribunals (CSRTs) were first implemented in July 2004 in response to the Supreme Court's *Hamdi* and *Rasul* decisions. The CSRTs conduct a one-time review of Guantanamo detainees to ascertain whether they are or are not enemy combatants by providing a venue for detainees to personally challenge (in a very limited way) their status as enemy combatants.

Administrative Review Boards (ARBs) conduct annual reviews to determine whether detainees are of any further intelligence value and whether they present a continuing danger to U.S. security.

suggest that these proceedings are far too superficial. My own suggestion, therefore, is that much more effort and expense should be given over to assisting the detainee in gathering any and all evidence he may require to prove that he is not a terrorist, when that is what he claims. The relation between the government and defense counsel should be much less adversarial in this regard than in the normal criminal-justice setting. As a country with the ability to "project" military forces anywhere in the world, the United States certainly has the wherewithal, if it chooses, to dispatch investigative teams anywhere in the world. As a liberal democratic government, it should do all it can to ensure that the detainees it holds indefinitely truly are the dangerous terrorists it claims. The United States should spare no expense in assisting a detainee's counsel in interviewing witnesses, collecting affidavits, and otherwise gathering evidence. Certainly, each detainee must be apprised of all the evidence against him and be allowed to confront witnesses and dispute any other evidence against him. The more effort and expense the United States undertakes to ensure that the detainees it holds truly are mega-terrorists, the more solid will be its moral position regarding their preventive detention.

To date, the indefinite detention of terrorist suspects has been associated with Bush Administration's unilateral and unreviewable determinations of detainees as "enemy combatants." But there is no necessary connection between preventive detention and abuse of power by the Executive branch. There is no reason why a system of preventive detention could not be subject to both judicial review and congressional oversight. The principle of checks and balances within the Doctrine of the Separation of Powers would require, at a minimum, that the courts have authority to review whatever detention proceedings are ultimately devised, as are detention proceedings in domestic law. Such provision for judicial review could only enhance the moral posture of the United States as it holds mega-terrorists in indefinite, preventive detention.

8   The Punitive Aspect

Although subject to continuing detention until the end of hostilities, regular prisoners of war (POWs) are not liable for punishment. They are not considered to be criminals; they are "privileged combatants." The attitude is that enemy soldiers in traditional wars are simply "poor sods" who had nothing to do with starting the war and who just happened to be on the other side. They are often regarded as morally innocent.[22] But this is not the case with terrorist detainees.

---

[22] Michael Walzer mentions this view in *Just and Unjust Wars* 4th ed. (New York: Basic Books, 2006), p. 36.

Terrorists are different from POWs and may be thought to deserve a punitive response on two grounds. First, they have undertaken past, wrongful (terrorist-related) activities, such as participating in a terrorist organization, training for terrorist actions, planning terrorist operations, and so on. Second, their dangerousness is their own doing. The terrorist poses a future danger because of his future voluntary actions. If released, he will engage in terrorist actions of his own free will. His dangerousness, it may be said, is his own fault. If this is right, there may be a punitive element that colors the preventive detention of terrorists (separate from any punishment for past wrongs). If so, this can only add to the moral justification of the detainee's indefinite detention.[23]

Nevertheless, preventive detention is not punishment for past wrongdoing. Although the preventive detention of a sex offender may carry a punitive implication, it is still the case that if he is cured of his sexual pathologies, he must be released. Similarly, if the terrorist detainee has a genuine change of heart and forswears any and all future terrorist activities so that he no longer presents a danger, then he too should be released.[24]

---

[23] Michael Davis has argued that some preventive detention can be justified as punishment for reckless endangerment. If a dangerous person is informed of his condition, but refuses to take measures that could eliminate his condition, then he is not exercising the care a reasonable person could be expected to exercise. As such, he is guilty of reckless endangerment—for which he deserves punishment. See: Michael Davis, "Arresting the White Death: Preventive Detention, Confinement for Treatment, and Medical Ethics," APA (*American Philosophical Association*) *Newsletters*, v. 94, n. 2 (Spring 1995), pp. 92–98.

[24] A possible example is that of Yaser Esam Hamdi. Hamdi was a U.S. citizen apprehended in Afghanistan and held as an "enemy combatant" in military detention in the United States. In June 2004, the U.S. Supreme Court ruled in *Hamdi v. Rumsfeld* that a U.S. citizen labeled "enemy combatant" could not be held indefinitely in a U.S. military prison without the assistance of a lawyer and without an opportunity to contest the allegations against him before a neutral arbiter. At that point, he was released to Saudi Arabia (October 11, 2004) without being charged. In exchange for this release, Hamdi agreed to renounce his American citizenship and to never engage in any terrorist activities. He agreed not to aid or assist the Taliban or any member of al-Qaeda or any terrorist organization designated as such by the United States. Furthermore, Hamdi formally renounced terrorism and violent jihad and promised to notify officials of Saudi Arabia and the U.S. Embassy in Saudi Arabia if he were solicited or came into contact with any known terrorists or terrorist organizations, or if he became aware of any planned acts of terrorism. *Yaser Esam Hamdi v. Donald Rumsfeld: Settlement Agreement* (September 17, 2004).

I leave aside here all questions about the possibility and morality of "brainwashing," reconditioning with or without psychotropic drugs, forceful indoctrination, hypnosis, brain surgery, and all other techniques of coercively reorienting a person's beliefs, attitudes, and commitments.

Chapter 11
The Great Right: Habeas Corpus

Wade L. Robison

We are in the midst of an uneasy period for liberty, with a President curtailing our liberties while invading Iraq to spread "the freedom agenda."[1] It is a period both paradoxical and frightening. For those whose country has been invaded? A fiasco leaving law and liberty there both chimeras. For us? Wiretapping without a warrant, refusing citizens entry into the country, denying citizens the writ of habeas corpus—the list is long. The Constitutional terrain we were in has been transformed, its familiar landmarks altered as though by an earthquake.

Of greatest concern is the failure to abide by the Constitution's requirement that the "privilege of the Writ of Habeas Corpus shall not be suspended." The writ is a judicial order directing officials holding someone prisoner to bring the prisoner before the court so the court can determine whether the prisoner is being unlawfully held because of a legal or a factual error.[2] The writ requires that a court, an authority independent of those doing the detaining, deem sufficient the reasons for detaining that person.

The writ is thus a bulwark against arbitrary imprisonment. Its suspension allows a government to detain anyone indefinitely, without charging the person with any crime, leaving the person without any recourse—helpless in the face of the government's power.

We might have thought it a settled matter of law that American citizens may invoke the writ of habeas corpus if detained by federal authorities unless "Rebellion or Invasion" require its suspension for public safety. Yet the matter has become unsettled, and will remain unsettled, even should the Supreme Court decide that the President lacks the authority to deny American citizens the writ. Court decisions contain their conditions, waiting to be exploited, opening new lines of attack even as they settle others.

---

[1] President Bush from a news conference the week of August 20, 2006.

[2] It was a factual error that led to Brandon Mayfield, a Portland lawyer, being detained as a material witness for two weeks without being charged. Fingerprints on a bag of detonators found after the Spanish railway attacks were misidentified as his (Eric Lichtblau, "U.S. Will Pay $2 Million to Lawyer Wrongfully Jailed," *New York Times*, November 30, 2006).

D.A. Reidy and W.J. Riker (eds.), *Coercion and the State.*
© Springer Science + Business Media B.V. 2008

Like a canary in a mine, the health of the writ in our Constitutional democracy is a measure of the health of the political system insofar as our liberty is concerned. I shall make three claims. First, the writ has a special Constitutional status. Second, it requires some such structural features within a constitutional order as the separation of powers, without which the privilege of the writ would be useless. Third, the scope of the writ should be determined not by the status of the person whose liberty is denied, but by the status of those denying liberty. Each of these claims has important practical consequences. Let us begin with Hamilton's understanding of the place of the writ in our Constitutional order.

1   Habeas Corpus

In Federalist Paper No. 84, Alexander Hamilton says that

> The creation of crimes after the commission of the fact, or, in other words, the subjecting of men to punishment for things which, when they were done, were breaches of no law; and the practice of arbitrary imprisonment have been, in all ages, the favourite and most formidable instruments of tyranny.

He then quotes Blackstone regarding arbitrary imprisonment:

> To bereave a man of life…or by violence to confiscate his estate, without accusation or trial, would be so gross and notorious an act of despotism, as must at once convey the alarm of tyranny throughout the whole nation; but confinement of the person, by secretly hurrying him to jail, where his sufferings are unknown or forgotten, is a less public, a less striking, and therefore a more dangerous engine of arbitrary government.

The "remedy for this fatal evil," Hamilton continues, is the *habeas corpus* act, "which… [Blackstone] calls 'the BULWARK of the British constitution.'"[3]

Hamilton is arguing against adding a Bill of Rights to the Constitution, and one reason is that the Constitution contains within its body the most important protections against arbitrary government. He thinks that adding a Bill of Rights would dilute the more important protections already in the Constitution: the privilege of *habeas corpus* and prohibitions against bills of attainder, *ex post facto* laws, and titles of nobility. Regarding the powers of Congress, the Constitution says in Article I, Section 9, Number 2 that

> The privilege of the Writ of Habeas Corpus shall not be suspended, unless when in Cases of Rebellion or Invasion the public Safety may require it.

A set of prohibitions follows in Number 3:

> No Bill of Attainder or ex post facto Law shall be passed.

And another in Number 8:

> No Title of Nobility shall be granted by the United States.

---

[3] Alexander Hamilton, John Jay, and James Madison, *The Federalist*, The Gideon Edition, ed. George W. Carey & James McClellan (Indianapolis, IN: Liberty Fund, 2001), p. 444.

The prohibitions in 3 and 8 are repeated in Section 10 regarding the powers of the States. The federal and state governments are thus prohibited from granting titles of nobility and from passing bills of attainder and ex post facto laws.

These provisions raise many questions. Why are these provisions, and these alone, internal to the Constitution, not tacked on like the Bill of Rights? Why are states not denied the power to suspend the privilege of habeas corpus? Why is it called a privilege rather than a right? How does the denial of titles of nobility protect our liberty?

However necessary answering these questions may be to a full examination of how these internal features protect our liberty, I shall focus only on "the privilege of a Writ of Habeas Corpus" and why it is thought so essential to our liberty that it is embedded within the body of the Constitution.

2   Constitutional Status of Habeas Corpus

Constitutional issues may be distinguished by the forms of argument that determine their answers judicially.[4] They fall into three classes:

1. Those concerning the legislative details, administrative enactments, and so on, within the framework of powers created by the Constitution, none of which are put into question.
2. Those concerning the provisions and implications of the Constitution itself.
3. Those concerning the conditions for having any constitution or the particular Constitution we have.

The last class in turn divides into two:

- The constitutive conditions for constitutions, such as the equality of the contracting parties
- The practical conditions for agreement among the contracting parties so as to have a particular constitution

Dred Scott is a classic case where the Court considered the constitutive conditions of having a constitution, arguing that the necessity for equality of the contracting parties made unconstitutional the regulation of slavery in the territories by Congress. The original states had the power to determine for themselves whether to be slave or free, and so, the Court argued, any new state would be denied an original power if unable to determine for itself whether to be slave or free. Chief Justice Taney's decision, I would argue, also considered the conditions for the adoption of our constitution, claiming that neither Southern states nor Southerners would have agreed to a constitution that made freedom possible for their slaves if they traveled into a free territory or state.[5]

---

[4] See my "Hard Cases and Natural Law," in *Law, Justice and Culture*, Vol. II, ed. Andre-Jean Arnaud & Peter Koller (Stuttgart: Fran Steiner Verlag, 1998), pp. 49–55.

[5] "Hard Cases and Natural Law," op. cit., pp. 50–52.

The advantage, and disadvantage, of such bedrock decisions is that no appeal is possible beyond them to any deeper principles. The conditions constitutive of constitutions and of their being adopted are as deep as one can go. Appealing to any other constitutional features would be trumped by those deep principles. Appealing to extra-constitutional matters would have no legal import. The only alternative is to provide another construction of those deep principles, meeting the decision head-on. That is often not a realistic possibility.

No Constitutional provision is clear on its face, and the provision for a writ of habeas corpus needs construction to determine its place.[6] Is it a constitutive condition of constitutions or their adoption, constitutive of our Constitution or its adoption, a provision of our Constitution, or something like legislation operating within our Constitutional framework? Its placement determines its Constitutional weight and thus its immunity, and vulnerability, to certain forms of argument. Being constitutive of all constitutions or of our Constitution, for instance, would immunize it from attack from all but other constitutive provisions and make its meaning key in constructing the meaning of all other provisions.[7]

We can, however, readily imagine constitutions without a writ of habeas corpus. We can imagine citizens adopting a constitution without a writ, under the real conditions in which having a constitution is judged far more important than ensuring that future abuse does not occur. So the writ is neither a constitutive condition of constitutions nor for their adoption. But it is in our Constitution, and there it presupposes the constitutive and structural feature of the separation of powers. The privilege is operative only if the judiciary is operating independently enough of the other branches to serve as a check on their abuse of power when used to detain individuals.

Locke argued that any form of government except an absolute monarchy is permissible, but also argued that the best form includes a separation of powers.[8] We can see one reason why it is best, given his stance. The main concerns of those in a state of nature are security and liberty. How are we reasonably to give up our natural liberty to be secure and yet maintain civil liberty? Choosing an absolute monarch would be to give up our natural liberty without any gain in security or civil liberty. We would put ourselves at the mercy of the absolute power of an individual

---

[6] As does every legal provision, I would argue, and everything that carries meaning. See in this regard Francis Lieber, *Legal and Political Hermeneutics* (New York: Legal Classics Library, 1994). Originally published in 1839, I shall assume its basic views in what follows—that anything can be a sign (Lieber, 17), that anything can be a sign of anything (Lieber, 22), that every sign requires interpretation (Lieber, e.g. 23)—and add only that understanding a provision depends upon seeing its function within the structure of a system, argument, or what have you, a requirement that we also understand the point or function of the system.

[7] The phrase "constructing the meaning" itself begs for constructive interpretation. It does not imply that readers may make something mean whatever they wish. Construction is a form of interpretation, neither literal nor extravagant, to use Lieber's terminology, highly dependent on structural features of the document in question, and subject to objective, and so public, criteria.

[8] John Locke, *Two Treatises of Government*, ed. Peter Laslett, 2nd ed. (Cambridge: Cambridge University Press, 1967), Book II, Chapter VII, Section 90.

who could deny us our liberty at will—as though prosecutor, judge, and jury all in one. Locke's solution to this problem is to make the choice of an absolute monarch unacceptable. Indeed, any solution granting such power is equally suspect whether the solution is an oligarchy or a pure democracy or anything else. The only way to ensure that those in power do not use that power to deny someone's liberty arbitrarily is to provide a check against such power. No paper guarantee is sufficient. That can be trumped by extravagant constructions. What is required is some structural feature such as the separation of powers.

Our Constitution embodies that structural feature in its very form, the first three sections setting out the three branches of government. Having a judiciary sufficiently independent to assess the claimed grounds for detention is a necessary condition for the writ. We could lose the writ by losing a sufficient separation of powers, and so the loss of the writ may be symptomatic of a major fault in our Constitutional order, a failure of one of its constitutive features. But locating the writ in that Constitutional landscape does not give us much sense of its Constitutional weight—how it fares in Constitutional arguments when weighed against other Constitutional provisions. We must look elsewhere for that.

3   Constitutive Conditions of Citizenship

Arbitrary imprisonment is a "fatal evil," Hamilton says, for which the writ is "a remedy." The concern, he says, is that individuals are imprisoned secretly and that their "sufferings are unknown or forgotten," without anyone the wiser about their status. Denying them access to a lawyer or visitors ensures the secrecy that Blackstone claims, and Hamilton agrees, is "*a more dangerous engine* of arbitrary government."

But there are two issues here we need to disentangle. The one concerns arbitrary imprisonment, the other, secrecy. Hamilton apparently thought the writ a remedy for both, ensuring that imprisonment is open to examination and thus censure from the public and that it must be justified to an objective and independent arbiter. Perhaps his world was too small for a government to seize and imprison an individual without it becoming public knowledge. Ours is not. There is no necessity that anyone other than the person detained and those detaining the person need know. Only those in the know are in a position to object to the imprisonment; but seized and held in secret, a prisoner cannot object and cannot inform anyone who might object.

The privilege of the writ would thus be lost even though a court stood ready to hear the evidence, factual and legal, that would, or would not, justify the imprisonment. So the loss of the writ does not necessarily put at risk the separation of powers. We could maintain a sufficiently robust separation of powers to allow a court to act independently of the other branches of government to assess imprisonment, and the other branches could still seize and imprison someone. All that is required is that the seizure and imprisonment be kept secret. Hamilton would seem to be mistaken. The writ of habeas corpus would seem to provide no remedy against someone being imprisoned secretly, their "sufferings…unknown."

Yet there is a way of understanding the writ that gives it the Constitutional weight Hamilton thinks it has. It is of no small importance that the protection provided by the writ is within the body of the Constitution, not an additional right added onto it, but internal to the document and internal to the Constitutional order created by it. The prohibition against titles of nobility is instructive here. It is a prohibition regarding the status of citizens under the new Constitutional order. No citizen is to be distinguished from any other citizen by titles of nobility. There are to be no Lords, no Counts, no Ladies, no Countesses. All are equal as citizens, none superior to any other in any way relevant to their position in the new Constitutional order as citizens. All are equally subject to the law. None can properly claim privileges or immunities that do not belong to all. So in our courts, for instance, no citizens can claim that their position in society favors them in any way. Each is a citizen, and only a citizen.

What we find in the Constitution, that is, are a set of internal features that give defining features to what it is to be a citizen of the United States. This should not be surprising. A constitution necessarily creates, besides a nation, a set of legal relations, changing the status of all subject to its scope. Individuals become citizens, constitutionally restricted in some ways, enabled to claim certain rights, entitled to certain privileges and immunities, immunized constitutionally in certain ways. Our Constitution created, besides the United States, citizens of the United States, and internal features of the Constitution make them, as citizens, forever immune from bills of attainder and ex post facto laws, forever immune from imprisonment without the privilege of the writ of habeas corpus except in the two conditions specified by the Constitution, forever equal to any other citizen in the eyes of the Constitution and so unable to claim privileges and immunities not available to every other citizen.[9]

These four internal protections against the power of the government are constitutive of what it is to be a citizen of the United States. They have been marked out as requirements within our Constitutional order, necessary even if, as Hamilton claimed, the government were granted only limited powers and a Bill of Rights were therefore unnecessary. It is their positioning within the Constitution that gives them special prominence and special Constitutional weight.

Nothing within the Constitution is to be construed so as to diminish the protections they afford. Constitutive, as they are, of what it is to be subject to the Constitution, they are constraints on governmental power. Neither the President, nor Congress, nor the Courts have the Constitutional power to restrict them. They are, Constitutionally, as weighty as any grant of power and so serve to restrict any grant of power.

In the upheaval of our Constitutional landscape we are now experiencing, we must thus ensure that the internal protections of our Constitution maintain their

---

[9] Gordon S. Wood's *The Radicalism of the American Revolution* (New York: Vintage reprint, 1993) is particularly helpful in explaining how revolutionary was the idea that citizens are equal under the law.

proper weight. We might have thought it a settled matter that citizens are not to be denied the privilege of invoking the writ of habeas corpus should they be detained by federal authorities. We now know that it is not. We might have thought it a settled matter that the writ may be denied only "when in Cases of Rebellion or Invasion the public Safety may require it." We now know that it is not. The issue is now open for adjudication, no longer a settled matter of law. That is a matter of no small regret. When settled matters of such moment become justiciable, events are set in motion which may alter the constitutional and political landscapes and not necessarily for the betterment of either.[10] But this President has unsettled the issue of whether citizens are entitled to the privilege of the writ of habeas corpus, and because unsettled, it is at risk. But its being unsettled also gives us a chance to understand how deeply grounded in our Constitutional system the writ is.

It would be unacceptable to claim that the denial of the writ is consistent with the Constitutional prohibition by claiming that we are now in a state of rebellion or have been invaded. Such interpretations would be extravagant, in Lieber's sense,[11] changing the commonly understood meanings of "rebellion" and "invasion." We might try to maintain the Constitution's requirement less dramatically by claiming that those are but two examples, among a longer possible list, of ways in which the public safety might be threatened. That would also be an extravagant interpretation, but even were it not, we ought to be chary of weakening the writ in such ways given that it is internal to the Constitution and has great Constitutional weight because of that placement.

The writ can only retain that Constitutional weight, its being constitutive of being a citizen under our Constitution, if there is a sufficiently robust separation of powers to permit an independent judicial review of any detention and if there are no secret seizures and detentions. We know how to ensure the former. Among other things, court hearings cannot be secret, and there must be public records of the decisions taken regarding writs. Otherwise, we citizens cannot be sure that the courts are responding, and responding properly, to writs of habeas corpus. Ensuring that there are no secret seizures and detentions requires, as we shall see in §4, an examination of the writ's internal logic and purpose.

We must keep in mind that the aim of the writ is to prevent those in positions sanctioned by our Constitution from abusing their power by imprisoning individuals without recourse. The focal point of concern is the massive power a government can bring to bear upon an individual. Any expansion of governmental power to deny the

---

[10] One of the more unfortunate legacies of Congressman Tom DeLay is the Texas reapportionment case. It had been a settled matter, not of law, but of custom, that states only reexamine congressional districts after the census every ten years. Challenging that custom produced a result with political implications some at least may deplore—an invitation to every legislature to reexamine congressional districts whenever they wish and certainly whenever the majority in the legislature changes parties. What was settled had some unfortunate consequences, but the change has arguably wrought more.

[11] Extravagant construction is "the attempt, by mal-construction, to carry designs into the sphere of the instrument," abandoning any attempt to construe it, but reconstructing it, as it were, to mean what you want it to mean. Lieber, op. cit., p. 81.

writ, any rereading of the carefully conditioned exceptions to the immunity embodied in it, comes at the expense of what it is to be a citizen. The Constitution was constructed to create a new kind of order, one predicated upon the citizens of this new order having a status unlike any other individuals in the world. A reinterpretation of any one of the internal protections of the Constitution will change the dynamics of the relation, altering constitutive features of American citizenship.

4   Scope of the Writ

Hamilton emphasizes, by quoting Blackstone, the secretive nature of arbitrary imprisonment. It is because the imprisonment is "less public" that it is *"a more dangerous engine* of arbitrary government." Individuals simply disappear. We know of them only if released or if information somehow slips out. So we do not know how many individuals are now being imprisoned by this government without being charged, for instance. Information comes out haphazardly.

It recently became public that two American citizens were detained in Iraq, neither with good cause. One was an FBI informer who kept pleading with his captors to check his computer and cellphone for his e-mails to his FBI contact. He became a suspect "for having associated with the people [he] tried to expose."[12] Denied access to legal representation, he was imprisoned for 97 days before officials let him go, without explanation.

Given how unsettled our Constitutional protections have become, it is perhaps not surprising that an American citizen can be held by American authorities, and repeatedly interrogated by, he was told, members of the FBI, the CIA, the Naval Criminal Investigative Service, and the Defense Intelligence Agency, all officials of the United States. However unsurprising, it is still constitutionally unacceptable.

What is required if we are not to have an erosion of what it is to be an American citizen is an understanding of both the internal logic and the purpose of the writ of habeas corpus and the other internal protections in the Constitution. Those protections mark legal relations. To say that citizens are immune from ex post facto laws just is to say that officials in the Constitutional order are prohibited from passing ex post facto laws. To say that titles of nobility are prohibited just is to say that officials of the Constitutional order are precluded from treating any citizen differently from any other citizen because of any title of nobility and that no citizen, as a citizen, is to be marked off legally from any other citizen by having a title of nobility.

Just so, the privilege of the writ of habeas corpus creates a legal relation between citizens and officials acting under the color of the Constitution. Citizens are immune from arbitrary imprisonment; officials are precluded from arbitrarily imprisoning citizens. It is one and the same relation. That is its internal logic.

---

[12] Michael Moss, "Former U.S. Detainee in Iraq Recalls Torment," *New York Times*, December 18, 2006.

In addition, and rather obviously, citizens would not be immunized from arbitrary imprisonment—the purpose of the writ—if governmental officials can seize and imprison them arbitrarily. The internal logic of the Constitution's internal protections guarantees that the purposes of those protections are achieved. Citizens are immunized from being subject to bills of attainder, ex post facto laws, differential treatment depending on status, and arbitrary imprisonment just because officials operating under the Constitution are prohibited from subjecting them to bills of attainder, ex post facto laws, and so on. To say that citizens are immunized in a certain way and that officials are prohibited in acting in a certain way is to refer to one and the same relation.

We can understand now why Hamilton thought the writ a remedy for both arbitrary imprisonment and for the imprisonment being done secretly—"confinement of the person, by secretly hurrying him to jail,…". Whether an official arbitrarily seizes and imprisons someone publicly or secretly, the official is acting in a manner prohibited by the Constitution.

Besides, the purpose of the writ would be denied if a citizen were Constitutionally immunized against arbitrary imprisonment, but could still be confined secretly. Secrecy makes the privilege otiose. Those detaining citizens might as well toss into their cells a Get-out-of-jail card from Monopoly for all the good the privilege of the writ will do them in such circumstances. To have the Constitutional weight its placement the Constitution gives it, the privilege must really immunize citizens from arbitrary imprisonment, and the only way to do that is to ensure that those acting under our Constitution, as employees or representatives of us, are prohibited from seizing and imprisoning individuals arbitrarily—a prohibition that would no doubt need to be backed by the force of the criminal sanction to be effective. When we look at the privilege as an immunization requiring that officials of the Constitutional system not subject a citizen to arbitrary imprisonment, we can see why it does not matter whether the imprisonment is public or secret: both are Constitutionally prohibited.

We ought to focus, that is, on the officials doing the detaining, not on the status of the person being detained. If individuals are acting under the color of law, as officials or employees, that is, of the United States government or, arguably, any of the states,[13] those whom they are imprisoning ought to have the privilege of the writ of habeas corpus, whether publicly or secretly imprisoned.

5   Non-Citizens

If the aim of the constitutive features of citizenship is to prevent officials acting under the color of our constitution from abusing the power invested in them by the Constitution, then anyone subject to the official authority constituted by that

---

[13] See in this regard Eric M. Freedman, *Habeas Corpus: Rethinking the Great Writ of Liberty* (New York: New York University Press, 2001), pp. 2–5, 9–46.

Constitution ought to be immune from the exercise of such arbitrary power—visitors and aliens, for instance. We should be equally aghast at a visitor to the United States being held for 97 days without access to a lawyer. When we permit someone into the country, we expect that person to follow our laws—not to drive, say, on the left side of the road just because that is the way it is done in their home country. Just so, they have a reasonable expectation that if they follow our laws, they will not be subject to arbitrary arrest. What would be abuse of power were it used against citizens would be equally an abuse against visitors and aliens.

The point of ensuring that those in government do not exercise arbitrary power is lost if it were only to ensure that they do not exercise arbitrary power sometimes, regarding some individuals, even if we can distinguish between citizens and non-citizens. That would be the legal equivalent of having titles of nobility, exempting some who live under the protection of the Constitution from the arbitrary power of government, treating them as a special class of individuals, while leaving others, such as visitors, also living under the protection of the Constitution, open to such power.

If only because any supposed distinction between individuals living under the Constitution will itself be questionable, making it unclear in at least some cases who is on one side of the line and who is on the other, a distinction subjecting some class of those living in the United States to arbitrary imprisonment makes fragile the security and liberty of each of us. None of us can know whether by some official's lights, in some circumstances, we might fall on the wrong side of the dividing line. That is all the more likely in the current situation, one fraught with great danger, where officials are decidedly risk averse, more nervous about not detaining someone who is a danger than about detaining an innocent by mistake. The chance of someone innocent being detained in such a situation is significantly higher than would be the case in a less risk averse situation where, say, the presumption of innocence operates. We would all live with a sense of fragility. Worse, we would have no recourse to a writ that would provide us with an opportunity to prove that we were citizens—and so entitled to the writ.

It might seem that those who are not citizens or visitors or aliens constitute a very different class. Not living within the United States, they are not living under the protection of our Constitution, and so, it may be thought, they may be seized and imprisoned without any recourse to a writ of habeas corpus. One feature of our modern world that Hamilton did not envisage is that governmental power would be so great that it could span continents. It makes no difference whether someone lives in Yonkers or York, Memphis or Milan. Each is subject to the power of our governmental officials who can, and apparently do, seize and detain those they wish.[14]

---

[14] Osama Mustafa Hassan was purportedly seized in Milan in 2003 by agents linked to the CIA (Ian Fisher, Mark Mazzetti, "Italians Indict C.I.A. Operatives in '03 Abduction," *New York Times*, February 17, 2007).

There are no doubt powerful incentives for such actions against those suspected of terrorism, whether they are foreigners or citizens. The risk is that terrorists will cause even worse harm to American citizens than was caused by targeting the World Trade Center. Seizing suspected terrorists and imprisoning them, and then either torturing them to obtain information about terrorist activities or detaining them so that they are prevented from acting might seem not unreasonable, at least on some utilitarian calculation where we must weight the possible harm, potentially catastrophic, against the harm to those being detained, even if indefinitely.

But, first, the likelihood of innocents being detained given such a policy would be high given the risk averse mindset of the officials doing the seizing and detaining. No one in the CIA or the FBI or whatever other organizations in our government are authorized to seize and detain individuals would want to be the one who decided not to detain someone who later did catastrophic damage.

Second, and more important, an utilitarian argument for preventive detention is not limited in its scope by the status of those being detained. The argument justifies preventive detention for those suspected of terrorism. What gives the argument its rhetorical weight is that the terrorism may produce catastrophic damage. The status of the suspect is not thus a weighty consideration in the calculus, and so the argument applies to anyone—citizen, visitor, alien, foreigner—within the reach of those governmental officials charged with seizing and detaining suspects.

An utilitarian calculation is thus, thirdly, wildly inappropriate here. It undercuts the Constitutional weight of the constitutive features of citizenship we find in the body of the Constitution. We would need to read the Constitution as saying that citizens are immune from arbitrary arrest unless some official, acting under the Constitution, decides that they may be terrorists. Citizens are immune from arbitrary arrest, that is, unless an official decides they are not. In that case citizens may be seized and imprisoned, without any chance of obtaining a writ that would require those doing the seizing and imprisoning to prove to an independent body that the the seizing and imprisoning was justified. What matters on a utilitarian calculation, that is, is the potential for catastrophic terrorism, not the status of those suspected of intending it.

What matters for the Constitutional immunity to have its proper Constitutional weight is that it not be subject to such utilitarian calculations and that officials authorized under the Constitution be prohibited from using such calculations to justify seizing and detaining individuals. Such officials are, after all, *our* officials, acting as *our* agents in furthering Constitutionally acceptable ends, and they ought then to operate within the confines of the Constitution.

They ought to operate within those confines whether they are seizing and imprisoning citizens or non-citizens. What matters constitutionally is the status of those doing the seizing and imprisoning. They have no authority to seize and imprison anyone on their own. Whatever authority they have comes from our Constitution, and there is no good reason to suppose that they can retain their authority, outside our borders, without being restrained by the Constitutional provisions that operate within our borders. Besides, it is not as though other countries are completely lawless, unable to retain themselves those suspected of terrorism. The cleric seized on the streets of Milan, purportedly by CIA agents, was under investigation by the Italian government for terrorism.[15] Some may regret their not seizing the cleric and imprisoning him, but they perhaps thought that they should have some evidence to justify detention.

In the situation we are now in, with our Constitutional protections unsettled, it will take more than such considerations to settle matters so that we do not live in fear of arbitrary detention, without recourse. But however much more is required, we need to keep in mind that at issue is arbitrary state power, that the power is immense, and that it can be exercised against anyone who happens to fall into the hands of those with the power to imprison in the name of the state. If the writ's purpose is to protect individuals against such power, its scope is not to be limited by any characteristic of those the power is exercised against. Someone held by authorities of the United States government ought to have such a privilege to ensure that their detention is lawful, is, that is, justifiable because subject to the review of an independent arbiter.

6 Deep Constitutional Commitments

The writ of habeas corpus is not just an appendage to the Constitution, readily removable, like an appendix, whenever a President wishes. It is reflective of deep Constitutional commitments. The placement of the privilege within the body of the Constitution carries with it the vision of a new creation, a citizen of a nation with all the rights and privileges and immunities any other citizen has and officials with constitutionally limited powers and authority. Its placement is reflective of a concern that no citizen can withstand the power of a government bent on using that power to the citizen's detriment and that all governmental authority is constituted authority. The placement is thus reflective of concern about how to protect citizens from the government they have created, and the immunity it creates to government power is thus reflective of deep Constitutional commitments—deep enough to trump any other considerations, of any sort except other Constitutional provisions of equal depth or "Rebellion or Invasion."

The writ's Constitutional depth has enormous practical implications. First, though not itself constitutive of the Constitution or of its adoption—though we might now wonder if those about to become citizens would have adopted the Constitution without such an immunity—its health is a mark of a healthy separation of powers. Necessary to maintain it is an independent judiciary, and arguably necessary to maintain an independent judiciary is that no court's deliberations be secret, that its decisions and the grounds for them be publicly accessible so that all may assess the court's independence from Congressional or Presidential pressures. It is

---

[15] Ibid.

unacceptable to have any court keep its decisions from public scrutiny. Without public exposure to ensure independence, we risk just the sort of secretive imprisonments that Hamilton and Blackstone warned against.

Second, because the privilege is constitutive of what it is to be a citizen, no citizen ought ever to be denied the privilege—whether in the United States or abroad. We now know we have had instances of both. More important, because the aim of the privilege is to immunize those at risk of governmental power from being imprisoned arbitrarily, without recourse and perhaps without reason, what matters to giving the privilege its privileged place is the use of governmental power, by any official of the government. The scope of the privilege should be determined not by the status of the person whose liberty is denied, but by the status of those denying liberty. Citizens and non-citizens alike are to be afforded immunity from imprisonment that may be arbitrary, and so imprisonment requires assessment by an independent body, sufficiently robust and separate from those doing the imprisoning, to make an objective judgment.

Part V
Coercion and the International Order

Chapter 12
Coercion Abroad for the Protection of Rights

Steven P. Lee

Coercion is necessary to protect rights, including human rights. Protecting rights requires a political organization that respects and promotes respect for the rights of all members of society. Many rights must often be coercively enforced if respect for them is to be generally expected. There must be a power that not only *respects* but also *protects* the rights of citizens by requiring all citizens to respect them, prohibiting citizens from taking actions that would violate them, and punishing citizens who fail to honor these prohibitions.[1] While there are forms of coercion that do not involve physical force, force seems necessary for any widespread and effective coercive system for protecting rights, including human rights, given that individuals are often moved by various considerations to violate them. In this essay, I will discuss coercion that involves physical force (and the threat of such) and consider the agent of coercion to be the state.

1 Humanitarian Intervention

Human rights should be respected and protected, so every state may be required (or at least permitted) to use force to promote that respect among its citizens. But what about protecting human rights beyond its borders? Human rights are, I will assume, universal values applying to all individuals. But many individuals live under governments that systematically fail to respect (an oppressive state) or to protect (an inept or failed state) their rights. While it is the duty of each state to respect and protect the rights of its citizens, when it fails to do so, as is often the case, are other states ever justified in using force to remedy the situation? This is the issue of humanitarian intervention (HI).

---

[1] The distinction between respect for and protection of rights reflects Henry Shue's point that the duties corresponding to a right include both the nondeprivation of what the right guarantees individuals (what I call the rights' being respected or not violated) and protection of the right against the holders' suffering such deprivation (what I call the rights' being protected). (He includes a third obligation, one of aid, if the right is neither respected nor protected.) See his *Basic Rights: Subsistence, Affluence, and U.S. Foreign Policy*, 2nd ed. (Princeton, NJ: Princeton University Press, 1996). Note that legal arrangements to protect rights can involve tort law as well as criminal law.

D.A. Reidy and W.J. Riker (eds.), *Coercion and the State*.
© Springer Science+Business Media B.V. 2008

HI, as I will discuss it, is the use of military force by a state, P, against another state, V, due *not* to V's having aggressed against P (or a third state), but instead to V's violations of, or failure to protect, its own citizens' *basic human rights*. A main purpose of P's use of force is to rescue the citizens of V and protect them from further rights violations.[2] By basic rights, I understand, following Henry Shue, those moral rights that are fundamental, in the sense that they are necessary for the realization of any other moral rights. Basic rights are a "moral minimum" and include rights to subsistence and security.[3] HI is concerned with on-going rather than past violations of these rights. HI is a matter of *rescuing* individuals from a current pattern of rights violations, not punishing a state for its past violations.

Much has been written about the justification for HI in the past several years. My discussion will be different from many earlier discussions of HI in two ways. First, I will offer a different approach to the justification of HI; I begin the discussion of justification at a different point.[4] Second, I will expand the traditional discussion of HI to cover an area not usually addressed, namely, the question of the *scope* of justified HI. Is HI ever justified? If so, is HI justified only *in extremis*, in a humanitarian crisis such as genocide, or also short of this? This is no mere academic question, given that states fighting wars on other grounds will sometimes seek to rationalize their military adventures by claiming that they are cases of HI.

Most believe that HI is justified in at least some cases. These include cases of extreme human rights abuses, such as genocide or ethnic cleansing. The challenge is to find an account of HI that *shows how* it is justified in these cases.

Because it risks initiating war, HI is usually morally understood in terms of just war theory. Just war theory assigns a prominent role to state sovereignty. State sovereignty seems obviously morally salient. The main objection to HI, then, has been that it violates this principle. But approaching HI through the principle of sovereignty (what I will call the *standard approach*) makes the justification of HI problematic. A corollary of the principle of sovereignty is the nonintervention principle, which precludes all use of military force that is not a response to external aggression. HI apparently violates this corollary since it involves the use of force against a state that has not committed external aggression. If HI is justified, then, it must be as an exception to this corollary principle of nonintervention. As one theorist recently put it: "Humanitarian intervention is generally treated as an exception to the nonintervention principle, which requires us to respect the integrity of a foreign country and not to interfere in matters of domestic jurisdiction."[5]

---

[2] While threatening the use of force can be an instrument to deter other states from violating their citizens' rights, in examining HI in this essay, I will not directly address the deterrent use of force.

[3] Shue, *Basic Rights*.

[4] While the protection of rights is normally an obligation, I ask only if HI is permissible. The reason, in my view, is that the morality of the use of military force is an all-things-considered matter that cannot be determined by the moral requirement to protect rights alone.

[5] Carla Bagnoli, "Humanitarian Intervention as a Perfect Duty: A Kantian Argument," in Terry Nardin and Melissa Williams (eds.), *Humanitarian Intervention* (New York: New York University Press, 2006), p. 117.

How is this HI exception to the nonintervention principle justified? Most often, the justification is simply asserted. "Grievous violations of human rights, including ethnic cleansing, massacre, and other acts that 'shock the moral conscience of mankind,' are just too serious to be regarded merely as a matter of domestic jurisdiction."[6] It is natural to sympathize with this claim, but still, an argument is needed. Perhaps a different approach would work better, an approach that does not assign state sovereignty, and thus the principle of nonintervention, so basic a status.[7]

The *alternative approach* I will develop considers matters from the other end, so to speak. The standard approach assumes a *moral discontinuity* between the domestic and foreign use of force by a state, a discontinuity represented by state sovereignty and the nonintervention principle. According to the standard approach the use of force must, morally speaking, be considered differently at the two levels, and an HI exception requires backing down from the sovereignty inspired rule that only defensive military force is justified. The alternative approach understands a state's use of force to protect human rights abroad as morally continuous with its domestic use for the same purpose, in that the same basic justificatory principles apply. The *scope* of justified force may be different in the domestic and international cases due to empirical differences between them. But the limitations applying at the international level are of the same kind as those applying at the domestic level. There is no principled difference, as implied by the principle of sovereignty, and thus no moral discontinuity between the two levels.

The difference between the standard and the alternative approaches is evident in the different domestic analogies to which each may appeal. The standard approach likens the cross-border use of military force to individual self-defense. As an individual is morally entitled to use force against another individual only in self-defense, a state is morally entitled to use force against another state only in self-defense. State sovereignty is analogous to individual autonomy. Perhaps the only way to eke out a justification for HI on this analogy is to liken HI to paternalistic interference at the individual level. On the other hand, an analogy for the alternative approach is that between a state's domestic use of force to protect rights and its international use of force to protect rights. In the first analogy, the analogue is a different form of agency (the individual, in contrast with the state), whereas in the second analogy, the analogue involves the same form of agency (the state) acting in a different way or at a different level. This difference between the analogies reflects the moral discontinuity of the standard approach and the moral continuity of the alternative approach.

---

[6] Bagnoli, "Humanitarian Intervention," p. 118.

[7] Some authors criticize contemporary accounts of just war theory, such as Michael Walzer's *Just and Unjust Wars* (New York: Basic Books, 1977), for their legalistic reliance on the idea of sovereignty. These authors point out that pre-modern accounts of just war emphasize achieving human goods instead of respecting sovereignty. So, an approach based on these earlier accounts may avoid the criticism in this paragraph. See, for example, Joseph Boyle, "Traditional Just War Theory and Humanitarian Intervention" and Anthony Coates, "Humanitarian Intervention: A Conflict of Traditions," both in Nardin and Williams (eds.), *Humanitarian Intervention*.

Let me mention briefly another way to approach the HI issue that is similar to the alternative approach, though it adheres to the rhetoric of sovereignty. According to this other approach, sovereignty is not absolute, but morally conditional. A state is regarded as sovereign only when it respects the fundamental rights of its citizens. If it does not do so, then there is no moral bar to outside interference such as sovereignty imposes under the standard approach. It may not be inaccurate to speak in this way, but it seems unnecessarily round-about. In making justified intervention conditional on the absence of sovereignty, and making sovereignty conditional on a state's respecting its citizens' rights, it simply adds an unnecessary and potentially misleading step to the account. It is clearer, more straightforward, and ethically more revealing to say outright that justified intervention is conditional on a state's failure to respect its citizens' rights.

The second aspect of my discussion is the proper scope of HI. What is the extent of the human rights violations necessary to justify foreign military force to avoid them? This issue is not often addressed by those discussing the moral justifiability of HI.[8] An answer to the scope question is one of the main results we should expect from an account of HI. The stipulation of an HI exception under the standard approach seems especially ill-suited to answer the question of what, if any, justification there could be for HI beyond a response to the sort of extreme human rights violations represented by genocide. Having a clear answer to the scope question, or at least a clear understanding of how one goes about finding an answer, is practically important because of the inherent danger in allowing states permission for intervention without a clear appreciation of the facts necessary to justify it. Without a proper understanding of the scope of justified HI, it would be easier for states to claim a humanitarian purpose to rationalize a military adventure. One way to approach the scope question is to consider different regimes arrayed in terms of the degree to which their populations are subject to human rights violations, in this sort of way:

	Rwanda in 1994	Iraq in 2003	Rawls's Kazanistan[9]	
gross violations	×—————————————	×—————————————	×————————	minor violations

When is HI appropriate? Our intuitions are probably clear for Rwanda (intervene) and Kazanistan (don't intervene), but likely not for cases in between. We need a theory to explain these intuitions and to clarify our thinking about the in-between cases. While the scope question is often posed in this way by asking for the point on such a line that distinguishes permissible from impermissible HI, as we will see, this is a somewhat misleading way to consider the matter.

---

[8] One exception to this is Boyle, "Traditional Just War Theory," pp. 49–50.

[9] John Rawls, in *The Law of Peoples* (Cambridge, MA: Harvard University Press, 1999), introduces a fictional, nonliberal nation, Kazanistan, that is non-democratic and hierarchical, but is nonaggressive and recognizes many of the individual rights recognized in a liberal state, in particular those that are basic human rights.

2 An Alternative Account

My alternative normative account of HI starts with the limitations on the justified use of force by a state to protect human rights in the domestic case and then generalizes to corresponding limitations in the international case, treating the two cases as morally continuous. The basic idea behind my alternative approach is that the universality of human rights implies that borders do not mark a sharp moral discontinuity, as the principle of sovereignty implies. Borders do not have basic moral importance, though they do have secondary moral importance.

The scope question arises at the domestic level as well as the international level. There are moral limitations on the use of force to protect rights in each. Even when state force is used to protect rights domestically, the scope of its justified use is limited. It is clear that force should not be used by a state to protect individuals from *all* moral rights violations, for some such use would be morally counterproductive, that is, it would make the situation morally worse. *Counterproductivity limitations*, as I shall call them, fall into two general categories: (1) *efficiency limitations* and (2) *rights-balancing limitations*. Efficiency limitations concern factors such as:

(1a) The value of the protection of the rights in question and the state's ability to provide that protection (through force)
(1b) The cost in scarce resources of the state's attempt to provide that protection (through force)

Rights-balancing limitations involve the costs in rights violations that accompany efforts to protect rights through force, and require that we balance such violations against the rights violations avoided. Rights violations may follow from use of force by a state to protect rights because of:

(2a) The prospect that use of force by a state to protect rights will itself violate other rights
(2b) The prospect that giving the state the powers it needs to protect the rights will lead to its using that power for domestic oppression

Efficiency limitations are a consequentialist matter, while rights-balancing limitations are a deontological matter.[10]

Following this idea of counterproductivity limitations, the justifiability of a state's use of force to protect rights in a particular domestic context may be determined by the application of the *efficiency-limitation test* or the *rights-balancing-limitation test*. In these tests, factors such as those listed above are assessed, and a determination is made as to which side the balance of factors favors, that is, whether the use of force in question is justified ("passes" the test) or is not justified ("fails" the test). When the use of force in question fails the test, it falls under a moral limitation on the state's use of force

---

[10] I will assume, though it is controversial, that it makes sense to balance rights violations and rights protections in this sort of way.

to protect rights. If the use of force in question passes one test but fails the other, which is possible, then it is impermissible. To be permissible, it must pass both tests.[11]

To see how the limitation tests work in practice, consider lying. Let us assume that each person has, in general, a moral right not to be lied to. Still, no one thinks that force should be used by a state to suppress lying (apart from special cases). This intuition may be explained by either sort of counterproductivity. Applying the efficiency-limitation test, it seems clear that it would be inefficient for a state to use force to protect a right not to be lied to because (1a) the state is unlikely to be very successful at achieving this goal and (1b) the extent of resources involved in a serious effort by the state to achieve this goal would likely be disproportionate to the value of the rights-violations avoided. It seems clear that a use of force by the state to suppress lying would fail the rights-balancing-limitation test as well because (2a) the right against being lied to could be protected only at the expense of the extensive violation of other rights, especially the privacy rights that the intrusiveness of such a use of force would violate and (2b) the extensive power that would have to be assumed by a state in any serious effort to suppress lying could easily be used for oppression. In failing both tests, the impermissibility of a state's use of force to suppress lying is overdetermined.

3   Rights and Social Groups

But the best way to show the basis of the moral continuity between the domestic and international cases is to consider domestic examples where the state intervenes to protect individual rights within a *social group* in civil society. The reason is that HI is also a matter of a state's intervening to protect individual rights within a social group, specifically, another state. In the domestic case, a state's use of force to protect rights within a social group is often legally limited. It is my contention that these legal limitations reflect moral limitations and that the moral limitations apply to the international case as well, thereby demonstrating the moral continuity between domestic and international levels. This would demonstrate, by showing that such moral limitations do not always apply, that HI is otherwise justified.

Consider limitations, implicit in family law, on the state's use of force to protect individuals from rights violations that occur within families. Activities go on within families that violate the rights of their members, for example, the mistreatment of wives by their husbands, but the state is not always legally justified in intervening to protect those rights, though the extent of these limitations is a matter of controversy

---

[11] This is akin to the feature of traditional just war theory requiring that, to be justified, a war satisfy the conditions of both just cause and proportionality.

and changes over time.[12] One sign of these limitations (and their changing parameters) is the doctrine of "oneness" in family law, according to which the law should treat the family as a unit rather than a collection of individuals, though this doctrine has been in decline as the rights of family members have received greater recognition.[13] The rights of children are also often as risk in families. Parents have considerable discretion in how they treat their children, and the allowable discretion encompasses parental behavior that would be a violation of the children's rights. As an example of a legal limitation on the state's ability to protect children in families, children are sometimes precluded from bringing tort suits against their parents.[14] The state thus sometimes denies children (or their representatives) the ability to use tort law to draw on state resources to protect themselves from their parents.

These sorts of limitations on the state's intervention to protect rights within social groups apply to a variety of domestic groups beyond the family, such as, for example, religious groups. The legal limitations can, in many cases, be shown to be morally justified by an application of the limitation tests, and this shows that there are factors involved in the activities within social groups that entail moral limits on state intervention to protect rights beyond those applying to individuals outside the context of their group memberships. In terms of the efficiency-limitation test, the moral appropriateness of these limitations is shown by a variety of factors. Interpersonal relations within a social group would make outside force to protect rights less likely to succeed and make the resource cost of attempting the protection greater (as when, for example, battered spouses refuse to testify against their batterers). Another factor impeding efficiency is the tendency of the victim and victimizer within a social group to join forces in opposition to the state's attempt to protect the victim's rights. Outside of social groups, victims of rights violations will almost always cooperate with the state's efforts to prosecute the victimizer, but within social groups, often not. A vivid illustration of this is that domestic partners sometimes team up to resist the enforcement efforts of police called to the scene of a domestic dispute.

In terms of the rights-balancing limitation test, the moral appropriateness of the legal limitations is shown by the tendency of state intervention in domestic social groups to protect rights of some members to violate the rights of other members. This is due to the way that social groups are created and sustained through the choices of their members. People value social groups and their membership in them; for most people, group membership is of major importance in their lives.

---

[12] For example, in the name of "family values" some would deny the state access to the inner workings of the family in order to protect the male privilege that is the flip side of the rights violations of the women involved. Others would endorse an increase in state power to interfere in families to root out that old form of privilege. This is, I take it, the import of the feminist slogan, "the personal is the political."

[13] Harry Krause, *Family Law in a Nutshell*, 2nd ed. (St. Paul, MN: West Publishing, 1986), p. 116.

[14] Krause, *Family Law*, p. 196.

People choose to join, remain in, and leave social groups, and an important part of protecting their rights in general is protecting these choices. Because a group can be very important to its members, they will often choose to stay in the group even when they are being mistreated in a way that, absent their consent, would count as a rights violation. They make this choice for the sake of the group and its importance to them, often out of concern that their refusal to consent to the mistreatment would damage the group or alienate them from it.

Given this, two factors create a tendency for state intervention to violate rights. First, it is often very difficult to tell from the outside whether or not group members' mistreatment by other group members is consented to by the victims (whether wisely or unwisely) for the sake of the group or their continuing membership in it. When such consent exists, there has been no rights violation, and the state should not intervene. But when the state mistakenly believes that no consent to mistreatment has been given, and so intervenes when there has been no rights violation, it violates the rights of the members who had chosen to tolerate the mistreatment. The members' rights are violated because intervention shows the state's lack of respect for their choices; the state intervention undoes the good they had chosen to try to achieve, and may, more generally, do harm to the group for which they sacrificed in making those choices. The second factor is that some particular form of mistreatment within a group may be directed at a number of its members, some of whom will consent to it and some of whom will not. If the state intervenes to protect the rights of the latter, it necessarily violates the rights of the former. If it does not intervene in order not to violate the rights of the former, it fails to protect the rights of the latter.

4   Limitations on Intervention

My argument is that HI may be justified on the same basis as a use of force by the state to protect rights within domestic social groups. From a moral perspective, the same sorts of efficiency and rights-balancing limitations that restrict the domestic use of state force by a state to protect rights within social groups also limit states' efforts to protect the rights of citizens of other states. Overall, HI is justified because some state efforts to protect rights of those abroad are not covered by the limitations. Some HI can pass the limitation tests.

The limitations in the international case are generally stronger than the limitations in the domestic case because the differences between states as social groups and domestic social groups imply stronger limitations in the case of states. One important difference, relevant to the efficiency-limitation test, is that HI would be the initiation of war. States are organized to mount military resistance to outside military intervention—on many views this is the primary *raison d'etre* for the state. This is not the case with social groups in civil society because an aspect of the state's internal sovereignty is its practical monopoly on the use of force. In addition, the citizens of a state are, in general, highly motivated to support military resistance to foreign intervention, even when its purpose is to protect some of them against rights violations. Military resistance is to be expected even when it is not justified (when it is not morally speaking self-defense), which presumably it is not when the HI itself is justified. Another difference relevant to the efficiency-limitation test is that the achievement of rights protections through force is generally much more difficult in the international than in the domestic case.[15]

This high degree of citizen support for military defense on the part of a state against which a HI is directed is due to the high importance citizens place on their state and their membership in it, as well as their strong identification with it, as represented by the powerful forces of nationalism. Like members of domestic social groups, citizens of states are often willing to consent to mistreatment that would otherwise be a rights violation for the sake of the group or their membership in it. But the strength of nationalist passions shows that this willingness is generally stronger for states than for domestic social groups. Citizens are generally more likely to tolerate mismitreatment by their states than mistreatment by the domestic social groups of which they are members. Consider what this means in terms of the rights-balancing-limitation test. Roughly, a proposed case of domestic or foreign intervention by the state to protect rights would pass the rights-balancing-limitation test only if more of the victims of the mistreatment did not consent to it, and so would have their rights protected by intervention, than did consent to it, and so would have their rights violated by intervention. Also roughly, the more severe the mistreatment, in either the domestic care or the international case, the more likely its victims are not to consent to it, that is, the greater the balance of nonconsenters to consenters to the mistreatment. This all means that to get a positive balance of nonconsenters to consenters, which is generally necessary to pass the test, the severity (as opposed to the extent) of the mistreatment would have to be greater in the case of the state than in the case of domestic social groups. So, in general, the threshold at which the severity of the mistreatment justifies intervention is higher in the case of the state than in the case of a domestic social group. So, the limitations on state intervention are greater in the international case than in the domestic case.

Compare this account of the moral limitations on HI with Michael Walzer's. He argues that resistance to outside military intervention is almost always justified because intervention is *ipso facto* a violation of a special right of a community to determine its own political fate (this right being a composite of the rights of individual citizens to live in a political community of their own choice).[16] This special right, which I will call the "right to political community," is apparently what others have called the right of national self-determination.[17] Walzer argues that a use of military

---

[15] Daniel Kofman refers to the view that HI is unlikely to succeed it protecting rights as "feasibility skepticism;" see his "Moral Arguments: Sovereignty, Feasibility, Agency, and Consequences," in Thomas Cushman (ed.), *A Matter of Principle: Humanitarian Arguments for the War in Iraq* (Berkeley, CA: University of California Press, 2005), p. 131.

[16] Walzer, *Just and Unjust Wars*, pp. 53–54.

[17] I ignore in this discussion the fact that the state and the nation are two different things.

force that is not defensive is morally precluded in almost all cases because no amount of rights protection through intervention could trump this right, which intervention would violate. The application of a rights-balancing test could not show HI to be permitted. Walzer does allow HI *in extremis* as an exception by claiming that when genocidal rights violations are going on in a state, the political community within that state has effectively ceased to exist, and without the community, there is no special right the violation of which would morally stand in the way of HI.[18] HI is permissible only when the right to political community does not apply.

But Walzer's mistake is not to recognize that the right to political community does not trump in all cases because it must be weighed against the rights protections that a HI could achieve. Intervention may be permitted because the rights-balancing-limitation test does not necessarily yield a limitation on the state's use of force abroad to protect rights. The special right to political community does not always trump other rights considerations because the rights protection that would be achieved by a particular HI may outweigh the violation of this special right. The mistake is obvious once the state is seen as akin to a domestic social group. The individual rights of which Walzer's right to political community is a composite are the rights involved in the choices individuals make to consent to mistreatment by the group, as discussed earlier. Because the violation of these rights must be balanced against the protection of other rights that intervention would achieve, as revealed in an application of the rights-balancing-limitation test, these rights violations do not invariably trump other considerations in either the domestic case or the international case. The plausibility of Walzer's claim that the right to political community trumps other considerations is a result of the tendency of the rights of which this right is a composite to be collectively weightier in the international case. The strength of nationalist sentiments skews the results of the rights-balancing-limitation test against intervention. The *reductio* of Walzer's claim that such a right always trumps other considerations is that, if it were to do so it would do so at the domestic level as well, and the state would then be morally impossible because a government not permitted to intervene in domestic social groups could not exercise control over a territory.

5 Sovereignty and the Scope of Humanitarian Intervention

Sovereignty is a legal concept, and, as such, it is not sufficient to show that HI is not morally acceptable. The claim that sovereignty has moral force as an embodiment of a right of national self-determination fails to recognize that the permissibility of intervention depends on balancing rights protections and rights violations, not

---

[18]Walzer, *Just and Unjust Wars*, p. 101. This argument strikes me as ad hoc. Was the political community broken in Nazi Germany during the Holocaust? Empirically, it seems not. One could stipulate that when genocide is occurring, the community had broken down in a moral sense, but then the argument becomes question-begging.

on taking one sort of right as a trump. Sovereignty does not show that we need to adopt the standard approach and begin with the assumption that HI is not justified. The question is whether HI is morally justified, not whether it is legally justified. Arguments about HI make a moral, not a legal, appeal. The moral claim is that human rights should be protected and that it is sometimes permissible to use force across borders for that purpose. As such, the above argument is not falsified or shown to be irrelevant by the fact that the globe is divided into legally sovereign states. Though a state has legal authority to coerce its own citizens, while lacking legal authority to coerce individuals in other states, the questions if and when such use of force is *morally* justified is another matter.[19] Legal sovereignty may be of instrumental moral value, but, as such, respect for it would be at best a defeasible moral rule of thumb. The fact that sovereignty is widely recognized and often fiercely defended affects the moral argument not as an independent principle, but by contributing to the circumstances to which our moral principles must be applied. I have emphasized the expectation of resistance as a factor leading to an efficiency limitation on the justifiability of use of force to protect human rights, a factor that applies at both the domestic and international levels. But because sovereignty is widely regarded as legitimate, this factor plays a much stronger role at the international level than at the domestic level. Sovereignty cannot, however, show HI to be always unjustifiable. As a principle of international law, sovereignty is, like any other principle of law, domestic or international, subject to moral criticism. To the extent that HI is disallowed by the legal principle of sovereignty, a state's practice of HI, when it is morally justified, is like a citizen's justified practice of civil disobedience on the domestic level.

How does this account help with the question of the proper scope of HI? Where on the line of severity of mistreatment does HI become justified? The first thing to note is that this is a misleading question. There is no sharp point, or even fuzzy interval, to be found on the line because the justifiability of each potential HI depends on circumstances peculiar to that situation.[20] The reason is that the permissibility of HI is determined in at least two dimensions, the severity of the mistreatment (genocide, slaughter of political opponents, authoritarian rule, etc.), and the extent to which the victims consent to the mistreatment. These are the two sorts of factors balanced in the application of the rights-balancing-limitation test. A line of

---

[19] All along, I have been writing as if the agent of HI is an individual state, but this need not need be the case. An HI can be authorized and/or undertaken by a regional association (as with NATO in Kosovo) or the United Nations (as with the intervention in Somalia). In many cases, this would be a morally preferable arrangement, were it, in the circumstances, possible. Indeed, the increasing feasibility of this option may well be an indication of the extent to which international law is moving in the direction of regarding sovereignty as not providing legal protection of a state from intervention when it violates the rights of its citizens. It may be the beginning of the evolution of legal authority for HI.

[20] The line, though it is characterized in terms of three particular cases, Rwanda, Iraq in 2003, and Kazanistan, is meant to be general. The three cases are examples only.

severity, such as that between Rwanda and Kazanistan produced earlier, considers the problem in only a single dimension. The need to consider more than one dimension is clear in the application of the efficiency-limitation test, where many sorts of factors must be taken account of. The result of applying the limitation tests lies in the details rather than the general features of each case. So, the alternative approach provides a means of determining the scope of justified HI, one lacking in the standard approach. But it also reveals that it is difficult to make general pronouncements of proper scope, that scope must be determined on a case-by-case basis.

One cannot, for example, make a blanket pronouncement that HI is always permissible to stop a genocide or always impermissible to overthrow an authoritarian regime. Intervention to end a genocide would always pass the rights-balancing-limitation test, because, since it may be presumed that no one would consent to such mistreatment, there would be few rights violations from intervention to balance against the rights protections intervention would achieve. But such intervention might not always pass the efficiency-limitation test, given, for example, a risk of nuclear war. On the other hand, intervention to put an end to an authoritarian regime would normally fail both limitation tests, but not necessarily. If a large portion of the population were making clear their opposition to the regime, intervention could well pass the rights-balancing-limitation test, given that one could infer that only a small portion of the population had consented to their mistreatment by the government, implying that the balance of rights protections to rights violations would favor intervention. In addition, given the widespread opposition to the regime, the military efforts of the government to defend against intervention might well be quite weak, and the intervention may pass the efficiency-limitation test as well.

Thus, the alternative approach provides a method for determining the scope of justified HI (however difficult it might be to apply in particular cases), but implies that this scope cannot be determined in a general way, that is, exclusively in terms of the severity of mistreatment to which citizens in another state are subject. But, if we are forced to make a general statement about the permissibility of HI for the sake of providing a rule-of-thumb, there are reasons to be restrictive and to adopt the earlier suggestion that respect for sovereignty may be treated as such a rule. Given the grim consequences of war and the risk that a general rule might be misused or abused by powerful states to rationalize military adventures, it may be appropriate to accept a defeasible rule that HI is justified only when severe and widespread rights violations are in progress.

Chapter 13
Transnational Power, Coercion, and Democracy[*]

Carol C. Gould

1 Introduction

In this paper, I want to consider some directions for transforming transnational power from a power over people's lives to something more democratic. This issue is posed concretely by the development of economic and technological globalization led by large transnational corporations that move freely around the world, new multilateral institutions like the WTO and the IMF, emerging forms of cross-border political linkages and also new global threats of violence and environmental degradation. We can observe that these contemporary developments have not been accompanied by democratic control or even accountability of new political, social, and economic institutions to the people operating within them, despite the modes of transnational communication that this globalization may introduce. The question before us, then, is whether transnational forms of social, political, and economic power can become more responsive to people's individual and collective decisions, such that the institutions can facilitate people's *power to* act together rather than exercising *power over* them. But in order to deal with the question of how this transformation might occur, we need a clearer understanding of the nature of transnational power, and even more basically of power itself. This will also entail distinguishing power from coercion, with important implications for understanding the forms that transnational democratic governance might take. These implications concern the degree to which democratic transnational power has to be exercised through coercive means or instead whether it can operate in a way more congruent with people's equal freedom and their social cooperation, rather than depending so heavily as at present on either state power or juridical supremacy.

[*] Earlier versions of this essay were presented at the AMINTAPHIL National Conference, Washington University, St. Louis, MO, November 4, 2006; as the Annual Peace and Justice Lecture, Michigan State University, East Lansing, MI, February 20, 2007; and at the University of Pennsylvania, Program in Philosophy, Politics, and Economics, and the Department of Philosophy, March 15, 2007. I would like to thank the participants in those sessions, my research assistant Francis Raven, and the editors of this volume for helpful comments and criticisms on the manuscript.

D.A. Reidy and W.J. Riker (eds.), *Coercion and the State.*
© Springer Science+Business Media B.V. 2008

The nature of power has not recently been the focus of much social and political philosophy (though it was the main subject of a recent annual meeting of the American Political Science Association). So for the most part we need to reach back to earlier analyses of the concept to get a start here. In the course of this discussion, I want to raise some hard questions about power and its transnational manifestations and then consider the role of so-called countervailing power as well as the possibility of certain democratic but noncoercive forms of social power, in which it is transformed from "power over" people's lives to their "power to" act effectively in individual and collective contexts. I will go on to suggest that there are three transformations of social power that are normatively required in transnational interrelations, and that these modes partly address the current problems associated with the exercise of power and the use of coercion. These transformations go beyond the more customary emphasis on NGOs or on resistance movements or other sorts of cross-border social movements, though these are important as well. I argue that the three required transformations are: (1) the broad democratization of decision-making within economic, social, and political institutions, including those that are cross-border and transnational; (2) the implementation of regional human rights protections; and finally (3) the cultivation of transnational solidarity, where this can be seen as a complement to transnational power, and perhaps also as a form of power itself. I will conclude by briefly highlighting the ways in which this conception makes it possible to avoid to a significant degree a coercive approach within social and political organization, and to substitute instead a largely voluntaristic model of democratic social and political association. The proposal of more voluntaristic forms of political organization and the critique of coercion have previously been associated with either libertarian or anarchist approaches to states. Without fully adopting either of these approaches, the conception of transnational power and democracy introduced here also seeks to minimize coercion as the means or the motivation for social and political order.

2   Analyzing Power

In order to analyze transnational power, which clearly has a structural and institutionalized dimension, it will be helpful to begin with the earlier discussion of power in political philosophy. Instead of the classic discussion of power as the *ability to* effect something, the discussion in political theory in the 1970s framed the issue in terms of the various *faces* of power, and understood it as centrally entailing *power over* others. Moreover, power was conceived individualistically as that of an agent A over an agent B. Initially, as in Robert Dahl's early account, this was understood in behavioral terms as one agent causing another to do something. The assumption here was that there is a conflictual situation in which A gets B to do something that B does not want to do. As Jeffrey Isaac points out in his helpful analysis of the history of this debate, this empiricism was subsequently modified by Bachrach and Baratz in their addition of power's second face. In their account, power often involves the suppression of conflict, and does not necessarily require getting someone to do something but rather limiting what they can do. This pointed to a structural feature of power as embodied in institutionalized practices, where these practices often operate to benefit some at the expense of others.[1]

As Isaac further recounts, and as also discussed in Clarissa Hayward's helpful historical account,[2] Steven Lukes went on to add the notion that power involves an ability to exclude potential issues from the political process by influencing, shaping, and determining the perceptions and preferences of others. At that point and more recently as well, Lukes speaks of interests and not only revealed preferences, where interests are necessarily understood counterfactually. Lukes writes, "A exercises power over B when A affects B contrary to B's interest."[3] Accordingly, preferences can themselves be understood as an effect of power's exercise, and may not involve overt conflict at all. Lukes appeals here to an idea of objective interest—what an agent would do under ideal democratic circumstances. In a later article, Lukes clarifies that power is an "agency" concept not a "structural" one, yet it "is held and exercised by agents (individual and collective) within systems and structural determinants."[4]

At that point, Lukes was not very concerned with "power to" but rather in analyzing "power over" (though he has more recently emphasized this more positive conception). To this idea of power over, Jeffrey Isaac added the idea of *enduring powers to act* that are possessed by A & B and brought to bear in their interaction.[5] Power here appears as having a structural nature and specifically as an enduring capacity in virtue of the social relations that structure interaction. Social power refers to capacities to act possessed by social agents because of the enduring relations in which they participate. They are relations of interdependence. Isaac speaks in this context of structurally distributed powers. He also proposes that we can speak of people's real interests as motivating their accession to such power. These real interests refer to the norms, values, and purposes implicit in the practice of social life and associated with social roles as principles of action. His favorite example is teacher-student relations. It's not obvious, however, how relations of this sort can be extrapolated to understanding transnational power. In transnational contexts, we want to speak not only of agency and roles, but of the power of institutions, including especially corporations, as well as nation-states and international associations of states.

Clarissa Hayward's discussion of power in terms of networks of social constraints is probably more relevant to this latter context, but her approach in contrast seems to leave little room for agency.[6] She seeks to eliminate the emphasis on the "faces of power" in favor of a more fully structural account of social limits. In this way, Hayward's approach appears to hark back to Foucault's early notions of biopower

---

[1] Jeffrey Isaac, "Beyond the Three Faces of Power: A Realist Critique," *Polity*, v. 20, n. 1 (1987), 4–31.

[2] Clarissa Rile Hayward. "De-facing Power (Social Authority)," *Polity*, v. 31, n. 1 (1998), 1–22.

[3] Steven Lukes, *Power: A Radical View* (London: Macmillan, 1974), 27.

[4] Steven Lukes, "Power and authority," in *A History of Sociological Analysis*, ed. Tom Bottomore and Robert Nisbet (New York: Basic Books, 1978), p. 635, cited in Isaac, "Beyond the Three Faces of Power," 14.

[5] Isaac, "Beyond the Three Faces of Power."

[6] Hayward, "De-facing Power (Social Authority)."

and power as constraint, though Foucault's later works on governmentality open more room for agency and even for selves in countering the power of institutions and of their embodiment in everyday life through a range of practices.[7]

Foucault's later work helpfully distinguishes between power, coercion, violence, and authority. A focus on these distinctions is also important in the work of Hannah Arendt, who importantly saw power and not violence as the essence of government. For our purposes in this essay, we can emphasize the contrast between power and coercion. On my view, coercion involves the use of force or violence to get people to do things against their will. Standardly, in the political domain, the threat of coercive force is used to produce compliance of people with the laws of a state or a more local entity. Derivatively, the term coercion has also been applied not to the use of force and violence directly but to the implicit or explicit threats of the use of these means that may enable people or institutions to get others to do their bidding.

In contrast to either of these readings of coercion, it is evident that power, even in its sense of "power over" others, can operate with means or instrumentalities other than force and violence and the threats that may be applied can be other than appeals to force. In this sense, the concept of power focuses on the relative standing of people towards each other, in virtue of certain background conditions. Thus, whereas the general definition of power is the ability to effect something—whether as "power to" or "power over" (including the control of some people's actions by others)—I think coercion is most helpfully understood in terms of the notion of enforcement, as Scott Anderson has emphasized,[8] and derivatively also as threats of force. And although a certain sort of power can draw on coercive background conditions, whether understood as force directly or its threat (and this has been especially important in international affairs), we can say that at the limit coercion as the use of actual force or violence can serve to eliminate the possibility of power itself in its destructive moment. It is this fact, along with the important recognition that power can operate with means other than coercive ones, that suggests that the concepts of coercion and power, even taken as power over others, need to be kept distinct.

3   Power and Freedom

In an important way, Hannah Arendt's conception of power as inherently social contrasts with the conceptions of power in political theory discussed earlier, namely those of Dahl, Bachrach, Lukes, and Isaac. Whereas these theorists attempt to

---

[7] Michel Foucault, *The Archeology of Knowledge* (New York: Pantheon, 1972); *Discipline and Punish* (New York: Vintage, 1979); Michel Foucault, *The History of Sexuality*, Volume I, Part Five (New York: Vintage, 1977); "Governmentality," trans. Rosi Braidotti and revised by Colin Gordon, in *The Foucault Effect: Studies in Governmentality*, eds. Graham Burchell, Colin Gordon, and Peter Miller (Chicago: University of Chicago Press, 1991), 87–104.

[8] Scott Anderson, "Toward a Better Theory of Coercion, and a Use for it," http://ptw.uchicago.edu/Anderson02.pdf.

account for structural power, they leave considerable room for the exercise of power by an individual alone, and in fact seem to derive their model from relations between individuals, in which someone has power over another. By contrast, for Hannah Arendt, power does not apply to individuals at all (who ought rather to be characterized in terms of strength). For her, power in social relations results from the human ability to *act in concert* in order to persuade or coerce others. In this way, her account not only emphasizes the social dimension of power but its status as a sort of "power to."

Arendt's emphasis on collective action introduces an important normative possibility, but we can doubt that such action in concert is sufficiently explanatory of the sorts of structural power of institutions and elites over others that are characteristic of existing forms of corporate (or increasingly political) transnational power. Whether one takes a Marxist approach or adheres to newer views of empire in which a hegemonic state is given a leading role, power seems to be exercised less by individuals (individually or collectively) than by structures and institutions. Thus, to give an account of transnational power we would need an understanding of institutionalized power, as well as a further comprehension of what is involved in collective or shared social power in this arena (beyond the general idea that it is exercised in concert).

Before considering further the status of transnational power and its democratization, we can take note of an additional conceptual problem involved in the basic analysis of power, a problem hinted at in Arendt's approach. Whether understood as exercised by individuals or only collectively, the positive conception of power as an ability or capacity to act raises the issue of its relation to freedom. If power is fundamentally the ability to act without external constraint, how does it differ from freedom as an ability to act without external constraint? Interestingly, in contrast to the first understanding of power as power over others which clearly limits people's freedom (whether understood as the ability to pursue their interests or to develop themselves), we are faced with the possibility that "power to" as an ability to act becomes assimilated to freedom as such a capacity. This seems to render the account paradoxical or at least puzzling.

The distinction between power to and freedom does not seem to lie in the fact that power is a disposition or potential or capacity whereas freedom is a state of affairs, because freedom can also be a capacity. And while the freedom to do something does presuppose being able to do it or the power to do it, so having the power to do something presupposes the freedom to carry it out. Furthermore, the distinction cannot lie in the connection to responsibility, because both freedom and power, at least in their application to individuals, presuppose that the agent is capable of being held morally responsible for the action.

I pose this paradoxical issue here without attempting to fully resolve it. But it may be that this coincidence of freedom with power as the ability to act is not in fact philosophically problematic with regard to the deep meaning of these concepts. Indeed, we can observe a similar assimilation of the power to act with the freedom to act in several earlier political philosophers who regarded this as a positive indication of the centrality and force of these basic notions.[9] It is clear in any case that this reading of power contrasts with more recent approaches that hold freedom to be the very opposite of power. In these latter approaches, power, taken in the sense of "power over," essentially stands in need of being checked or limited, if freedom is to be protected.

On my view, normatively acceptable power involves both *freedom from* the sort of domination in which one person or group exercises *power over* others; and positively, as *power to*, it involves the equal *freedom* of people *to* act (individually or jointly), to develop capacities, and to realize individual or joint projects. Further, for people to have opportunities to exercise this power in relatively equal ways in their personal lives, they would need equal access to the social and economic conditions of action. Beyond this, the power to act can be seen to imply a requirement for democratic control over collective actions and the need for democratic accountability of social and political institutions. This is because in acting in concert people ought to be able to co-determine the course of the action, if they are to be equally free or self-determining. In my view, such a right of co-determination of the course of common or joint activity by participating in decisions about it is precisely the meaning of democracy. The power to act, therefore, if it is interpreted in accordance with the norm of equal freedom, entails overcoming situations in which some exercise power over others, and requires the introduction of democratic decision-making concerning the aims and methods of common action and the direction of the various institutions that are designed to carry common activity forward. The implications of this notion of power will be considered further in the final part of this essay.

We can observe finally that from this normative standpoint, both *power over* and coercion, understood as involving force and violence or the threat of such means, can be criticized as limitations on freedom. Nonetheless, the requirement of equal freedom can sometimes legitimate minimally necessary coercion (at least as states are presently constituted), in order to protect people's equal ability to act and their equal access to the conditions for self-transformation and development.[10] Yet, I would suggest that this norm of freedom requires limiting the use of coercion to the degree possible. It likewise requires action to eliminate or mitigate the power of some over others, where these others are constrained in their capacities or development. Whereas coercion operates with force and violence, I have suggested that this power over others can be wielded through other means as well, and often operates "behind the backs" of agents through institutional frameworks in social, economic, and political life. We have seen finally that the transformation of "power over" to "power to" requires attention to the conditions for effective action at individual and collective levels, including opportunities to decide on the course of these activities and co-determine their direction democratically.

---

[9] See, for example, John Locke, *An Essay Concerning Human Understanding*, Essay II, xxi, 7–13, Echo Library, 2006.

[10] See the article by Alistair Macleod in this volume for an argument connecting coercion to the requirements of justice, which he understands as equal opportunity.

4   Faces of Transnational Power

This essay thus far has distinguished *power over* from *power to*, and has related power in this latter sense to freedom. In the transnational context, examples of *power over* are rather easy to find. Thus, the problematic impact of multinational organizations on workers and on labor standards both in the US and abroad has been widely explored and documented, e.g., in the use of sweatshops, child labor, or the massive outsourcing of jobs; and the environmental impacts of multinationals have been criticized, including for example, the role of large oil companies in preventing awareness of, and action on, global warming. The IMF and WTO also have played a significant role in constraining the life options for people in developing countries, for example, through the "resource privilege" that Thomas Pogge has emphasized. The exploitation of natural resources in these developing countries by well-off Western countries is facilitated by the international practice of recognizing corrupt rulers, rather than the people themselves, in developing countries as the rightful owners, and thus the only legitimate sellers, of these resources. A particularly clear cut example of IMF exercise of *power over* is the case of its 1998 loan to Bolivia, requiring as a structural reform that Bolivia sell off its public enterprises. Bolivia accordingly transferred its Cochabamba local water agency to a multinational consortium of private investors (including a subsidiary of Bechtel), with the consequence that water prices rose drastically, and legislation was enacted that would charge peasants for the use of water from local wells.[11] The mass protests spawned by these actions, along with the support of some journalists and media outlets in the US and elsewhere, and the eventual agreement to have the private consortium withdraw are also of interest for our purposes in pointing to a possible role for social movements in countering transnational corporate and multilateral "power over" others. We will consider directions for transforming such power in the next section.

In order to more fully theorize the case of transnational power, we can introduce here two additional sets of distinctions from the international relations literature that can be brought to bear on our analysis. The first set is found in Kenneth Boulding's work, who still retains a focus on the "faces of power." After characterizing power's general meaning as the ability to get what one wants, Boulding goes on to discern three types. First, there is destructive power, as primarily military or threat power—the power to destroy. This is closely related to what we might call coercive power, or the sort of power over others linked to coercion as force and violence, or the threat of such coercion. Second, Boulding describes productive power as economic power (to produce and exchange). Of course, this may also involve a threat or a coercive element, though Boulding did not theorize it that way. And third is what he calls integrative power—as the power of bringing people together. This is power based on mutual trust, which he also saw as legitimating power generally.[12]

---

[11] http://www.pbs.org/frontlineworld/stories/bolivia/timeline.html

[12] Kenneth E. Boulding, *Three Faces of Power* (Newbury Park, CA: Sage, 1989).

Yet another contemporary distinction that may be of help in this connection is that between hard and soft power. According to Joseph Nye, "Soft power is the ability to get what you want by attracting and persuading others to adopt your goals. It differs from hard power, the ability to use the carrots and sticks of economic and military might to make others follow your will."[13] Although presently understood as wielded by states, the contrast is extendable to international institutions. Nye and others attempt to clearly demarcate the persuasion and public relations involved in soft power from propaganda and insist that soft power needs to be based on credible claims.[14] Nonetheless, this is not always easy to accomplish, and more generally it isn't clear that soft power constitutes a departure from *power over* towards *power to*. Rather, it seems an alternative and less objectionable way of wielding power over others. Accordingly, beyond both hard and soft power, it has been suggested by Peter Ackerman that we recognize another type, which he calls "civilian-based power." This third conception, associated with social movements and perhaps also NGOs and other civil society organizations, involves a more "ground up" and people-based conception. It could perhaps be regarded as a species of the integrative power that Boulding has described.

In transnational contexts then, we can as before distinguish *power from* and *power to*, and also distinguish power from coercion. This noncoercive sort of power has thus far been mainly characterized here in terms of Boulding's integrative power, and as the intention, if not the reality, of soft power. Importantly, it has been identified with some forms of power found in transnational civil society associations and social movements that aim at social transformation and that attempt to proceed in relatively participatory ways. In contrast, transnational coercion is manifest in the use of force or violence, exercised directly through war and in political violence more generally. But to the degree that coercion can also be involved in the mere threats of force or violence as well, it can also lie behind the sanctions implied in international law, where such law has developed growing scope and effectiveness in the past decades. Although still derived primarily from agreements among nation-states, international law is increasingly coming to have important sway on its own, especially through the development of the institutions of global governance. Such law is manifest in new transnational forms in the European Union and in some other regional contexts as well. And although the development of international law is highly significant in ordering previously anarchic relations between states and especially in providing an important frame for human rights protection, it nonetheless might be held to reproduce in the international sphere the traditional issues concerning the legitimacy of the exercise of coercion heretofore centered on nation-states. And it raises new questions of its own concerning the seemingly

---

[13] Joseph S. Nye Jr., *The International Herald Tribune*, January 10, 2003, reprinted at http://www.ksg.harvard.edu/news/opeds/2003/nye_soft_power_iht_011003.htm. See also Joseph S. Nye, *Soft Power: The Means to Success in World Politics* (New York: Public Affairs, 2005), and particularly chapter 4.

[14] *Ibid.*

undemocratic adoption of much of international law, especially insofar as those affected by it currently lack a say in constructing it. Indeed, even regimes of human rights, to the degree that they are legally binding and not only moral requirements, come up against the difficulties of justifying the use of means of coercive force in order to protect them. I will return to these issues in the concluding section of the essay.

5 Democratizing Transnational Power

In considering the modalities for democratizing transnational power, the account given thus far suggests that the issue can helpfully be framed in terms of moving from *power over* (i.e., of some over others, or of institutional power over individuals) to *power to*, where, moreover, this "power to" is understood as a shared social power. The question of precisely *how* to move from power over to power to, in terms of the strategies and tactics required to accomplish this transformation, along with the particular institutional changes needed, is too large and difficult a question for this essay. Some modalities that have been advanced by critical social theorists include various forms of resistance and direct action and especially nonviolent civil disobedience, other types of countervailing power, and more democratic modes of transformation (which I favor).

Here, I will briefly highlight three elements of a more democratic conception of transnational power, understood as a shared power to achieve socially beneficial ends and advance common interests. I focus on these not only because of their centrality, but because these three directions are most often omitted in current discussions of how to come to grips with and to transform transnational power. I would argue that each of the elements sketched here is essential in order to tame the various sorts of corporate and hegemonic power that dominate transnational associations in the present. My emphasis on these factors is not meant to imply, however, that other directions, and especially proposals for global distributive justice, are in any way less important. The others have simply been more often discussed and emphasized.

The three elements, which I see as crucial ingredients in this transformative process, all of them large and aspirational at present, are (1) the democratization of the range of economic, social, and political institutions, whether local, cross-border, or transnational; (2) the development of regional human rights agreements and institutional protections; and (3) the cultivation of new forms of transnational solidarity. Each of these addresses some of the problems with "power over" that I sketched earlier, while also serving to promote something like Boulding's integrative power. I believe that although these directions are rather comprehensive and demanding, taking them seriously may be the only way to achieve any real breakthrough in overcoming the dominating modes of power characteristic of the contemporary situation.

First, then, democratic deliberation and participation in the range of economic, social and political institutions, for which I argued in *Rethinking Democracy*,[15] contrasts with the power of some over others within these institutions, and gives expression to an idea of shared social power in which each participant is able to co-determine with others the course of the activity. While the academic and popular emphasis on democratic management of firms and social institutions has diminished in recent years, I suggest that it is normatively required, in that it allows people to co-manage their social lives insofar as they are engaged in joint or common activities. In my view, there is no principled difference between the requirement for political democracy and these other sorts of democratization. In terms of justification, the same considerations of equal rights to participate in determining the course of joint or common activities pertain, where such rights of participation constitutes the core meaning of democracy on my view. In terms of forms and procedures, the often smaller-scale contexts of economic and social life admit of more informal procedures than have characterized the political domain, but similar opportunities for participation and representation (in large institutions) are in order. The claim here is that not only is democratic participation normatively required in the range of social and economic institutions, as of political ones, but that the practice of democratic modes of decision making in these other contexts can facilitate participation in politics. It does this by being educative, as Carole Pateman has argued,[16] particularly in affording opportunities to practice equal and reciprocal treatment. It may also help to counter the apathy that besets politics, inasmuch as it is easier for people to make a difference in decisions in these smaller-scale institutional settings.

An especially noteworthy example of democratic management in a major corporation is Mondragón Corporación Cooperativa (MCC), currently the sixth largest corporation in Spain. MCC impressively combines modern management techniques and high efficiency and profitability with such factors as flattened hierarchies, participatory quality initiatives, and considerable equality and democratic decision-making at its workplaces.[17] Although based in the Basque region of Spain, it is increasingly transnational in scope, although many of its foreign subsidiaries are not yet cooperatively run. But it should be emphasized that the proposed self-management model does not only pertain to large firms, but applies to smaller scale ones, and in different ways to social and cultural institutions as well.

In *Globalizing Democracy and Human Rights*, I have argued further that rights of democratic participation also pertain to newly emerging cross-border communities, whether political, ecological, technological (via the Internet), in addition to such

---

[15] Carol C. Gould, *Rethinking Democracy* (Cambridge: Cambridge University Press, 1988), especially chapters 1 and 9.

[16] Carole Pateman, *Participation and Democratic Theory* (Cambridge: Cambridge University Press, 1970).

[17] Francisco Javier Forcadell, "Democracy, Cooperation and Business Success: The Case of Mondragón Corporación Cooperativa," *Journal of Business Ethics*, v. 56, n. 3 (2005), 255–274.

economic corporations, whether relatively local or more fully transnational.[18] In these various contexts, democratic forms of organization permit power to be exercised jointly by the participants in these various communities. These forms apply not only to the formalized regional association of states of the European Union, but also to more localized cross-border communities, such as exist between the US and Canada. Cooperative projects and attention to the needs of local and regional stakeholders are already fairly well advanced in some cases, particularly when there is some degree of economic integration, as in the Pacific Northwest Economic Region (PNWER), or increasingly where there are shared ecological problems.

In these contexts, I would also suggest that new forms of transnational participation and representation need to be devised. Thus, forms of transnational representation are relevant for current multilateral institutions like the WTO, so that they can take better account of the effects of their policies on those at a distance, particularly in regard to human rights impacts. But new modes of transnational representation also need to be implemented for relatively permanent regional and global assemblies that may be introduced. The Internet is of some help in gaining input from remotely situated people, but it cannot entirely replace opportunities for more face-to-face discussion, even assuming fuller technological integration of video capabilities in the coming period. In order to facilitate online input into decisions from people situated at a distance, new software has to be developed to make full use of the networking possibilities that exist. Discourse will need to be facilitated among people who have not only very different views and positions, but also different cultural frameworks and languages.

The second element in transforming transnational power is the development of human rights frameworks at the regional level. For power to be democratically shared in cross-border communities, it is necessary to enable and protect the power of individuals operating within them, as well as to devise social and economic institutions that can more adequately meet basic needs, and new political modalities of guaranteeing the possibilities of democratic decision making. A human rights framework is required for all these purposes, as well as to insure a principled exercise of power within transnational associations that will be both legitimate and nondominating. The suggestion is that if we hope to see these new associations and communities become democratic, then we need regional human rights agreements and institutions to protect the basic rights of people taking part in them. This would in turn seem to entail new human rights conventions and courts, perhaps on the European model. One of the main functions of such courts would be to permit appeals by citizens even against decisions of their own governments, in cases in which human rights are violated. In addition, such regional agreements and courts could provide appropriate frameworks for appeal for members of those communities that spanned borders. As to whether such new frameworks can also make a contribution to realizing human rights taken not only as constraints on, but as the goals of,

---

[18] Carol C. Gould, *Globalizing Democracy and Human Rights* (Cambridge: Cambridge University Press, 2004), especially chapters 7 and 9.

transnational associations is a more difficult issue. For that to happen, regional associations would have to become more fully politically organized, as is the case in the European Union, and that possibility is one for the longer term.

Human rights frameworks contribute to the transformation from "power over" to "power to" by protecting and enabling the equal freedom (positive and negative) of the members of transnational associations. They can do so by insuring the conditions of relatively equal power to act, both politically and otherwise, and by attempting to insure that social forms of power will be exercised democratically, as well as by providing an appeal in case basic rights are ignored or violated. Since many of the new transnational linkages are themselves regional rather than fully global, inasmuch as they often stem from economic (or increasingly ecological) cooperation in cross-border contexts, it is appropriate that the human rights agreements and enforcement should also be regional in the first place (although they may draw on universal declarations of human rights or on global covenants). Beyond this, such regional arrangements have two additional advantages over more global ones, at least for the near term, if not indefinitely. First, they permit some scope for interpretation of universal and abstract norms in contextual ways that reflect regional cultural backgrounds (so long as the egalitarian thrust of these rights would be respected to a large degree). Further, they enable a diversity of spheres for the further development of human rights law. Such a multiplicity of arenas for appeal and innovation may itself be desirable in order to guard against human error or against pernicious political constraints which could undercut human rights conventions and jurisprudence.

The final element of this demanding picture of the transformation to *power to* is the cultivation, where possible, of transnational solidarities. This refers to cross-border relations and networks of active support for the basic interests and human rights of distant others, so as to help overcome oppression and suffering and to meet needs.[19] Solidaristic relations eschew power over others and place weight on a shared commitment to justice. Indeed, we can see solidarity in this sense as itself a form of power that does not deny the interests and needs of others or force people to act contrary to their own interests, but is deferential to these others, and is ready to act to help them as they require. Such solidarity also has potential reciprocity implied within it, so that it does not require pure altruism on the part of the members of the solidarity group. To the degree that it is exercised across varying individuals and associations, it can be denoted a conception of *network solidarities*. A small example of such solidarity can be seen in the Cochabamba case discussed above, in which Pacific News Service correspondent Jim Schultz and colleagues helped to publicize the Bolivian protests and organized a mass email campaign to Bechtel to object to the company's actions and to influence the consortium to withdraw from Cochabamba.[20]

---

[19] Carol C. Gould, "Conceptualizing the Role of Solidarity in Transnational Democracy," *Journal of Social Philosophy*, Special Issue on Solidarity, eds. Carol C. Gould and Sally J. Scholz, v. 38, n. 1 (2007), 148–164.

[20] http://www.pbs.org/frontlineworld/stories/bolivia/timeline.html

As in this example, transnational forms of solidarity currently often involve lending the power to act of the relatively powerful to those who are needy and relatively powerless to meet their own needs without such help. Yet, I have argued elsewhere that it requires *deference* to these others in determining how they should be helped.[21] In putting the others and their needs into consideration, solidaristic action can contribute to integrative power, in a way that is extendable beyond traditional borders. Indeed, we can propose that just as democracy is the political opposite of power over others so solidarity is its moral opposite, and that both are required to transform power into a genuinely shared social phenomenon.

6   Transnational Power and Coercion

I have suggested some ways in which transnational power can eventually come to take more of the form of the power of people and associations to meet needs and develop capacities rather than the power of corporations and hegemonic states over individuals. But the transformations I have discussed and particularly new human rights regimes at regional and transnational levels raise the question of whether they might introduce new forms of transnational coercion as well. The strengthening of international law and even the eventual development of a system of global law, e.g., regarding the environment, raise difficult questions of a possible extension of the coercion that serves to enforce law within nation-states to an international level.

From my standpoint, although it may be necessary to use coercion in the service of duly constituted and democratically formulated law, it nonetheless constitutes a constraint on the freedom of individuals, even if it is in the service of justice or other values. Anarchists have alerted us not only to excesses of coercion exercised by nation-states, but to the ways that coercive mechanisms necessarily limit the scope of individuals' agency and that of groups.[22] So what can we say about the new forms of transnational coercion that the juridification of regionally-binding human rights will introduce?

We can observe first that democratically arrived at agreements and cross-border constitutions can help to make the threat of coercion more legitimate in these cases. In addition, I would suggest that there are two cautionary implications of the recognition of the negative aspects of coercion in this new context. First, it reminds us that it is a mistake to see human rights as implemented exclusively or even mainly by means of law. Rather, as I have argued, the fulfillment of people's human rights in transnational domains requires in the first instance certain fundamental social and economic changes to make it possible for people to realize these rights in more egalitarian and voluntaristic ways. Thus the nonpolitical domains have to be transformed in their

---

[21] Gould, *supra*, note 19, esp. 157.

[22] Emma Goldman, "Anarchism: What It Really Stands For," in *Red Emma Speaks: An Emma Goldman Reader*, ed., Alix Kates Shulman (Amherst, NY: Prometheus, 1996).

functioning to help meet the needs specified by the (so-called) positive basic human rights, including rights to means of subsistence and to health. Along these lines, too, democratization of cross-border associations can help in the achievement of the human rights that are linked to notions of democratic governance itself. Beyond this, a second implication of this analysis is that there needs to be a presumption in favor of the minimization of coercion wherever possible. The sorts of excesses of state power and violence that we have recently witnessed must not be replicated in the new forms of transnational democratic governance for which I have argued. How to accomplish this, however, is a difficult and pressing issue, but one that in many ways lies beyond our comprehension at present.

Chapter 14
A Developmental Approach to the Legitimacy of Global Governance Institutions[*]

Monica Hlavac

Criticism of the legitimacy, or better, illegitimacy, of global governance institutions (GGIs) is common. Yet, there has been little systematic theorizing on the subject. The primary objective of this paper is to provide a conceptual and structural framework for understanding and assessing judgments about the legitimacy of GGIs. GGIs include multilateral organizations such as the World Bank, World Trade Organization (WTO), and International Criminal Court (ICC), as well as various less formal transnational judicial and regulatory networks. The framework I articulate and defend falls short of a general theory of legitimacy for GGIs. We do not yet know enough about GGIs to work out a general theory. But we do know enough to work out a partial theory, one that might frame and render more productive further investigations into GGIs and their legitimacy.

The framework I develop takes a novel approach to GGI legitimacy. This "developmental approach" begins with the fact that we lack developed norms regarding how GGIs ought to regard those individuals most affected by their activities. It addresses this lack, which I refer to as "the problem of normative unclarity," by adopting a more personal, agent-sensitive, rendering of legitimacy. This in turn grounds one provisional condition for legitimacy—robust transparency—to be realized at the loci of specific GGIs. This criterion enhances GGI legitimacy by placing GGIs in environments of local participation where the currently lacking norms regarding how GGIs ought to regard those most affected by their activities might develop under conditions of inclusion, reason-giving, and attention to the full range of relevant interests. In due course, with these norms in hand, we can then turn to a more complete and general theory of GGI legitimacy, with more stringent standards.

One virtue of this proposal is that by focusing on a single and minimal necessary condition of legitimacy, the door is left open with respect to the further demands of legitimacy on GGIs. These further demands may well vary given what I call "GGI diversity." GGIs will vary in their functions and operations, in the modes of their impacts on individuals, and accordingly in the norms to which they are properly subject. The proposal advanced here is consistent with developing out of the diverse

[*] For their helpful comments on earlier versions of this paper, I am delighted to thank Allen Buchanan, Matt DeCamp, Erich Gerlach, George Rainbolt, David Reidy, Walter Riker, and David Wong.

and locally fecund sites of GGI activity a plurality of legitimacy standards, each well-tailored to the specific normative context to which it applies.

1 The Problem of Normative Unclarity

Critics who bemoan the lack of legitimacy of GGIs often cite a highly idealized list of conditions that GGIs ought to satisfy—accountability, fairness, equality, inclusiveness, etc. These conditions accompany the spread of democratic norms to an increasing number of countries and reflect an attempt to implement these norms at the international level.[1] Since no GGI can likely satisfy each and every one of these conditions, the current global climate raises an important question: Are there any *necessary* conditions that *any* GGI must satisfy to be *legitimate*?

1.1 Putting the Cart Before the Horse

Authority can be legitimated in a variety of ways and sources of legitimacy can be grouped into three basic types: source-based, procedural and substantive. Proposals for GGI legitimacy have tended to focus on *substantive* legitimacy-making conditions, such as environmental protection or compatibility with human rights, and various *procedural* protections, such as accountability or inclusiveness, or some combination of these two sources.[2] For example, Keohane and Nye cite three ways in which GGIs experience a "democratic deficit," suggesting that they implement various procedural protections, such as transparency and participation, and address their insufficient politicization, i.e., the lack of effective politicians linking organizations to constituencies. Alternatively, Buchanan and Keohane offer a Complex Standard of legitimacy with three elements: first, GGIs should enjoy on-going consent of democratic states; second, GGIs must satisfy the three substantive criteria of minimal moral acceptability, comparative benefit and institutional integrity; third, GGIs should possess certain epistemic virtues needed to achieve on-going contestation and critical revision of the most basic features of the institutions.[3]

---

[1] Keohane, Robert O. and Nye, Joseph S. Jr., "The Club Model of Multilateral Cooperation and Problems of Democratic Legitimacy," in Robert O. Keohane, *Power and Governance in a Partially Globalized World* (New York: Routledge, 2002), p. 225.

[2] A GGI might be legitimated by its *origin or source*. Buchanan and Keohane call legitimacy derived from state consent the 'International Legal Pedigree View.' They argue that the Pedigree View fails given that many states are themselves illegitimate. Further, the idea that the Pedigree View provides a check on stronger states is flawed. Weaker states are protected only at that cost of allowing tyrannies to withhold consent, and therefore legitimacy, from GGIs. Allen Buchanan and Robert O. Keohane, "The Legitimacy of Global Governance Institutions," *Ethics & International Affairs*, v. 20, n. 4, 2006, pp. 405–437. See pp. 412–414.

[3] *Ibid*, pp. 432–433.

While it would be ideal, from a moral standpoint, if GGIs exhibited accountability, inclusiveness, or ensured compatibility with human rights norms, it is less clear why these standards serve to *legitimate* the particular activities of GGIs. Before we can debate the merits of various standards, and demand that GGIs make institutional modifications in the name of legitimacy, *the problem of GGI legitimacy* must be made sufficiently precise. We must have a concrete notion of what it is about the nature and conduct of these entities—as institutions that rule involuntarily over millions of people—that calls for their legitimation. Insofar as certain proposed conditions are to be recognized as principles of legitimacy, and not merely good features for GGIs to embody, this suggests that there is something about GGIs that motivates the problem of their legitimacy. We must give content to our concerns and understand how and why they threaten GGI legitimacy.

1.2 The State: A Paradigm Conception for GGI Legitimacy?

An institution is legitimate in the normative sense if it has the right to rule, but what this means for an institution depends on the authority it purports to wield.[4] In the case of the state, the problem of legitimacy is to explain how a state can have the moral authority to do the kinds of things that are involved in its governing. Just as in the problem of state legitimacy, we must first consider what the right to rule amounts to in the case of the GGI—what rights, privileges or powers the GGI should exercise—and only *then* can we consider under what conditions the GGI would be legitimate. However, we must not be misled by our familiarity with the case of domestic states—a familiarity that has lent itself to a general inquiry into their legitimacy—into thinking that we are familiar enough with GGIs to undertake a general inquiry into their legitimacy. For we face at least two substantial problems in this endeavor that do not arise in the case of states, both of which are overlooked in the present debate about GGI legitimacy.

First, it is far from clear what feature(s) of GGIs motivate(s) the problem of their legitimacy. Obviously GGIs have growing powers and privileges, but what are they, exactly? Which, if any, are common to all GGIs? Which *ought* they have? Second, once we have a proposal for what the legitimacy of a particular GGI should consist in, we must show that it is applicable to *all* GGIs despite their varying goals, functions and domains of activity, in order to assess the prospects for a general theory of GGI legitimacy. I will explore the first of these problems in the remainder of this section, and I will discuss the latter, what I call the fact of GGI diversity, in Section 2.

---

[4]Like Buchanan and Keohane, I am here interested in the normative sense of legitimacy as opposed to its sociological meaning. According to Buchanan and Keohane, "An institution is legitimate in the sociological sense when it is widely *believed* to have the right to rule. When people disagree over whether the WTO is legitimate, their disagreements are typically normative." *Ibid.*, p. 405.

1.3   Motivating the Problem of GGI Legitimacy

With regard to domestic government, the problem of legitimacy is motivated by the fact of coercion. Rousseau familiarly implored, "If men are born free, what can justify their chains?"[5] Obviously GGIs do not have a coercive structure analogous to that of the state; for example, they lack a legislature or effective police capacity. So while a state's legitimacy right is the correlate of the set of political obligations incumbent upon its subjects, a weaker conception of legitimate authority is appropriate for GGIs. But the content of this weaker conception depends on the powers wielded by GGIs. So what fact or condition motivates the problem of legitimacy in the sphere of global governance?

Interestingly, most critics fail to mention explicitly what, exactly, prompts their concern about GGI legitimacy. They cite troubling moral defects of GGIs (e.g., disproportionate domination by wealthy nations) but fail to connect these defects to the issue of GGI legitimacy. The particular critique that GGIs lack *legitimacy* embodies a very specific concern, that GGIs wield power by directing rules toward states that adversely affect people, yet they are not accountable for this power. This concern specifically targets GGI activities occurring beyond the control of those affected by them.[6] Theorizing that abstracts away from this obscures the root of calls for legitimacy.

For example, Keohane and Nye touch upon the peculiarity of the problem of the legitimacy of GGIs in their discussion of the WTO:

> So what is the problem? From one democratic perspective, the WTO is almost the ideal design of an international institution. The international bureaucracy is weak; the organization is responsive to (mostly) elected governments. The escape clauses and dispute settlement procedures allow domestic political processes to prevail when severely challenged by international integration without at the same time destroying all rules and procedures.[7]

Thus, Keohane and Nye acknowledge that GGIs are weak relative to the governments of rich, powerful states, and so raise the important question as to just what the fuss regarding the legitimacy of GGIs is all about. But while they raise this important question, they nevertheless fold in the face of critics, urging GGIs to meet the procedural standards of democracy without providing any argument as to what it is, exactly, that demands legitimation. Just because GGIs exhibit a *democratic deficit*, a lack of transparency, participation, and sufficient politicization, why do these deficiencies imply a *legitimacy deficit*? While most might agree that it would be ideal if GGIs were accountable and sufficiently politicized, why are these necessary conditions for the legitimacy of any GGI?

One promising suggestion is that the worry motivating the problem of legitimacy is not one of *hard power*, defined by Nye as "command power that can be

---

[5] Jean-Jacques Rousseau, *The Social Contract*, book 1, ch. 1. Many editions.

[6] For example, activist movements such as "Global Exchange" accuse the WTO, IMF, and World Bank of increasing inequality and hunger and destroying the environment; they critique their policies for being written with little input from citizens and seek to increase local action. See http://www.globalexchange.org/index.html.

[7] Keohane, Robert O. and Nye, Joseph S. Jr., *supra*, note 1, p. 227.

used to induce others to change their position," but rather *soft power*, which flows from the ability to convince others that they want what you want. As Nye states, soft power "co-opts people rather than coerces them."[8] While most GGIs are not coercive in the same manner as states, they make significant rules that are essentially involuntary, so the concept of legitimacy certainly seems applicable. For instance, the former general counsel of the World Bank, Andres Rigo, notes substantial harmonization among national laws, harmonization that is not part of the World Bank's mission but that nevertheless frequently results from World Bank activity.[9] In Anne-Marie Slaughter's discussion of Rigo's research, she suggests that it reflects the "hard impact of soft law," in the form of principles, guidelines, codes, standards, and best practices. She states, "Where states seek to create new legal rules and policies in the face of a dearth of local knowledge and expertise, they often seek to borrow from other states or internationally renowned experts. The World Bank is an obvious source from which to borrow."[10]

Thus, upon further exploration, it may turn out that it is GGI influence through soft law that needs legitimation, as it reflects power wielded by GGIs that is largely unrecognized and unregulated. However, this claim is, at present, controversial and merits further argumentation and explication. We need to know more specifically *how* soft power affects both states and individuals, and we need to inquire as to whether or not GGIs *should* be having such an influence.

1.4   The Problem of Normative Unclarity

Before we can assess the appropriateness of particular legitimacy standards, we must carefully consider what we can and should expect of GGIs. While this project of determining what it is, exactly, that is motivating the problem of GGI legitimacy is partly empirical, it is most essentially *normative*. While we need to understand more about how GGI rules negatively impact people's economic, social and political life, we ultimately need to assess whether their current activities are necessary for their proper functioning; this requires that we consider what their function *ought* to be. For example, while harmonization or convergence among national laws is not part of the World Bank's official mission, it frequently results from the Bank's activity. As Slaughter notes, the World Bank provides guidance, saves transaction costs, and offers the luxury of security.[11] This guidance which the World Bank provides is often informal and of great influence. While we are just now starting to draw our attention to the

---

[8] Nye, Joseph S. Jr., *The Paradox of American Power: Why the World's Only Superpower Can't Go It Alone* (New York: Oxford University Press, 2002), p. 9.

[9] Andres Rigo, "Law Harmonization Resulting from the Policies of International Financial Institutions: The Case of the World Bank." (Speech delivered at a conference on Globalization and the Evolution of Legal Systems, University of Ottawa, October 2000.)

[10] Slaughter, Anne-Marie, *A New World Order*. (Princeton, NJ: Princeton University Press, 2004), p. 179.

[11] *Ibid.*, pp. 178–181.

de facto influences of GGIs, the important question yet to be addressed is whether or not the World Bank *should* be serving as a legislative model in this manner.

There is a potential disconnect between what GGIs claim to be doing, what GGIs actually do, and a considered understanding of what they should be doing. As Steve Charnovitz argues, one of the biggest challenges facing the WTO is to determine its own mission.[12] David Vines has suggested that, given that too many of the Bank's projects and programs appear to fail or under-perform, the function of the World Bank should not be to lend money but to encourage trade liberalization.[13]

The fundamental problem is that we lack normative clarity regarding many GGIs, and it is this *normative* deficiency that presently encumbers the task of choosing appropriate standards for GGI legitimacy. With the phrase '*normative unclarity*' I gesture toward a general deficiency of developed norms regarding how GGIs ought to behave as ruling institutions that can adversely affect many people through their activities. In other words, we do not know, with respect to many GGIs, what to expect of them, normatively speaking.[14] Our lack of deliberation as to what roles and responsibilities GGIs ought to assume leaves us without appropriate standards by which we can assess their legitimacy. The problem of normative unclarity is an important—and heretofore unrecognized—consideration that should frame the current debate on the legitimacy of GGIs.

2   The Fact of GGI Diversity

2.1   A Diversity of Challenges

One oft-cited challenge to their legitimacy is that some GGIs significantly constrain state sovereignty.[15] Buchanan and Keohane accurately target usurping the authority of democratic states as a relevant type of threat to the legitimacy of some GGIs. So

---

[12] Charnovitz, Steve, "Triangulating the World Trade Organization," *The American Journal of International Law*, v. 96, n. 1, 2002, pp. 28–55.

[13] David Vines, "The WTO in Relation to the Fund and the Bank: Competencies, Agendas, and Linkages." In Anne O. Krueger ed., *The WTO as an International Organization* (Chicago, IL: University of Chicago Press, 1998).

[14] We have normative unclarity with regard to *many* GGIs, not *all* GGIs. Normative unclarity is a matter of degree; certainly we have more normative clarity with regard to some GGIs than others. However, I am concerned with the many GGIs for which there is far less moral clarity—the World Bank, the IMF, the WTO, etc.

[15] Buchanan and Keohane, *supra*, note 2, p. 407. I would reply that these reasons have, for the most part, not been sufficiently spelled out as concerns about GGI legitimacy, and so the problem of normative unclarity does, indeed, enter here. What rules do societies accept and what rules should they accept? How do these institutions affect people and should they so affect them? Perhaps they can point to certain GGIs, for example, the UN Security Council, where we have some moral clarity, but the general nature of these reasons merely provides further evidence of the problem I have isolated.

have they successfully identified a general feature of all GGIs that merits legitimation? Certainly their critique needs a bit more fine-tuning, both empirically and normatively, before we can propose an appropriate legitimacy standard. However, this highlights a further problem hindering prospects for a substantively robust, general account of GGI legitimacy.

Some GGIs appear to transgress democratic sovereignty, and if we assume that democratic states are legitimate, this is a clear challenge to GGI legitimacy. However, is this concern applicable to all GGIs and to the same degree? For some GGIs the primary worry is that they transgress democratic sovereignty (for example, the ICC). But for others, it is that they adversely affect the well-being of millions of people. For still others, it is a combination of worries—regarding their impact on state sovereignty as well as individual well-being.

If we specify broad conditions for GGI legitimacy we run the risk of abstracting away from important differences among GGIs. For instance, some argue that the WTO should promote narrow economic goals, i.e., it should maximize economic efficiency in cross-border trade. Others propose that the WTO should include other goals as well, for example, environmental protection. If the latter is the case, then perhaps legitimacy requires a certain relationship between the WTO and multilateral environmental agreements. If we generalize over all GGIs, then we miss the opportunity to engage in discussions that are particular to the WTO.

2.2 Is the Problem Generalizable?

Suppose that the use of soft power is the primary threat to the World Bank's legitimacy. It would remain to be argued that this is also the primary threat to the legitimacy of the WTO and the ICC. Knowing that certain GGIs involuntarily impose rules on certain states is not sufficient to make choices about what conditions are desirable legitimacy-making features for *all* GGIs. I refer to this problem as that of 'GGI diversity'—GGIs differ a great deal from one another in their goals, actions and domains of activity, and so they have a differential impact on various peoples.

Given the multitude of problems that motivate what is oft-discussed as a singular 'problem of GGI legitimacy,' we should not expect a single, unified standard for assessing the legitimacy of all GGIs. Even if it turns out that every GGI transgresses state sovereignty to some degree, the degree will likely vary and sometimes fail to give rise to legitimacy worries, depending on what other values are in play.

3 The Dilemma of GGI Legitimacy

Given the problems of normative unclarity and GGI diversity, we face what I will call 'the dilemma of GGI legitimacy': Either we prematurely make a substantively robust, general legitimacy judgment, or we withhold the legitimacy judgment, taking what I call a 'wait-and-see' approach to legitimacy.

3.1 The Substantively Robust, General Account of GGI Legitimacy

The prospects for identifying a robust set of necessary conditions for the legitimacy of any GGI appear dim given the severity of the problems of normative unclarity and GGI diversity. The dominant approach to the legitimacy of GGIs, as exemplified by Buchanan and Keohane, is to proceed with our theorizing despite these problems. The implementation of accountability mechanisms will likely require substantial institutional development on the part of many GGIs, and in order to demand this we need to be confident that these mechanisms respond to the *right problem* motivating our need for the legitimacy of GGIs. And in order to identify the right problem, we first need to figure out what we should want of GGIs; only then can we be sure that accountability is not just good for GGIs but rather is a suitable feature for the legitimacy of each and every GGI.

3.2 The Wait-And-See Approach

If normative unclarity precludes a substantively robust, general account of legitimacy, such as that offered by Buchanan and Keohane, it might seem that we are left with a *wait-and-see approach*— of waiting until we know what sorts of roles and responsibilities these diverse and underdeveloped GGIs are *supposed* to assume before theorizing about their legitimacy. This is an unappealing solution, as it raises the problem of how we will know when we have achieved "satisfactory" normative clarity for work on legitimacy to commence. It seems that we are on the path toward achieving pockets of normative clarity in certain domains, led by work like Rigo's on the World Bank, while we have yet to do similar exploration in other domains.

There are two principal problems with the wait-and-see approach. First, this solution assumes that there is nothing we can say right now to constitute a *provisional threshold* for legitimacy. While it is important to frame our theorizing about legitimacy within the problem of the lack of normative clarity, this wait-and-see approach ignores certain features of the notion of legitimacy. Legitimacy is a *threshold notion*—it constitutes a ground such that any GGI that stands on or above it is legitimate. This requires that we temper our demands, for if complete justice was a necessary condition for legitimacy, legitimacy would function as an unattainable ceiling rather than as a floor. In addition, legitimacy is *dynamic*—institutions change in their capacities and functions, and as they do what legitimacy demands of them may change too. So, legitimacy standards must be *provisional*. Higher standards may become applicable as institutional capacity develops or functions change.[16]

Second, this solution not only overlooks the fact that we *can* say something to constitute a provisional threshold for legitimacy, but perhaps even more importantly, fails to recognize that we *must* make legitimacy judgments—first, to give a voice to those people involuntarily disadvantaged by GGI rules, and second, to help set the GGI on a path to normative development. GGIs make significant rules often negatively impacting tens of millions of people without allowing them to have a say in the process. At best many GGIs are following an inapplicable "norm of confidentiality," inapplicable because task expansion suggests that GGI activities no longer relate directly to national security or the stability of the state system.[17] At worst GGIs expose millions to a procedurally unjust system that is difficult to consider voluntary. Those who are adversely affected by compliance with rules that are not of their making desperately need the language of legitimacy.

4   Legitimacy and Agent-Sensitivity

While normative unclarity and GGI diversity characterize our theorizing in the realm of GGIs, I argue that we do have some idea about what would set us on the path toward normative development and increased legitimacy. While we are not prepared, at this stage, to inquire generally into GGI legitimacy, we can begin by

---

[16] Buchanan and Keohane also lay emphasis on this important feature of GGIs, and it is one of their desiderata for a standard of legitimacy, "It must properly reflect the dynamic character of global governance institutions: the fact that not only the means they employ, but even their goals, may and ought to change over time." *Supra*, note 2, p. 417. But while we agree that it is important to recognize the dynamic nature of GGIs, I believe that these institutions are even more dynamic than Buchanan and Keohane recognize, which is why I take the problem of normative unclarity as my point of departure. Normative unclarity means not only that we need ongoing contestation and critical revision of the standards of legitimacy, but that we have uncertainty regarding even the most basic standards of GGI legitimacy. Thus, making available the possibility of revision and increased stringency of standards will not suffice; we must focus on the development of norms so that we can continue to hold GGIs to higher standards of legitimacy. This feature of GGIs gives rise to the problem which I will describe as GGI dynamism, and I discuss this problem in the final section of the paper. By *higher standards* I include both the possibility of (1) an increased level or stringency of a provisional condition as well as (2) additional necessary conditions. For example, in "Political Legitimacy and Democracy" Buchanan argues that democracy is required for political legitimacy when democracy is feasible. Similarly for GGIs, the conditions for legitimacy must be dynamic depending on institutional capacity. See Buchanan, Allen, "Political Legitimacy and Democracy," *Ethics* v. 112, n. 4, 2002, pp. 689–719.

[17] Alasdair Roberts, "A Partial Revolution: The Diplomatic Ethos and Transparency in Intergovernmental Organizations," *Public Administration Review*, v. 64, n. 4, 2004, pp. 410–424.

exploring the concept of legitimacy, identifying what we can say about GGIs in the paradigm case, and ultimately get a better understanding of how the concept applies to GGIs.

4.1 Justification and Legitimacy

A. John Simmons illustrates the unique nature of the legitimacy judgment by distinguishing it from that of the justificatory judgment. The project of *'justifying the state'* is one of showing that some realizable type of state is on balance *morally permissible* and *rationally preferable* to all feasible non-state alternatives. Justifications of the state are not typically offered to the participants in states but rather to those moved by certain objections to the state as an institution. In particular, the background objection motivating attempts to justify the state comes from the anarchist, who denies that any state can be morally and prudentially justified.[18]

According to Locke, who supported such a distinction, this justification does *not* show that any particular state is *legitimate*, that any state has the right to rule over any or all persons within its claimed domain. The question of the state's legitimacy is a second stage in the argument. One is likely to raise the question of why this distinction is necessary—is it not the case that arguments that demonstrate that a state is justified also demonstrate its legitimacy? If the state is morally acceptable and prudentially preferable, should it not be accepted by those subjected to it? The Lockean maintains that from the fact that a state treats its subjects well and provides benefits for them it does *not* follow that those states have with any particular subject the kind of *morally significant relationship* that could ground a state's right to impose duties.

4.2 An Agent-Sensitive Approach

Simmons worries about the Kantian tendency to conflate justification and legitimacy for at least two reasons. First, it ignores the Lockean premise of the natural freedom of persons. According to Simmons, something more than justification is needed to engender political obligation, as it represents a departure from the moral condition into which each person is born. Second, legitimacy draws attention to particularizing, duty-creating circumstances that justification does not bring into account. Kantian theorizing is not responsive to the common intuition that states must stand upon something more personal if they are to exercise legitimate authority over individuals.

---

[18] Here I am aided by Simmons' illuminating discussion. A. John Simmons, "Justification and Legitimacy," *Ethics* v. 109, n. 4, 1999, pp. 739–771.

Given his strong conception of legitimacy, in which a state imposes binding duties and has the right to use coercion to enforce those duties, Simmons requires a consent account of political obligation, maintaining that only voluntarily assumed transactional bonds legitimate the state. But because GGIs do not claim such strong authority and do not wield coercive power, I argue that the voluntarist approach is not the appropriate point of departure when it comes to GGIs. Insofar as voluntarism means actual choice or consent, I do not in this sense advocate a voluntarist position with respect to GGIs.[19]

However, I do wish to endorse Simmons' distinction between justification and legitimacy, as it reveals something valuable about the relationship between institutions and their subjects that we must consider in our theorizing about GGIs. The approach that I take, which I call an *agent-sensitive* position, attempts a more personal rendering of legitimacy but is not motivated by the voluntarists' desire to square natural freedom and political obligation. My reason for defending agent-sensitivity is to ensure that GGIs register the fact that they constrain the actions of agents, as opposed to the mere behaviors of things.

There is a tendency to assume that if one does not accept voluntarism as Simmons does, and its gold standard of consent, one must endorse the Kantian generic rendering of legitimacy in which actual choice is left behind in favor of hypothetical "reasonable" choice. We do not have to demand consent but nor should we accept generic moral principles which generalize over people. The agent-sensitive approach focuses not on one's actual choice but on the fact that persons are *choosers* who are capable of consenting. The point is not to respect each wish that an agent might have—not only is this not morally necessary, it is practically infeasible—but rather to recognize and treat the affected person as a concrete particular *agent*.

4.3 The Relationship Between the GGI and 'Those Most Affected'

Simmons' point illustrates why I think we should focus attention on those people most affected by the GGI, even though GGIs largely direct their rules toward states.[20] Legitimacy traditionally has to do with the nature of a state's rights over any particular subject; to achieve legitimacy the institution must interact with the

---

[19] And so insofar as voluntarism ultimately leads to philosophical anarchism, I escape the latter conclusion with regard to GGIs by denying the former. My hope is to maintain the distinction between justification and legitimacy in a way that does not fall prey to Simmons' critique of the Kantian but nevertheless avoids the philosophical anarchist conclusion.

[20] Of course, once it is agreed that we need to forge such a relationship, the question then arises as to how we can best encourage substantive participation by those groups most affected, in the most efficient and morally acceptable manner as possible. While this subsequent question is beyond the scope of this paper, I imagine that current work on participation in the development literature will prove invaluable. See, for example, Michael M. Cernea, *Putting People First: Sociological Variables in Rural Development* (New York: Oxford University Press and World Bank, 1985); and, The World Bank's "Participation Sourcebook," available at http://www.worldbank.org/wbi/sourcebook/sbhome.htm.

subject in a way that confers this right. However, while the subjects of GGIs are often states, it is the affected people whose well-being is compromised. I maintain that there are at least three reasons to focus attention on the people most affected by a GGI's operations.

First, as I mentioned above, we must be careful not to hastily analogize to states. The problem of normative unclarity is a serious impediment to our theorizing on the subject of legitimacy with regard to GGIs. It seems that those affected by a GGI's operations would be in a good position to assist in this normative work and so it would be a strategic move to take advantage of this insider perspective. Likewise with the problem of GGI diversity—if we are to determine which worries most pressingly ignite the problem of legitimacy with respect to a particular GGI, who better to decide than those who are impacted by its pernicious activities? These institutions are so new and, as I will discuss in Section 7, they are highly dynamic, and so the affected people can best attest to the changing roles and activities of the GGI.

Second, one concern that underlies all the worries about GGI legitimacy is that these institutions affect the well-being of millions of people. We are worried about GGI intrusion into society, and their usurping the authority of democratic states, because this eventually impacts the people of those states. From the fact that a GGI protects the least controversial human rights, or delivers unsolicited benefits, it is not clear why, exactly, it follows that individuals must accept its authority. The latter demand has to do with the GGI's special moral relationship to the affected individuals, and it seems that the proposed standard must address this particular interface.

Finally, while GGIs often design their rules for states rather than individuals, this merely reflects the conventional nature of the system. Ultimately it is individuals that are impacted. Impacted individuals may or may not fall within the borders of all the states party to a GGI agreement or policy initiative. Often those impacted will be scattered across several states, many of which may play no part in the underlying GGI activity. Poverty, education reform, etc., are often regional issues. GGIs working in these areas should address all the groups of individuals they intend to benefit. This may mean addressing groups outside of, or not well-represented within, states participating directly in the GGI activity.[21]

4.4 Legitimacy and Participation

The Lockean maintains that from the fact that a state treats its subjects well and provides benefits for them it does not follow that those states have with any particular subject the kind of *morally significant relationship* that could ground a state's right to impose duties. Simmons, speaking on behalf of the Lockean, says that "Only

---

[21] For instance, many environmental decisions, such as pollution and climate change, have impacts on many states. While voters in a certain state may favor pollution, as they do not suffer the ill-effects, the decision to pollute must involve those affected by the decision. For example, at the First Millennium Conference of Indigenous Peoples in Panama City in 2001, indigenous leaders charged that the policies of the IMF and World Bank harm indigenous communities around the world and fail to take into account the cultural reality of these communities.

interacting with you—and in a way that we normally suppose gives one party a moral right to expect something of another—will seem to 'legitimate' its imposition and/or enforcement of duties on you."[22]

If we must legitimate a particular GGI in an agent-sensitive manner, and with respect to those most affected, then it seems that an appropriate first step toward conferring legitimacy would be to build a foundation upon which such a special moral relationship could take root. Any solid moral relationship must have at minimum, in order to even get off the ground, firm uncoerced participation by both parties. Insofar as one party is uninvolved, in the dark, or involuntarily engaging with the other party, one can hardly claim to have a *relationship* of any sort, as opposed to mere *interaction among parties*. The GGI must create opportunities for individuals to become *participants* in its activities, toward the end of eventually creating a significant relationship through which the right to rule can be conferred.

The cornerstone of this agent-sensitive approach is the notion of participation. Therefore, I recommend that we recognize a *continuum of meaningful participation*, with the GGI's aim being to create stronger and more meaningful avenues through which subjects can participate. The weakest form of participation is mere availability of information, or *transparency*, while a slightly more meaningful form of weak participation would be information that is available without undue burden, what I will call *"robust" transparency*. A slightly more substantive relationship would involve a two-way transferring of information, as opposed to the one-way offering of information from the GGI to its subjects; an example would be the creation of a national institution which would allow individuals to *petition* the GGI. Finally, an even stronger form of participation would be all inclusive and full participation, namely, *equal voting rights*.[23] If all GGIs start out by encouraging the weaker forms of participation, they will be on their way to building a more substantive moral relationship with those they affect.

5 Robust Transparency

In the remainder of this paper I set out a compromise position between the substantively robust, general approach and the wait-and-see view. This developmental approach is based on the insight that while theorizing about legitimacy is problematic because of the lack of normative clarity regarding many GGIs, the process of making legitimacy judgments itself constitutes an essential part of the solution. The approach is *developmental* in that the provisional condition for legitimacy also provides one necessary ingredient for the development of norms regarding certain GGIs, paving the way for the development of *higher standards* for their legitimacy.

---

[22] A. John Simmons, *supra*, note 18, p. 752.

[23] One might plausibly argue that the strongest, most meaningful relationship between a GGI and its subjects—the gold standard—is *consent* of the governed. While there is much to be said about consent as a standard—what it entails, whether it is an achievable condition and whether it is even desirable (is it getting too close to justice?)—such a discussion is beyond the scope of this paper.

5.1   Escaping the Dilemma

We escape "the dilemma of GGI legitimacy" by first recognizing the two features of the legitimacy judgment highlighted in sub-section 3.3. Legitimacy is a *threshold notion* and the legitimacy of GGIs must be *provisional*; given the nature of GGIs as institutions under continual change, higher standards for legitimacy will become appropriate as institutional capacity and function develops. The second step is to embrace the core spirit of agent-sensitivity—we need to set the GGI on a path toward developing a significant relationship with those whom it affects.

5.2   Robust Transparency: A Necessary Condition for GGI Legitimacy

The developmental approach defends one necessary provisional condition for the legitimacy of GGIs: robust transparency. I defend a *robust* notion of transparency as a condition for legitimacy which urges that GGIs do not merely make information *available* in assessments and reports but actually make this information *accessible, without undue burden*, to the affected parties.[24] For instance, Slaughter proposes the creation of a virtual public space, suggesting that by making information available on a website, an organization would provide a central forum for citizens and groups and convince officials that they are under scrutiny.[25] By contrast, I require that this information not only be available in this way but accessible to all without undue burden.

Robust transparency confers legitimacy upon GGIs for both intrinsic and instrumental reasons. Transparency is *intrinsically valuable* insofar as it is a part of the substance of legitimacy. It is through the process of giving those affected by the GGI's activities a *voice* that the GGI is legitimated. While I have argued that there is not much that we can say about what roles and responsibilities any GGI should assume, there is at least one condition that we can demand of *all* GGIs, namely, that they should make information readily accessible for their assessment. By making this information available the GGI encourages a certain type of weak, two-way, relationship between it and those individuals most affected by its activities. By explicitly engaging these people, the GGI judges them worthy of certain information and it suggests a willingness on the part of a GGI to be subjected to assessment by reasonable agents. While we might not be clear as to what, exactly, motivates the problem of legitimacy as it pertains to GGIs, and so the manner in which GGIs ought to be assessed remains an open question, we are clear on the need for GGIs

---

[24] Transparency only confers its full benefits if affected parties can get hold of the information *without undue burdens*. While many GGIs make a claim to transparency, they (at best) refer to a much weaker form of transparency—mere *availability* of information.

[25] Slaughter, Anne-Marie, *supra*, note 10, pp. 235–237.

to be willing to be assessed in some fashion or other.[26] Thus, robust transparency confers legitimacy upon GGIs, not because it is a democratic norm that has been gaining global momentum, but because it initiates a weak relationship with those people most affected by its activities. While this is only the first step in identifying the *particular* morally significant relationship that is necessary to *fully* legitimate the GGI's right to rule, it is, indeed, a necessary one.

Transparency is *instrumentally valuable* insofar as it guarantees *responsiveness* by the GGI to the needs of those whom it affects.[27] Participation by a GGI's subjects ensures that the GGI can properly respond to their needs. Instrumentally, robust transparency offers important epistemic benefits which are paramount for at least two reasons. First, information about the GGI is a prerequisite for other procedural protections, such as accountability, and so transparency sets the stage for the GGI to meet higher standards for legitimacy. Second, as I discuss in the next section, this information is necessary for the development of norms regarding GGIs.

It is important to note that I am concerned primarily with the development of norms governing the relation between GGIs and those individuals most affected by them. I make no claim about the types of norms or norm complexes governing other categories of relationships: standards of conduct among GGIs for their dealings with one another, rules governing the relation of GGIs and all states, etc.[28]

---

[26] While the World Bank can claim to meet certain elements of a weak transparency, for instance, by pointing to numerous final reports that study the effectiveness of its developmental assistance, it does not satisfy the demands of a more robust transparency. The achievement of even a weak transparency would require numerous institutional adjustments within the Bank; for example, I propose more transparency regarding Board discussions and operations, including a formal and open record of deliberations and votes. In order to achieve robust transparency, and so fulfill my proposed necessary condition for legitimacy, the World Bank must not only make reports and minutes of meetings available to the public, it must make them accessible without undue burden. For example, this might entail that the World Bank focuses more of its resources on the development of knowledge fairs or town hall meetings. Slaughter, Anne-Marie, *supra*, note 10, pp. 235–237.

[27] Therefore, my view is plausible whichever view of transparency one holds. If it turns out that transparency is intrinsically valuable for legitimacy, as I suggest, it will only strengthen my case if it is also of instrumental interest in bringing about the development of norms.

[28] Here one might object that there is a fair amount of literature regarding international norms pertaining to the interaction of groups of states, notably, as Charles Beitz discusses, the emerging role of human rights as a moral touchstone in international life. See Beitz, Charles, "Human Rights as a Common Concern," *The American Political Science Review*, v. 95, n. 2, 2001, pp. 269–282. However, GGIs are not states (nor are they reducible to interactions among groups of states) and so they demand the development of norms regarding their particular issues, roles and responsibilities. One might certainly attempt to make the case that the role of human rights is not limited to interaction between and among states, and that human rights should also be recognized as presenting standards of evaluation for GGIs. Two points are especially relevant in response. First, those who claim that human rights should play a role much broader than that of standards of assessment and criticism for domestic institutions must present an *argument* for this extension of human rights to the realm of GGIs. While Beitz claims that the role of human rights is broad in this sense, he, like most others in the literature, tends to restrict his examples and evidence to cases in which human rights are used as standards of evaluation for domestic institutions. Second, even if it might be successfully argued that human rights standards can be extended to the domain of GGIs, we still need increased normative clarity regarding GGIs to determine *which* particular human rights standards serve as desirable legitimacy-making features for GGIs.

5.3   Will Robust Transparency Impede the Successful Operation of GGIs?

One might object to my emphasis on transparency for GGIs, claiming that GGIs are so *successful* precisely because they are not subject to intense public scrutiny. One can expect an objection along these lines to be raised by Anne-Marie Slaughter who argues that GGIs such as the WTO are *effective* precisely because they are exclusive.[29] The problem with this Slaughter-like objection is that it *assumes* that "effective operation" ought to be the goal of all GGIs, and that "effective" ought to be understood as speedy and efficient. I have argued that we lack normative clarity regarding how GGIs ought to operate; we don't yet know how various GGIs ought to function with respect to those they impact, and so on. So while we will hopefully start to gain increased normative clarity once we set GGIs upon a more transparent path, for now, Slaughter's focus on speed and efficiency as the goal for all GGIs remains controversial.[30]

5.4   Is Robust Transparency a Premature Concern?

In a similarly practical vein, one might object that my emphasis on transparency is premature, that we have more pressing concerns about basic human needs with which we should be concerned. Such an objection might take two forms. The stronger claim is that this goal of meaningful participation is a luxury problem and that we should set our sights on addressing more pressing matters, viz. meeting people's basic human needs, such as food and water. However, I would argue that these efforts need not be conceived as separate concerns, but rather, they can be pursued in tandem. Our choice is unduly restricted if it is between aspiring toward meeting people's basic nutritional needs and creating an environment in which they can meaningfully participate.

The weaker claim is that in order for the affected people to participate meaningfully they will need to have their basic needs met—food, shelter, education, etc.—and so these needs must be met *first*. In contrast to the stronger claim, this objector agrees that we should maintain our goal of meaningful participation but argues that, as a matter of practice, we must first meet people's basic needs. In response to this claim I would argue that not only *can* we jointly pursue these goals, it would

---

[29] Slaughter, Anne-Marie, *supra*, note 10, p. 145.

[30] Supposing that Slaughter's normative aspirations for GGIs are on target, one might argue that the provisional threshold of transparency will not necessarily undermine the speed and efficiency of the GGI. First, I have argued that for provisional legitimacy, a GGI must focus on being transparent to those *affected*—not *all* international actors. Hopefully this subset will be more probing in their analysis, given what is at stake, then the broader global public, who would be likely to focus only limited attention on the GGI. Second, while the affected people will have a voice in *normative development*, the GGI will presumably still be exclusive in *rule design*.

perhaps be *best* if we did so. The effort of meeting people's basic needs is likely to be much more successful if the affected parties are actively involved in the process; there are limits on what external experts can know about such things.[31]

6   The Developmental Approach to GGI Legitimacy

6.1   The Developmental Approach

Withholding the legitimacy assessment until we achieve increased normative clarity is precisely the wrong way to address our normative haziness. The practice of making legitimacy judgments plays a crucial role in the process by which we come to develop basic norms. Legitimacy attributions and normative development give rise to one another.

There are two crucial features of the developmental approach: (1) the provisional threshold for legitimacy, robust transparency, conditions the development of norms regarding the GGI, and (2) the very practice of making legitimacy judgments focuses attention on the GGI's activity, establishing a weak relationship between the affected individual and the GGI that likewise encourages normative development.

6.2   Robust Transparency and Normative Development

Robust transparency creates an environment ripe for the development of norms in two ways. First, as suggested in Section 5, robust transparency confers *epistemic benefits* so that those affected by the GGI have the information they need about a GGI in order to evaluate it in a critical way. Much of our normative haziness stems from the fact that the affected peoples know so little about GGIs—how they function, over what domains—which makes it challenging to make proposals suggesting what they should be like. Developing a more intimate understanding of particular GGIs and how they affect the public is the first step toward normative clarity.

This is especially important because GGIs change rapidly, and one way to keep up with task expansion—what the GGI does and how it presents itself—is to necessitate a robust transparency. For example, the World Bank was conceived during World War II to help rebuild Europe after the war. Today's Bank, however, has sharpened its focus on poverty reduction as the overarching goal of its work.[32] These are starkly different ambitions. And to complicate issues, it matters not only what the Bank claims to do, but also what it actually does, as Rigo's research has illuminated. Inconsistencies between its claims and deeds render the development of suitable norms all the more challenging.

---

[31] Michael M. Cernea, *supra*, note 20.

[32] http://web.worldbank.org

We are not seeking information about each and every decision of a GGI, for example, the ecological and economic consequences of a particular climate regime in a certain place and time. Rather, the sort of information that must be made available will be that which is conducive to norm development. We are interested in getting answers to more foundational questions about the GGI as opposed to particular policy decisions, i.e., what powers are wielded, by which institutions, what the institution's role within the broader scheme of global governance is, etc.

It is no doubt true that information needed for the enforcement of standards might be more appropriately directed to groups adequately equipped to assess compliance. Just as obviously, we will need external actors or groups (for example, transnational networks) to help identify ways in which power is exerted and to properly communicate this to those affected. However, information regarding the potentially contestable values at the root of particular policy decisions must be made available to all affected peoples. For instance, those affected may not consider "economic efficiency" to be a supreme value although it is at the heart of the WTO's commitment to liberalized trade.

Second, by establishing transparency as a prevailing norm for GGIs, we have a sort of "stepping stone" for further normative development. Having this norm as a foundation will help developing norms gain recognition insofar as they *cohere* with transparency. As the foundational norm, transparency will guide and put constraints upon further normative reflection. This is analogous to the way that international law codifies emerging norms. Such norms must make the case that they are logical extensions or necessary modifications of the law. This preference for coherence renders norms that tend to be resistant to change.

I must note the limitations of my argument in this sub-section. I am arguing here that robust transparency is merely a *necessary condition* for normative development. Certainly a variety of other standards and considerations must be recognized for there to be fruitful public dialogue regarding what norms are appropriate for certain GGIs.[33]

6.3 The Process of Making Legitimacy Assessments and Normative Development

My developmental approach involves expanding our view of the legitimacy judgment, as not merely a "motivating tool" that encourages GGIs to embrace *existing* norms, but also as a "normative tool" for the affected peoples to develop *additional*

---

[33] Indeed, it is these conditions, necessary for the promotion of normative public debate, which are the focus of another, larger project, "A Dialogical Approach to Human Rights," unpublished. While robust transparency is crucial in the case of GGI legitimacy, there are certain normative conditions—such as respect for persons—as well as guidelines on the suitable institutional arrangements that will prove essential for the fair development of cross-cultural norms.

norms regarding GGIs. My claim is that the process of gathering people to assess the legitimacy of a particular GGI will provide a crucial foundation for the initiation of a *normative dialogue* among affected peoples. This dialogue is important because it will ensure that the developed norms are connected to the GGI's particular practices and relations with the public. The development and modification of norms will be constant, as new relationships and forms of interaction emerge between the GGI and various publics.

In the process of learning more about the GGI's activities and assessing its provisional legitimacy, the affected peoples will engage in conversation about how the GGI ought to behave. The provisional threshold for legitimacy encourages those affected by the GGI to explore its activities, assessing not only what it does, but crucially identifying the ways in which it *ought* to be functioning. Both the process of evaluating the GGI, as well as possibly comparing the GGI with other institutions, will encourage this dialogue that will provide fertile ground for normative development. For example, the creation of knowledge fairs and town hall meetings will provide opportunities for public dialogue, thus functioning as informal mechanisms for instigating normative debate.

7   Localizing the Legitimacy Judgment

In addition to the more obvious differences between GGIs, there are also differences in the rates and directions in which GGIs are *dynamic over time*, what I will call "GGI dynamism." This feature provides yet another reason for us to be suspicious of proposals for a robust, general standard for GGI legitimacy.

7.1   Restricting the Domain of Discourse

While the developmental approach leaves open the possibility of achieving a *general* account of legitimacy, it embraces the fact that it is best, as a matter of current practice, if we take a more *localized* approach to making legitimacy judgments. By this I mean that from a non-ideal standpoint we should start by making local legitimacy judgments, focusing our attention on certain GGIs, in the hope of achieving greater domains of normative clarity. One reason to take a localized approach is that we have not yet identified what general features of GGIs we are trying to ground; we do not have sufficient agreement on what GGIs, as a class of institutions, are doing, what their key features are, what their goals ought to be, etc. In fact, we cannot tell if GGIs are even a well-behaved "class" over which generalizations are appropriate. Thus, the developmental view suggests that it is most effective if we proceed by using the legitimacy term on a case-by-case basis.

One way this works is by establishing specific or particular GGIs as *loci of activity*. For example, it is likely that it will be easier for certain GGIs to meet the minimal threshold for legitimacy than others, and so these GGIs will become established as sites of investigation. Once attention has been focused on the particular GGI, there are likely to be disputes about whether or not it should meet even higher normative standards due to its unique functions and institutional capacities. So while the goal is to uncover additional norms that regulate any GGI, the approach works best by first targeting key institutions.

7.2   The Fact of GGI Dynamism

Another reason to take a localized approach is that once we focus attention on one or another GGI we encounter the problems that accompany the fact of *GGI dynamism*— the on-going issue of GGI evolution due to institutional growth, task expansion, etc. This dynamic nature of GGIs demands an ever-vigilant debate regarding the current and potential activities of individual GGIs. This debate will elicit subsequent dispute regarding whether or not certain GGIs ought to meet even higher normative standards, above the threshold of robust transparency.

The problems that accompany GGI dynamism are distinct from the problem of normative unclarity. *Normative unclarity* is a problem, for the most part, because the practice of making legitimacy judgments regarding GGIs is still in its infancy. However, even if we achieve a substantial degree of normative clarity, and the threshold for legitimacy is raised, we nevertheless will, for the foreseeable future, continue to face the problem of *GGI dynamism*. This is not only because GGIs change over time, as they achieve greater institutional capacity and task expansion, but also because there will be normative disagreements as to what any individual GGI should be expected to achieve, given these tasks and capacities.

Consider, as an example, the large degree of overlap in the activities of the IMF and the Bank that has evolved since the mid-1970s. Jong-Il You notes two problems with this increasing overlap—"the possibility of conflict between the two and the possibility of each institution losing sight of its core mission."[34] You argues that a sharper division of labor is needed, as maintaining the pretense of consensus precludes the possibility of correcting flawed policies and undermines the legitimacy of the programs. I would argue that we will not be able to assess the full legitimacy of the IMF and the Bank until we sort out this relationship, which requires us to clarify the roles each institution should have in the realm of international finance. All that we can demand for now is that each institution is sufficiently transparent so that we can set about clarifying its roles and facilitate the development of norms. This process of clarification and development is a matter of *localized discourse*.

Therefore, the fact that GGIs are presently underdeveloped not only helps to explain the difficulty in generating a general theory of GGI legitimacy; it also

---

[34] Long-Il You, "The Bretton Woods Institutions," in *Governing Globalization*, Deepak Nayyar, ed. (Oxford: Oxford University Press, 2002), pp. 231–232.

presents the question of how these institutions might legitimately develop. Theorists must inquire into the legitimacy of the *process* through which individual GGIs transform themselves, as they develop institutionally and undergo normative development.

Conclusion

In summary, an appropriate response to the current diffuse and unfruitful debate about the legitimacy of GGIs is (1) development of a provisional legitimacy standard that lays emphasis on the eventual *participation* of those most affected by the GGI, toward the end of *normative development*, and (2) a properly constrained use of the term in more *localized* domains of discourse.

Chapter 15
Global Economic Justice, Partiality, and Coercion

Bruce Landesman

1 Two Liberal Views

My subject is global economic justice, the division of economic resources among human beings. Questions of non-economic justice involving rights to security, liberty of action, freedom of speech, religion, and political participation, will come into the picture now and then. But my central focus is economic justice.

Two liberal views about global economic justice are currently being debated by political philosophers. Cosmopolitanism holds that the most basic principles of economic justice apply directly to individuals across the globe, and require a just division of economic resources among all human beings. As Kok-Chor Tan puts it,

> principles of justice ought to transcend nationality and citizenship, and ought to apply equally to all individuals of the world as a whole...cosmopolitan justice is justice without borders.[1]

The other view—let's call it Liberal Nationalism[2]—holds that the most basic principles of economic justice apply to individuals *only within particular societies*. Economic justice is first and foremost about the division of resources within a sovereign state. It is 'domestic', rather than 'global'. Principles of global economic justice exist, but they primarily focus on relationships among states, not among individuals.[3]

---

[1] Kok-Chor Tan, *Justice Without Borders* (New York: Cambridge University Press, 2004), p. 1.

[2] Perhaps the first use of this phrase is in Yael Tamir, *Liberal Nationalism* (Princeton, NJ: Princeton University Press, 1993). Tan, *op. cit.* follows this usage. The same theory is called Social Liberalism by Charles Beitz, "Social and Cosmopolitan Liberalism," *International Affairs*, v. 75, 1999: pp. 515–530. Thomas Nagel calls it the Political Conception of Global Justice in "The Problem of Global Justice," *Philosophy and Public Affairs*, v. 33, 2005: p. 120. This is his name for the sort of theory put forward by John Rawls in *The Law of Peoples* (Cambridge, MA: Harvard University Press, 1999). The Rawlsian account has recently been defended by David Reidy in "Rawls on International Justice: A Defense," *Political Theory*, v. 32, 2004: pp. 291–319, and "A Just Global Economy: In defense of Rawls," *Journal of Ethics*, v. 11, 2007: pp. 193–236.

[3] This is a simple statement of liberal nationalism. Some complexities will be addressed below.

D.A. Reidy and W.J. Riker (eds.), *Coercion and the State.*
© Springer Science+Business Media B.V. 2008

On the cosmopolitan view, sovereign states play a derivative or instrumental role, as necessary agents for producing global justice among individuals. On the liberal nationalist view, states play a fundamental role. They constitute the primary context for economic justice.

Because it locates justice first and foremost at home, liberal nationalists will think it often more important to attend to the needs of the members of their own society, even if this means neglecting more urgent needs of those in other societies. Partiality towards the interests of co-nationals is a fundamental implication of the view. Cosmopolitans deny that this ordering is just. They can, however, allow partiality as an instrumental matter, when it is the only or best means for bringing about just economic relations among individuals as such.

Both of these views are liberal views. Liberal political theory embraces a deep-seated commitment to human equality that has been expressed in different ways, e.g. that people are of equal moral worth, that they must be treated as equals, and that they are entitled to equal concern and respect.[4] Liberals also hold that all people possess certain basic rights, e.g. rights to security, to liberty, and to a minimally decent level of material welfare.

Liberal nationalists therefore tend to endorse *cosmopolitan* (or *universalist*) principles about human rights that apply to all, independently of their nationality. Both views agree that states and individuals have obligations to ensure that all people can exercise these basic rights. Because of this, cosmopolitan and liberal nationalist views have similar practical implications in the current world in which a large percentage of the earth's population lacks basic human rights and live in dire poverty.

In *The Law of Peoples*, John Rawls expresses a liberal nationalist view. He argues, however, that well-off societies have a duty to help burdened societies become well-ordered. He also thinks that all humans have a right to sufficient material goods "to enable them to make intelligent and effective use of their freedoms."[5] This linking of freedom to a decent level of economic goods means that well-off countries have stringent obligations to those in poorer countries. Given the widespread poverty and misery in our world, both theories require aid to the global poor significantly beyond what well-off countries currently supply.

The primary competitor to both liberal views on global justice is the idea that affluent citizens and countries either have no obligations to the global poor or have only minor ones. Such a view has no agreed upon name and is not currently under serious debate by political philosophers. It is analogous to views on domestic justice that emphasize libertarian rights or desert: rich countries or well-off individuals either have rights to keep what they have earned through their individual efforts or deserve to do so.

---

[4] Ronald Dworkin has made "treatment as an equal" central to the liberal idea. For an early expression of this see "Liberalism", in Stuart Hampshire, *Public and Private Morality* (Cambridge: Cambridge University Press, 1978).

[5] John Rawls, *The Law of Peoples*, op. cit., p. 14

There are obligations to provide some help to foreigners in need, but these obligations are a matter of charity, not justice. Although not debated much by philosophers, this 'libertarian'-like view is probably much closer to conventional opinion than either liberal view.

For this reason the debate between cosmopolitan and liberal nationalist views tends to be 'academic' in the pejorative sense of that word—having no practical interest or import. Thomas Nagel has argued, however, that our thinking about global justice is at a very early stage. Domestic political theory is well understood but, by contrast,

> the concepts and theories of global justice are in the early stages of formation and it is not clear what the main questions are, let alone the main possible answers. […] The need for workable ideas about the global…case presents political theory with its most important current task, and even perhaps with the opportunity to make a practical contribution, though perhaps only in the long run.[6]

If Nagel is right, continuing the theoretical discussion may help.

Further, the two liberal views have serious and conflicting practical implications both for individuals and for states. I can give to either domestic or international charities. I can engage in political activity on internal or international matters. My nation may have to choose whether to provide better health care for its own poor or allocate resources to diminish AIDS in Africa. How to answer these urgent questions will depend to some extent on whether one inclines towards cosmopolitan or liberal nationalist ideas. It is therefore worth debating the issue, even though the world is far away from living up to the demands of either account of global justice.

2   Contrasting Inclinations

I find myself with conflicting inclinations about these matters. On the one hand, I tend to identify with my own country and its citizens and to be identified with it by others. Because of this, I find its injustices more troubling than similar injustices elsewhere. Further, morality includes special obligations to family and friends; special obligations towards those whose community one shares seem natural. This suggests attending first to domestic justice, and makes the liberal nationalist view attractive.

On the other hand, it is obvious that one's life chances are deeply affected by where one is born, which is a matter of pure contingency. Nothing about me, an American, justifies my wealth, compared to a person with equal potential in a very poor country. The resources of the earth are divided arbitrarily. The existing global distribution of property rights is a matter of history and chance, not justice. This suggests that justice should be global, taking all humans as individuals.

---

[6] Nagel, op. cit., p. 114.

To try to decide between these moral views, I am going to examine Michael Blake's very interesting and rich paper, "Distributive Justice, State Coercion, and Autonomy".[7] This is a recent expression of Liberal Nationalism that identifies coercion within sovereign states as the basic reason that economic justice is fundamentally a domestic matter.

3 Autonomy as a Universal Right

To understand how Blake understands the significance of coercion, we must first understand the importance he gives to the value of autonomy. For Blake autonomy is a central value of Liberalism. Equality is also central to liberalism but, as we shall see, it is autonomy and the way coercion violates it that enables us to show that economic justice is fundamentally a domestic, rather than a global, matter.

Autonomous agents, says Blake, are able to pursue self-chosen goals and relationships free from coercion; they are "part authors of their own lives" (267). Certain additional conditions must exist for a person to be an autonomous agent. An autonomous agent must have the mental ability to engage in complex planning; must be able to see himself or herself as an agent; and must have adequate options to choose among. In Blake's view, every human being is entitled both to autonomy and to the conditions necessary for it. His liberalism thus embraces the following principle:

> All human beings have the moral entitlement to exist as autonomous agents, and therefore to those circumstances and conditions under which this is possible. (267)

He is committed to "the global protection of individual autonomy" (268).

Since every human being has a right to autonomy, and the conditions necessary for it, Blake has a *cosmopolitan view* with respect to this right. The principle of autonomy

> mandates…that all individuals, regardless of institutional context, ought to have access to those goods and circumstances under which they are able to live as rationally autonomous agents capable of selecting and pursuing plans of life in accordance with individual conceptions of the good…[so] a consistent liberal must be as concerned with poverty abroad as that at home, since borders provide no insulation from the demands of a morality based on the worth of all autonomous human beings. (271)

This principle implies positive steps to promote autonomy, not just lack of interference. The principle also has implications for economic goods: all people have a right to the economic goods required for autonomy. If put into effect, this principle would satisfy the most important demands of cosmopolitan theorists.

---

[7]Michael Blake, "Distributive Justice, State Coercion, and Autonomy," *Philosophy and Public Affairs*, v. 30, 2002: pp. 257–296. References to page numbers of quotations from his essay will appear in parentheses.

While Blake endorses equality with regard to the right to autonomy, he rejects any stronger notion of global economic equality. He distinguishes between *absolute* and *relative* deprivation. People suffer absolute deprivation when they live below the level required for autonomous functioning. It is unjust for anyone to be allowed to live this way. Relative deprivation is economic inequality in contexts in which no one suffers from absolute deprivation. If everyone on the globe lived in conditions that allowed for autonomous functioning, relative deprivation or economic inequality among societies, would not constitute global injustice, since relative deprivation, he argues, is a concern only within societies. In that context it can be just or unjust, depending on whether the economic inequality is justifiable. To understand why economic inequality is only a domestic concern, we can now turn to what Blake says about coercion.

4   Coercion

Blake's main argument is this: Economic inequality matters within societies only because they are systems of coercion. Global community is not a system of coercion. Therefore economic inequality is not a global concern.

Blake's reasoning has several stages and has two starting points: a commitment to autonomy as a fundamental liberal value, and a thesis about the nature of moral justification. I will consider each in turn.

Autonomy. Blake begins with the premise that coercive restrictions on autonomy "are prima facie prohibited by the liberal principle of autonomy". Both the criminal and civil law involve such restrictions. The question, then, is how legal coercion can be justified, given that it violates autonomy.

The answer Blake gives relies heavily on the notion of hypothetical consent. A restriction on autonomy is justified only if free and rational people could consent to it, if it "would be consented to, ex ante, under some appropriate method of modeling rational consent." (274) John Rawls's original position provides such a model. T.M. Scanlon's notion of principles no one could reasonably reject is a slightly different expression of the idea.[8] So a system of coercion is acceptable if and only if it could be agreed to or not reasonably rejected by free and rational persons, and could thus be "justified to each and every one of those so coerced" (282). *Only then is a restriction on autonomy compatible with the value of autonomy.* Blake elaborates these familiar ideas at some length.

---

[8] Blake sometimes refers to principles all rational persons could consent to; sometimes to principles no one could reasonably reject. The distinction between these two ways of putting the matter was introduced by T. M. Scanlon, "Contractualism and Utilitarianism," in Amartya Sen and Bernard Williams eds., *Utilitarianism and Beyond* (Cambridge: Cambridge University Press, 1982). See also Scanlon's *What We Owe to Each Other* (Cambridge, MA: Harvard University Press, 1999), esp. chs. 3 and 4. The distinction between these formulations is not important for either Blake's discussion or mine.

Moral Justification and Inequality. A legal system tends to protect unequal shares of economic goods. Inequality is problematic because it is in tension with the liberal commitment to equality. That commitment does not mean that economic inequalities are unjustified. It means that they require justification, a justification compatible with each person's being treated as an equal, a justification no one could reasonably reject.

Blake argues there is a special need for such justification because coercion is involved in the maintenance of unequal shares and this coercion is a prima facie violation of autonomy. He does not explicitly say why this is so. The most obvious account is that when property is protected, people are prevented from taking from others what they need or want. You cannot have what is mine and thus your autonomy, your freedom of action, is prima facie violated. You need to be given a justification for this restriction. The system of unequal property rights is thus a coercive violation of autonomy and must therefore be justifiable to each and every person who falls under it.

Following this, Blake suggests that Rawls's difference principle is best understood as providing a justification for legal coercion:

> We have to give all individuals within the web of coercion, including those who do most poorly, reasons to consent to the principles grounding their situation by giving them reasons they could not reasonably reject…A principle that would allow material inequality greater than that of the difference principle, on this reading of Rawls, would be a principle that some members of society could reasonably reject. (283)

In Blake's view, Rawls sees, "coercion not cooperation [as] the sine qua non of distributive justice" (289).

Blake's conclusion, then, is that relative deprivation or economic inequality requires justification among people bound together under a system of coercion. Within such a system, inequality can be wrong even if the minimal conditions for autonomy have been secured for all. Inequality can be unjust, even if no one is poor.

When people are not bound by a system of coercion, inequality presents no such issue. Global institutions, says Blake, do not involve systems of coercion. Thus global inequality is not unjust, if no one suffers absolute deprivation. To defend this, Blake asserts that global institutions "do not engage in coercive practices against individual human agents" (286). The difference between domestic and global institutions is that only

> the former engage in direct coercion against individuals, of the sort discussed…in connection with criminal and civil law. There is no ongoing coercion *of [that] sort* in the international legal arena. (280, emphasis added).

Blake believes either that (i) global institutions do not involve coercion or (ii) they involve coercion but coerce only states, not individuals. (I will return to these claims later.) Thus, the conditions that make economic inequality a problem within a state do not apply to the conditions that exist among states.

> Material equality becomes relevant only in the context of certain forms of coercion, forms not found outside the domestic arena. […] Among persons who do not suffer absolute deprivation, economic inequality raises questions of justice when and only when those persons live under the same system of coercion (284–285).

5   Justice, Coercion, and Autonomy

Blake's account, in my view, raises three questions:

First, how do systems of coercion raise questions of justice about economic inequality?

Second, are there other conditions that also raise questions of justice about economic inequality? That is, is coercion the only relevant matter?

Third, is Blake right that international institutions do not involve the relevant kinds of coercion?

In this section I address the first two questions. I argue that Blake's emphasis on coercion misfires. It is not coercion that makes domestic inequality problematic. It is inequality itself.

Blake's main claim, as noted above, is that economic inequality within a society is maintained by coercion. Because of this, economic inequality is a prima facie violation of autonomy and needs justification to each and every person in the system.

We can see problems with this when we look more closely at what Blake means by autonomy. Blake oscillates between two different meanings of autonomy. When he first introduces the notion, it involves more than freedom to act. It requires having various mental capacities to deliberate about action and see oneself as an agent, as well as sufficient material means. Blake thus starts with a strong and rich notion of autonomy of the sort that Joseph Raz has developed.[9]

As Blake moves on, however, autonomy becomes a much weaker and thinner notion. In forming his central argument, he treats autonomy solely as freedom of action. Criminal and civil laws restrict a person's liberty of action. That's why they violate autonomy for Blake and require justification. *Autonomy has become mere liberty*, the right to act without legal sanction. This weak notion of autonomy as liberty is the notion of autonomy that plays the crucial role in his argument.

It is not true, however, that all restrictions on liberty of action are prima facie suspect. Human beings are social creatures and, as Blake himself admits, we need society to live. The state, he says, "is coercive and stands in prima facie conflict with the liberal principle of autonomy...[but] we cannot eliminate [it], given the (paradoxical) importance of government for the protection of autonomy" (281–282). It seems to me more plausible to hold that the restrictions on freedom of action needed to make human life in society possible violate no prima facie requirements. Restrictions on various forms of violence and injury do not violate any such demand. Recall John Locke's remark:

> Could they be happier without it, the law, as an useless thing, would of itself vanish: and that ill deserves the name of confinement which hedges us in only from bogs and precipices.[10]

---

[9] Joseph Raz, "Liberalism, Autonomy, and the Politics of Neutral Concern," *Midwest Studies in Philosophy*, v. VII (Minneapolis, MN: University of Minnesota Press, 1982). See also Joseph Raz, *The Morality of Freedom* (Oxford: Clarendon Press, 1986), esp. chs. 5 and 6.

[10] John Locke, *The Second Treatise of Government*, ch. 6, sec. 57, many editions, italics added.

Or consider John Stuart Mill's remark:

> All that makes existence valuable to anyone, depends on the enforcement of restraints on
> the actions of other people.[11]

It seems an overstatement to say that coercive restrictions on freedom of action which are absolutely necessary for human life are prima facie wrong and require justification.[12] The prohibiting of killing or injuring innocent people through law bears no such burden. There is no freedom to kill or harm that the prohibition on murder violates, prima facie or otherwise.

Let's consider a trivial example, given by Ronald Dworkin.[13] Some years ago New York City instituted a system of one way streets to improve traffic flow. Fifth Avenue is now one way downtown. One is not at liberty to drive uptown on Fifth Avenue. That restriction is coercively enforced. But it seems silly to say that there is any prima facie violation of autonomy or liberty here. This kind of restriction is a sensible way to meet human aims. It is an essential part of a practice that improves life.

Thus, the idea that any restriction on liberty of action is prima facie wrong and requires justification is mistaken, or at best an overstatement of the sensible idea that a just society needs to protect a broad area of liberty for its citizens. Blake's view on liberty of action fits much more comfortably into the Libertarian tradition than it does into the liberal democratic tradition he means to represent. On the libertarian view, any restriction on freedom of action is problematic. Starting from such premises, a libertarian like Robert Nozick finds no justification for anything more than a minimal state[14]. Blake, with his emphasis on both human rights and distributive justice, fits uneasily into that camp.

The real question to be addressed is this: *when exactly is a **restriction** on a person's liberty a **violation** of it, prima facie or otherwise*? The answer that makes most sense is that such a restriction is a violation when and only when it is arbitrary, irrational, senseless, unjust, discriminatory, etc. If this is correct, we must first decide if a restriction raises questions of justice or irrationality before we consider it problematic. Where it is a sensible part of an effective and fair practice, no such issues arise. Making Fifth Ave. one way raises no prima facie moral problems that signal the need for careful ethical deliberation.

This way of seeing things fits comfortably in the liberal tradition. As I have noted, that tradition emphasizes equality and the demand that all be treated as equals. A restriction on liberty is prima facie problematic only when it is arguably incompatible

---

[11] John Stuart Mill, *On Liberty*, ch. 1, many editions.

[12] We can also remind ourselves here of Hobbes's account of the state of nature where people have complete liberty of action. This leads to a "war of all against all," in which human life is "solitary, poor, nasty, brutish and short." *Leviathan*, ch. 13, many editions.

[13] Ronald Dworkin, "What Rights Do We Have?," *Taking Rights Seriously* (Cambridge, MA: Harvard University Press, 1978), ch. 12, pp. 266–78.

[14] Robert Nozick, *Anarchy, State and Utopia* (New York: Basic Books, 1971), esp. the Preface and chs. 1–3, 7.

with that equality. If anything is prima facie demanded, it is equality. For this reason, economic inequalities need justification, especially to those who are worst off.

Coercion is not the key concept. Economic inequalities require justification because they raise the question of whether people are being treated as equals. That's why we owe each and every person a justification of economic inequality. Coercion plays a secondary role in the story. It is only the means for maintaining the inequalities which demand justification on their own terms.

If this is correct, Blake cannot use coercion to distinguish domestic from global inequality. Since people need to be treated as equals, global inequality needs justification just as much as domestic inequality.

I do not deny that one might argue that in the absence of absolute deprivation, inequalities among societies can be justified because rational persons would consent to them or could not reasonably reject them. I take no stand here on this possibility. My point is that the hypothetical consent meta-ethics Blake endorses may still serve as a way of supporting his conclusion. Its power, however, does not rest on the claim of a strong right to liberty of action such that any restriction of liberty is a violation of that right. It rests, more directly, on the need to justify inequality to those who are equals.

6   Justice and Responsibility

I want to suggest another possible argument against Blake's appeal to coercion. I will only sketch out the argument. It will be incomplete and need more development to be fully persuasive. It expresses, however, a set of ideas Blake needs to address. Here is the argument sketch:

> Social and economic inequalities are human phenomena. They exist because of human conventions and can be altered by human decision-making. Inequalities are a problem from the point of view of liberal justice because we humans are responsible for them. They require justification because they are, in fundamental ways, a matter of human choice.

> This does not mean that human beings intentionally create inequalities. Inequalities arise through historical processes, affected by many contingencies. But we come to realize that the underlying conventions and norms on which they are based, including systems of property rights, can be altered or eliminated. In deciding not to change them, we are in effect choosing them. *We take responsibility for them when we do nothing about them.* Given our responsibility, a concern for inequality cannot be limited to domestic matters. Inequalities among people across the globe have arisen as a result of contingencies of many kinds. But they, too, can be altered. Domestic and international institutions can and do make decisions that affect the global distribution of resources. By not altering these inequalities, we choose them. In that regard, global inequality is no different from domestic inequality. If one is a concern of justice, so is the other.

To turn this sketch of an argument into a complete argument, I would need to say much more about responsibility. As formulated, the sketch assumes a strong idea of negative responsibility, that doing nothing to remove an alterable state of affairs makes one at least partially responsible for it. Some will reject this, and others will find it applicable in some conditions but not in others. The facts will be quite complex.

Blake himself seems committed to the view that citizens of affluent countries are responsible for *absolute deprivation* even if they have not caused it. To complete his argument, he would need to argue that affluent nations are not responsible for relative deprivation in other societies. His mode of doing this is to appeal to the coercion that underlies inequality within a society and makes that inequality problematic because it violates autonomy. I have argued that this mode of argument does not give him the criterion he needs to claim responsibility for domestic but not global inequality.

7 Global Coercion

Let me summarize my argument so far. My first question for Blake was "why do systems of coercion make economic inequality a matter of justice?" I have answered that inequality is not troubling because of coercion. For a liberal, it is troubling in itself; and some forms of coercion are not troubling. My second question was, "Are there conditions besides coercion that make inequalities a matter of justice?" I have answered affirmatively: From a liberal perspective that sees people as equals, inequality is troubling independent of coercion. It requires justification. It is also troubling insofar as it constitutes an alterable state of affairs that we are at least partially responsible for when we do nothing to change it.

My third question was whether Blake is right that international institutions do not involve the relevant kinds of coercion. If Blake is right that it is coercion that makes inequality problematic, is he also right that it does not do so globally as well?

It is hard to deny that there are numerous coercive relations between states. Aggression or the threat of it–coercive acts–may be resisted by force or its threat, including military attack, sanctions, embargoes, trade restrictions and the like, also coercive acts. Treaty violations can bring coercive sanctions. Individuals can be tried for various crimes against humanity under international law and imprisoned. Immigration policies prevent non-citizens from residing where they wish. Nations can demand favorable treatment from other nations by threatening various kinds of unfavorable actions. Coercion and threats of coercion among nations is common through history. Recall Hobbes view that the 'society' of independent nations is a state of nature and a state of war. One problem with Blake's thesis is that it is confined to the coercion that backs international law. But coercion in international matters comes in other forms, too.

Blake need not deny any of this. His main argument is given by the following remark:

> International legal institutions, in contrast [to states], do not engage in coercive practices *against individual human agents*…only [states] engage in *direct coercion against individuals*, of the sort discussed above in connection with the criminal and civil law. There is no ongoing coercion *of [that] sort* in the international legal arena. (280, italics added).

Thus the idea is that individuals are coerced only by states. The coercion that exists in the international arena is of a different sort—states coercing states perhaps, but not individuals.

Is Blake correct that international law does not coerce individuals? International criminal law as applied to war crimes provides one clear counter-example. In this case, however, there are international courts with the authority to prosecute violators, but there are few such institutions. More typically, when individuals violate international laws, it is expected that their own government will prosecute them. When an international intellectual property agreement prohibits pirated DVD's, the country where the piracy occurs is expected to punish its own citizens who violate the law. Thus Hollywood film companies expect China to crack down on piracy and the U.S. is aggrieved if it does not.

I suggest that the best way to describe such a case is that the international law does *apply* to individuals but the *enforcement mechanism* is left up to states. Enforcement could of course become internationalized over time as globalization continues and more international courts are instituted. For the present, Blake is right that international laws tend not to be enforced directly on individuals by international institutions. They are, however, indirectly enforced by their own states. And as such they play an important role in sustaining, through coercion, broad patterns of global economic inequality. It is hard to see, however, why the mere and contingent fact that international laws are typically enforced against individuals indirectly by their home states can have much weight in distinguishing the moral importance of domestic from international coercion.

Perhaps Blake means to appeal to an argument about the *effects* of coercion both domestically and globally. Since members of a single nation are bound together in one coercive system, one person's benefits can mean another person's loss and vice versa. Tax money spent on schools won't be spent on transportation systems. A tax decrease for some may mean a cut in benefits for others. Higher profits to share-holders can mean lower salaries for employees and higher prices for consumers. An economic system need not be a zero-sum system—some decisions may benefit all in the long run or help some without hurting others. But many decisions will involve a trade-off between interests and some will do better, while others do worse. In such a system of cooperation and community, the question of whether the distribution of economic goods is fair will emerge naturally.

If Blake emphasized this aspect, then his point would be that the international community is not so tightly connected. While international trade exists, it is not the dominant consideration and zero-sum trade-offs are the exception rather than the rule. Blake might find support in John Rawls's view about social self-sufficiency, as expressed in *The Law of Peoples*:

> the causes of the wealth of a people and the forms it takes lie in their political culture and in the religious, philosophical, and moral traditions that support [their] basic structure…as well as the industriousness and cooperative talents of its members, all supported by their political virtues. I would further conjecture that there is no society anywhere in the world—

except for marginal cases—with resources so scarce it could not, were it reasonably and
rationally organized, become well-ordered.[15]

A view like this raises enormous issues, both conceptual and empirical. The extent
to which the poverty of poor countries is due to local phenomena or is caused by
past colonialism and the exploitative economic power of rich countries is a matter
of intense dispute. Thomas Pogge, among others, has argued that the responsibility
of rich countries for poverty among the poor is significant enough to lay a heavy
burden on the affluent.[16] The role of coercion in determining people's lot throughout the world is a matter of great controversy. Blake must wade into these difficult
waters to show that there is a significant enough difference between domestic and
global coercion to justify the liberal nationalist view in his way.

In sum, I have argued that individuals can be coerced by international laws and that
this international coercion plays a role in sustaining global economic inequalities. The
fact that this coercion is often indirect—states coerce their own members into compliance with international legal norms—is morally insignificant. Blake's best tactic
would be to appeal to the causal role of a national community in determining who gets
what. It is, however, arguable that similar global interaction plays a similar role.

8   Impartiality and Partiality

Blake introduces his paper by noting that liberalism is committed to moral equality
and impartiality, and this commitment makes partiality towards one's own society
problematic. He says that liberals have responded in one of two ways, either by
trying to make particularist commitments compatible with liberalism, or by abandoning such commitments entirely and embracing cosmopolitanism.

Blake aims for a third way that avoids *both* particularistic commitments and
cosmopolitan neutrality. He claims that "a globally impartial liberal theory is not
incompatible with distinct principles of distributive justice applicable only within a
national context." (258)

> What a principle demands changes depending on the context in which it is applied; that we
> owe distinct things to fellow nationals need indicate not partiality towards those nationals,
> but rather a more sophisticated understanding of what impartiality *really* demands. (258,
> italics added)

Thus when we are bound together under the same system of coercion, impartiality
demands a special worry about inequality within our system, but it is permissive of
similar inequality with respect to those not under the same system.

In the remark quoted above, Blake says that our owing "distinct things to fellow
nationals *need not indicate partiality towards those nationals*". This claim strikes

---

[15] John Rawls, *The Law of Peoples*, op. cit., p. 108.
[16] Thomas Pogge, "A Global Resources Dividend," in David A. Crocker & Toby Linden eds.,
Ethics of Consumption: The Good Life, Justice and Global Stewardship (Lanham, MD: Rowman
& Littlefield, 1998), pp. 501–536.

me as word-play. What we owe distinctly to our fellow nationals is a special concern for their interests when similar efforts on our part could help others instead, perhaps to a greater degree. In any literal sense of the word, this is partiality towards co-nationals. Blake does not want to call it "partiality." Why?

My suspicion is that Blake fears that an acceptance of partiality leads to a radically particularist understanding of moral relations which denies human equality. Such a view holds that we have numerous strong duties to those closely related to us, fewer and weaker duties to those just outside our inner circle, and only a handful of very weak duties to those distant from us. Few people hold this radically particularist view. The notion of human equality is deeply engrained in the idea of morality, and in modern cultural understanding. It is difficult to give sense to the idea that some people are inherently better and others inherently worse. At the same time, partiality—the idea that that we have stronger obligations to those to whom we stand in special relationships—is also an essential part of morality. Blake is right that there is a tension between partiality and the commitment to moral equality, but it is a tension that characterizes morality.[17]

The solution to the problem is to understand equality in an abstract way that is compatible with inequality in particular situations. People must be treated as equals, or treated with equal concern and respect, but favoring friends and relatives is compatible with this, while discrimination on the basis of race or gender, and denying opportunities to those who are poor is not. Much moral and political argument hinges on disagreement over whether some form of inequality is compatible with treating people as equals or not.

I have argued that Blake's defense of liberal nationalism fails and thus my argument has been negative. It is possible, however, to defend liberal nationalism in other ways. Thomas Nagel's defense of it—he calls it the political conception of international justice—is attractive. Nagel agrees with Blake that there are cosmopolitan obligations involving basic human rights. But he argues that

> socioeconomic justice is different…it is fully associative. It depends on positive rights we do not have against all other persons or groups, rights we have only because we are joined together with certain others in a political society under strong centralized control.[18]

We have special obligations to our fellow citizens because we live together in a common enterprise under sovereign authority. We are "joint authors of the coercively imposed system and subject to its norms". Because of this

> the society makes us responsible for its acts, which are taken in our name…. Insofar as those institutions admit arbitrary inequalities, we are, even though the responsibility has been handed to us, responsible for them…. The request for justification has moral weight even if we have in practice no choice but to live under the existing regime.[19]

---

[17] Samuel Scheffler has carefully examined this tension in morality in "Nationalism, Liberalism and the State," in Robert McKim and Jeff McMahan eds., *The Morality of Nationalism* (Oxford: Oxford University Press, 1997), pp. 192–208.

[18] Nagel, *op. cit.*, p. 127.

[19] Nagel, *op. cit.*, p. 129.

According to Nagel, we do not have similar responsibility for the arbitrary inequalities that exist among nations or within nations other than our own. The important point, as I understand it, is that as members of a nation and the cooperative enterprise it involves, we identify with it. As a result of our identification we take responsibility for its actions, both good and bad. As Nagel summarizes it, our involvement "comes from a special involvement of agency or the will that is inseparable from membership in a political society."[20]

This identification is an instance of associative obligation. We have such special obligations to family, friends and colleagues. This is sometimes through voluntary agreement, but not always. This kind of obligation is a form of partiality and, as I have said above, is an essential part of morality that exists alongside the more universal obligations we have to all human beings.

It is difficult to underestimate identification with one's country. I have been deeply embarrassed more than once in my life by the actions of my country, and I just mention briefly three examples: the long denial of basic rights to black Americans and to women; the Vietnam war and the death and destruction it wrought; and the current war in Iraq that we initiated and that has ruined countless lives and unleashed forces of chaos that will affect our lives and the lives of others for generations. I feel a much stronger obligation for these wrongs and a duty to prevent them than for similar wrongs by other countries. Those who support the war feel a similar identification and an urge for justification.

It may be countered that identification with one's country is a psychological phenomenon, and not necessarily a moral one, a sentiment best overcome. This view has appeal. Identity with one's country has been used to justify terrible atrocities as well as noble endeavors. The subject of associative obligation with respect to states is a complex one and I do not intend to add to that discussion here.

My main point is that Blake seems to rule out associative obligation because of a worry that its commitment to partiality is incompatible with a commitment to equality. But justified partiality *must* be compatible with abstract equality. Surely I can prefer my family and friends over strangers on many things without rejecting the idea that people are fundamentally equal. We do not need the machinery Blake gives us to recognize that both equality and partiality are essential to morality.

The main issue concerning the state is not about partiality but about the state itself—whether the state is a fit subject for partial concern. The state is not the same as a friend or family member, or an association one has voluntarily joined. It is one identity we have among others, and it can be a weak one for many people. In my view, probing the scope and limits of associative obligation with regard to the state is the most fruitful way of making progress on the controversy between cosmopolitanism and liberal nationalism.

---

[20] Nagel, *op. cit.*, p. 128. For a similar argument see also David Miller, *On Nationality* (Oxford: Oxford University Press, 1995).

Chapter 16
International and Cosmopolitan Political Obligations

Helga Varden

1 Introduction[1]

Over the last few years, there has been intense political debate concerning the rightful use of coercion in the international sphere. Strong political forces have maintained that in addition to being inefficient, the current international authority, the United Nations (UN), is neither necessary nor desirable for the realization of international justice. This is seen not only in how recent efforts to improve and strengthen the UN are met with considerable resistance from powerful nations, but also by the fact that individual nations claim it rightful unilaterally to use coercion to solve conflicts in the international sphere. Though many other voices have argued that we need the UN, especially to enforce human rights internationally, there is little explanation why justice *necessarily* requires an international authority, rather than merely one or more just, strong nations. Therefore, current sentiment in favour of maintaining the UN is rarely supported by cogent justification that the UN is in principle necessary for international justice. From a philosophical point of view, the state of the contemporary debate is good evidence that we need to rethink the status of a distinctly international authority.

In this paper, I take a first stab at this task by arguing with Kant that international justice is in principle impossible without an international and cosmopolitan authority. The proposed account can explain why due respect for human rights and mutual respect of sovereignty among internally just states is possible only through the establishment of a transnational authority. The implication of this argument is that the liberal ideal of international political obligations is non-voluntarist in nature,

[1] I am grateful to Arnt Myrstad, Arthur Ripstein and Shelley Weinberg for their generous help in writing this paper. I would also like to thank the editors of this volume as well as the audiences at the 23rd Social Philosophy Conference at the University of Victoria (Aug. 2006), the faculty of law at the University of Oslo (Aug. 2006), AMINTAPHIL at Washington University and Southeast Missouri State University (Nov. 2006), the APA Pacific Division (April 2007), and the 1st annual conference of the Northwestern University Society for Ethical Theory and Political Philosophy (May 2007) for their useful comments. Special thanks go to my commentators John Harris at the Pacific APA and Kyla Ebels Duggan at the 1st annual conference at Northwestern University.

D.A. Reidy and W.J. Riker (eds.), *Coercion and the State.*
© Springer Science + Business Media B.V. 2008

meaning that states do not in principle have the right to resist the establishment of an international authority to regulate their international interactions.[2] Moreover, the justification for an international authority is not linked to the typical aggressiveness of states. *Even if* all states are non-aggressive, I argue, they are still obligated to establish an international authority, since its establishment is a precondition for international justice. Only an international authority can enable rightful relations among states, because only it can put the interacting parties under universal laws and therefore also have standing to rightfully solve conflicts and use coercion with regard to states' interactions. In addition, I explore Kant's arguments that justice requires international trade as well as interactions between just states and visiting, alien private individuals to be regulated by a cosmopolitan authority.[3] Both arguments strengthen the conclusion that the liberal ideal of transnational political obligations must be non-voluntarist, even if, as Kant argues, it is prudent to pursue the establishment of this authority voluntarily. A particular advantage of the position is its promise for solving several recalcitrant problems in current international politics, such as issues concerning rightful borders, trade—including the operation of multinationals in illegitimate and aggressive states, and the rights of stateless persons. The argument defends the conclusion that coercion in the international sphere is rightful *only if* authorised by an *international* and *cosmopolitan* authority.

2   A Kantian Conception of Political Obligations

Kant claims that justice in the international sphere requires states and individual persons not only to adhere to some reasonable conception of international law, but also to establish a transnational, public legal authority to regulate their interactions.[4] The justification for this claim has its foundation in Kant's understanding of justice (political freedom), and I will use Kant's conception of political obligations at the

---

[2] I believe that Kant's account of the transnational public authority is non-voluntarist also in the sense that it does not consider the rights of an international authority as in principle co-extensive with those of individual nation states. Since I do not engage issues of legitimacy concerning the structure of the international authority here, but only the duty to establish it, I cannot engage this issue here.

[3] With Kant I will use the term 'international' authority when I talk about how the transnational, public authority regulates the relations between states (or nations), whereas 'cosmopolitan' authority refers to this authority when it regulates a relation that includes a private individual.

[4] I refer to Kant's work by means of the Prussian Academy Pagination (PAP) only. I have used Mary Gregor's translation of *The Metaphysics of Morals* (New York: Cambridge University Press, 1996), (PAP 6:203–493). Other works cited include "On the Common Saying: "'This may Be True in Theory, but It Doesn't Apply in Practice'", (PAP 8:273–313), and "Perpetual Peace—a Philosophical Sketch", (PAP 8:341–386). Both are printed in T. Humphrey (trans./ed.), *Perpetual Peace and Other Essays* (Indianapolis, IN: Hackett Publishing, 1983).

state level to model the structure of his argument at the international level.[5] This approach to Kant's texts seems consistent with Kant's own view. For example, the sections on "The Right of Nations" and "Cosmopolitan Right" constitute chapters II and III (respectively) of Kant's account of public right in "the Doctrine of Right" (DR) and so naturally lead us to think that the argument preceding it, namely the private right account regarding nation states, prepares the ground also for these chapters (as it does for chapter I on national public right). Moreover, this interpretation is confirmed in the introduction to "The Right of Nations", where Kant argues that the right of nations is "[t]he only difference between the state of nature of individual men and of families (in relation to one another) and that of nations is that in the right of nations we have to take into consideration not only the relation of individual persons of one state toward the individuals of another, as well as toward another state as a whole" (6: 343f). Here Kant sees the argument concerning the right of nations as structurally similar to that given in his discussion of private right at the nation state level. Part of the interpretative puzzle consists in figuring out how to think of this similarity. Below I suggest that the arguments for the 'private rights' of states outlined in chapter II of Public Right in DR ("The Right of Nations"), are structurally similar to the private right arguments concerning assurance and private property in Kant's account of national justice.[6]

The relations between individuals and states and between individuals of different states are discussed in chapter III of public right in DR ("Cosmopolitan Right"). Here we find Kant's discussion of international trade and visitors. The analogous private right arguments in the national case are those concerning contract right (trade) and those concerning how the innate right to freedom always secures people a right to exist (visitors).[7] The final category of private right in the national case, namely status relations, is not considered in Kant's writings on international justice, but I suggest that we can expand Kant's account to include these relations. Finally, though the argument concerning the international sphere is a 'public right' argument, Kant explicitly confirms my claim that we must analyse these relations as analogous to interactions between private individuals in the state of nature: "As nations, peoples can be regarded as single individuals who injure one another through their close proximity while living in the state of nature" (8: 354). For all of these reasons I find that highlighting relevant features of his account of justice in the national case illuminates the structure of Kant's account of international relations. Before turning to the international sphere, let us therefore briefly outline how Kant's non-voluntarist

---

[5] I am grateful to Barbara Herman for encouraging me to make explicit the textual basis for utilising Kant's arguments as presented in the sections on national justice in DR to understand his theory of international justice.

[6] Kant has parallel arguments in "Theory and Practice" (8: 307–313) and in "Perpetual Peace" (8: 341–386).

[7] Kant's discussion of the 'right to hospitality' in his political essays should be seen as complementary to his discussion of visitors in DR.

conception of political obligations at the state level follows from his conception of justice.[8]

2.1 National Political Obligations

In "The Doctrine of Right" Kant argues that justice is possible only within civil society, or within a liberal, legal framework. Civil society is an enforceable precondition for justice, and not merely a prudent response to the inconveniences characterizing the state of nature (8: 313, 8:354).[9] These conclusions are grounded in Kant's relational understanding of justice. Justice requires individuals' interactions to be respectful of their innate right to freedom, meaning that no one's freedom is subjected to the arbitrary choices of others but only to universal law (6: 230f, 237). The innate right to freedom gives all persons, as embodied beings, a right to exist and to bodily integrity. External freedom, or setting and pursuing ends of one's own, however, requires more than this—and it is these further considerations that make Kant conclude that rightful interaction is impossible in the state of nature understood as a condition without a *public* authority. Justice cannot be realized privately by *each individual* acting virtuously, since it is impossible for private individuals to provide rightful assurance and to overcome certain problems of specification characterising the acquisition of private property, contract relations and status relations. The problem, in short, is that property, contract, and status relations[10] among individuals cannot be both rightful, reconcilable with each person's innate right to freedom, and determined and assured by a *private* authority. And private authority is the extent to which there is authority in the state of nature. Indeed, there are universal principles, namely the Universal Principle of Right and what Kant calls the 'principles of private right' that determine property broadly construed (private property, contract and status relations) (6: 258ff, 271ff, 277ff). The difficulty, rather, is in providing assurance for property holdings and determining rightfully how these abstract universal principles should be *applied*

---

[8]One may see this paper as a response to A.J. Simmons's claim in *Justification and Legitimacy: Essays on Rights and Obligations*, Cambridge University Press, 2001, that Kant "never explains very clearly why I have an obligation to leave the state of nature and live in civil society with others, rather than just a general obligation to respect humanity and the rights persons possess (whether in or out of civil society)" (p. 140). In "Kant's Non-Voluntarist Conception of Political Obligations" (*Kantian Review*, forthcoming) I provide Kant's explanation of the obligation as it pertains to the national case, and here I explain the obligation in the international case. Together these papers argue why we should reject Simmons's claim—as well as provide us reasons to reject the Lockean claim that private individuals and states in the international sphere have a natural executive right.

[9]For an overview of prudential vs. non-prudential readings of Kant's philosophy of right, see my "Kant's Non-Voluntarist Conception of Political Obligations".

[10]Status relations are relations where one person has standing within another person's private life, such as parental relations.

in empirical cases so that the resulting set of restrictions constrains each person's actions universally or non-arbitrarily (symmetrically and non-contingently).[11] Even mutual agreement cannot make relations among individuals rightful, since everyone's freedom is still subject to one another's arbitrary choice, namely that we continuously choose consent on matters of the correct application of the principles.

Due to the problems of assurance and specification, therefore, to stay in the state of nature is to commit wrongdoing. It is to stay in a condition where we subject one another's freedom to one another's arbitrary choices rather than to universal law. At most, the state of nature is a condition *devoid of justice*, meaning that in the best scenario it is a condition in which particular individuals do not wrong *one another*, but yet in choosing to remain in the state of nature they renounce any concept of right (6: 312) or 'do wrong in the highest degree' (6: 307f). In order to interact rightfully with others we must establish a condition in which our interactions are subject to universal laws rather than to one another's arbitrary restrictions. And the only way to do this is by establishing a will that is the will of each and yet the will of no one particular private individual, that is, a *public* will or a public authority (6: 345f, 8:344, 351f). To refuse to enter civil society is therefore to refuse the condition under which interaction consistent with each person's right to freedom is respected, which is to commit wrongdoing in the highest degree. Thus, individuals have a strict or enforceable duty to set up a *public* authority to provide assurance and to specify the rules for their interaction (8:371, 6: 230, 232). Because consent cannot be a necessary condition for the establishment of a rightful state, the liberal ideal of political obligations at the state level is non-voluntarist in nature.

2.2   International Political Obligations

Kant's theory of justice requires a non-voluntarist conception of international political obligations for the same kinds of reasons it requires a non-voluntarist conception of national political obligations. Although the suggested scheme provides a way of conceptualizing solutions to certain contemporary problems, such as freedom from poverty, the argument establishes the necessity of an international legal order *even if* no such problems exist. As in the national case, the main problems that cannot be overcome in the state of nature, and which therefore call for an international public authority, concern the provision of assurance and the application of international laws to actual interactions. Let's start with the argument why a transnational, public authority, rather than a very powerful state, is necessary to provide assurance in international relations.[12]

---

[11] See "Kant's Non-Voluntarist Conception of Political Obligations" for further explication of these points.

[12] As mentioned above, this discussion loosely corresponds to Kant's discussion in DR of "The Right of Nations" (6: 343–351), which mainly concerns the issue of war (and so issues of assurance and border conflicts), and his discussion of "Cosmopolitan Right" in (6: 352–353), which focuses mainly on trade and visitors' rights.

First, a superpower cannot provide assurance in the international sphere since it lacks an impartial *form*. On the one hand, a superpower has its own national interests, and hence cannot reasonably be seen as impartial to particular disputes in the international arena. On the other hand, the superpower cannot provide assurance in its own relations with other states. In order to provide assurance for these relations, yet another stronger power is needed, leading to an infinite regress. Therefore, in order to provide assurance in the international sphere we need at the very minimum a conception of a *public* power, meaning a power that represents no national interests yet can be seen as representing the interests of each nation. Since only an international authority in principle has the impartial form, only it can provide assurance in international relations. This entails that no state can rightfully refuse to establish a public authority that can provide assurance in the international sphere and we have a first reason why international political obligations cannot be voluntarist.

The lack of the right kind of impartiality also explains why rightful relations between bordering nations require an international authority. Rightful relations require states to subject themselves to universal (symmetrical and non-contingent) laws. It is impossible, however, for any state to apply the Universal Principle of Right so as to make objective or non-contingent determinations of what constitutes the border between itself and its neighbours.[13] Any proposal here can reasonably be challenged by its neighbours, entailing that a state that uses might to defend its proposed border will subject other states to contingent and asymmetrical—or unjustifiable—restrictions.[14] Of course, neighbouring states may happen to agree on borders making coercion unnecessary.[15] But their relation is not thereby made *rightful*, since their peaceful co-existence is still subject to each other's consent. By refusing to enter an international civil society, or to establish a public, international

---

[13] Jürgen Habermas, "Kant's Idea of Perpetual Peace, with the Benefit of Two Hundred Years' Hindsight", transl. by James Bohman, in J. Bohman and M. Lutz-Bachman, eds., *Perpetual Peace*, pp. 113, 116, also argues that the problem of application is of particular interest to Kant's position, and he understands Kant to be arguing that even if states were to enforce *reasonable* conceptions of international law when interacting with other states the result is not rightful relations.

[14] This is why, in my view, Kant argues that "war is but a sad necessity of the state of nature (where no tribunal empowered to make judgments supported by the power of law exists), one that maintains the rights of a nation by mere might, where neither party can be declared an unjust enemy (since this already presupposes a judgment of right)" (8: 346). Moreover, it is important to note that passages such as the following seem to suggest that for Kant war is the only solution to conflicts in the state of nature: "[t]he concept of the right of nations as a right to go to war is meaningless (for it would then be the right to determine the right not by independent, universally valid laws that restrict the freedom of everyone, but by one-sided maxims backed by force)... Reason can provide related nations with no other means for emerging from the state of lawlessness, which consists solely of war, than that they give up their savage (lawless) freedom, just as individual persons do, and, to establish a *nation of peoples*... that (continually growing) will finally include all the people of the earth" (8: 356f).

[15] Note that the international authority is constitutive of rightful assurance and rightful borders even if the world comprises only internally just states and individuals who happen not to want to travel or trade with one another.

authority with standing to determine possible, future disputes in their relations, states commit the worst kind of wrongdoing.[16]

2.3   Cosmopolitan Political Obligations

Let us now consider Kant's account of relations involving "individual persons of one state toward the individuals of another, as well as toward another state as a whole" (6: 343f). That is, let us consider Kant's account of 'cosmopolitan right', including both global relations of trade and visitors and hospitality.[17] As usual, we will pay special attention to uncovering the reasoning supporting his claim that these relations cannot be made rightful in the state of nature. Specifically, we want to understand what Kant means when he says that with regard to trade, cosmopolitan right "has to do with the possible union of all nations with a view to certain universal laws for their possible commerce" (6: 352), and generally, that cosmopolitan right is an "amendment" to civil and international law since it is "necessary to the public rights of men in general" (8: 360).

Consider first Kant's account of visitors and hospitality. Kant argues that it is a matter of private right that citizens of just states are subject to the laws of the countries they visit. Furthermore, states have a general right to deny visitors access to their territories, but not when it is impossible to turn a visitor away "without destroying him" (8: 358). The reason why states cannot be seen as having a right to turn away a person who will thereby be 'destroyed' is simply that this is to deny this person his innate right to freedom, since it involves denying that person the right to exist (even though he has done nothing wrong). And this is never permissible.[18] Moreover, a visitor must obey the laws of the state he visits. Provisional justice is obtained in relations between states and visiting aliens when the state does not turn away stateless individuals and members of oppressive states and as long as visitors obey the state's laws when they visit (8: 357–360). In my view, the reason why these relations between individuals and states are still only provisionally rightful is that visitors, stateless persons and members of oppressive states are necessarily precluded from rightful relations with the state in question since they cannot be subject to universal law in their interactions with it. *Rightful* relations are impossible here, because any general will of a state of which they are not citizens is not a general will constitutive of them. And the only way to ensure that the general will is inclusive of them is to

---

[16] Kant argues that if two states choose to stay in the state of nature, they do not wrong each other, but staying in "this condition [the state of nature] is in itself still wrong in the highest degree and neighboring states are under an obligation to leave it" (6: 344). They do wrong in the highest degree because they remain in a condition where they are subject to one another's arbitrary choices (consent) rather than being subject to universal law. We find this expression that staying in the state of nature is to do wrong in the highest degree several places in Kant's texts, such as (8: 380) and (6: 308).

[17] In DR Kant treats the problem of visitors and hospitality only very briefly (6: 352f), whereas in "Perpetual Peace" it gets a more thorough treatment (8: 356–360). Both texts are utilized in my account below.

[18] Of course, this does not entail that states are obliged to assist fleeing, international criminals, but that is beside the present point.

institute a general or public, *cosmopolitan* authority, since only it, by representing the wills of all and yet no particular state or private individuals, can have the impartial standing requisite to subject the interacting parties (states and private individuals) to universal law.[19] The public, international authority represents the will of each interacting party and so is the means through which relations can be made rightful. In this way, visitors, stateless individuals and members of just states are given political freedom in their interactions with just states. The possibility of establishing rightful relations amongst states and private individuals interacting in the international sphere is therefore another Kantian reason why the liberal ideal of transnational political obligations must be non-voluntarist in nature.

Let us now turn to the other aspect of cosmopolitan right, namely that concerning the possibility of contract right.[20] As is the case at the national level, the Kantian account maintains that enforceable international trade contracts require a judge impartial in its form. Rightful contractual relations require more than a third-party private judge to settle disputes between contracting parties, no matter how impartial she claims to be or actually is. Allowing private adjudication merely reproduces the contractual problem, since either party to the dispute can reasonably disagree with the way in which the judge performs her contractual duty in settling the dispute. Only a judge impartial in its form, namely a public judge, can overcome this problem. Regarding international trade, this means that a public or cosmopolitan judge must be established and we have another reason why civil society is constitutive of rightful international relations.[21]

This argument becomes especially important when we appreciate that international trade today often consists in multinational organizations operating in oppressive states or in states that fail to meet minimal institutional conditions for a legitimate state. This yields a special problem for the Kantian account because the relation between multinational companies and their employees must be made rightful. The problem in the case of oppressive states is that there does not exist a legitimate civil public authority to regulate the relations between multinationals and their employees, and so even provisionally rightful relations between them in those oppressive states are impossible. In my view, the better interpretation of the Kantian position will here argue that internally just states cannot permit their companies to operate in such oppressive states unless they also establish a public, cosmopolitan legal framework that regulates those companies' operations there. This cosmopolitan

---

[19] We can make this point more strongly: Because a state assumes a right to exclude non-citizens from its territory, there arises an additional principled reason for establishing an international authority since the state must make the relation between itself and non-citizens rightful.

[20] International contract right is less strict in that it follows only under the assumption that international trade and travel is deemed desirable.

[21] A similar argument follows from Kant's analysis of status relations, or relations involving married couples, families and servants, and parents and their children. When these relations are inherently international in nature, as for example in cases in which spouses are from different countries and when children are adopted or servants hired from a different country, rightful relations necessarily require a cosmopolitan authority with standing in the relationship.

framework sets and enforces rules for trade in these countries, so that provisionally rightful trade relations are possible.[22]

2.4   A Textual Puzzle

Maintaining, as I have done, that in principle Kant *actually* defends and that the best Kantian conception *should* defend a non-consensual conception of international and cosmopolitan political obligations is currently controversial.[23] To argue in this way is challenging not only because at several places in his political essays Kant appears to hold a voluntarist view of transnational political obligations,[24] but also because the theory

---

[22] I believe that these relations are still only provisionally rightful, because there is no civil institutional structure in place to ensure true independence for the people. True independence requires not only that the national public authority is in charge of the economic and financial systems, but also that there is unconditional poverty relief and structures that make it possible for citizens to work their way out of poverty. Conclusively rightful relations require that the international trade is supported by legitimate national states, and so these relations between transnational companies and their employees in oppressive countries that are regulated by the cosmopolitan authority, are still only provisionally rightful. Unfortunately, I cannot engage these issues here.

[23] Contrast this reading with much secondary literature on Kant, including most of the articles in *Perpetual Peace* (1997). It is also interesting to note that although Höffe agrees that Kant's considered conception deems a world republic—and not only a voluntarist federation of nations—necessary to international justice, he claims that this is not Kant's actual view (Höffe 2006: 16, 127, 140, 169–172, 197–201). Moreover, he quickly dismisses an interpretation somewhat similar to the one I suggest below. As will be evident, contra Hoffe, we can provide an interpretation that reconciles what Kant's theory demands with the difficulties Kant acknowledges in actually instituting these demands.

[24] For example, after Kant emphasizes that states are under an obligation to leave the state of nature by establishing a league of nations, he argues that "[t]his alliance must, however, involve no sovereign authority (as in a civil constitution), but only an *association* (federation); it must be an alliance that can be renounced at any time and so must be renewed from time to time" (6: 344f). Similarly, after arguing that "[o]nly in a universal *association of states* (analogous to that by which a people becomes a state) can rights come to hold *conclusively* and a true *condition of peace* come about" (6: 350), Kant maintains that "[s]uch an *association* of several *states* to preserve peace can be called a *permanent congress of states*, which each neighboring state is at liberty to join…. By a *congress* is here understood only a voluntary coalition of different states which can be *dissolved* at any time, not a federation (like that of the American states which is based on a constitution and can therefore not be dissolved.—Only by such a congress can the idea of public right of nations be realized, one to be established for deciding their disputes in a civil way, as if by a lawsuit, rather than in a barbaric way (the way of savages), namely by war" (6: 350f). Finally, many pages after Kant states "each nation can and should demand that the others enter into a contract resembling the civil one and guaranteeing the rights of each. This would be a federation *of nations*" (8: 354), he refers us back to this federation of nations and explains that it must be understood as a free association: "There can be talk of international right only on the assumption that a state of law-governedness exists (i.e., that external condition under which a right can actually be accorded man). For as a public right, its concept already contains the public recognition of a general will that determines the rights of everyone, and this *status iuridicus* must proceed from some contract that cannot be founded on coercive laws (like those from which the nation springs), but can at best be an *enduring free* association, like the federation of different nations mentioned above. For in the state of nature, in the absence of a state of law-governedness, only private right exists" (8: 384). The controversy, in sum, may be seen as focusing on what 'at best' means here—and my suggestion below is that it refers to prudential considerations involved in establishing the international and cosmopolitan authority rather than an abandonment of the theory.

challenges deeply held intuitions that obligating transnational political institutions require voluntary consent, since anything else challenges state sovereignty. Nevertheless, I believe that in part it was exactly the theory's challenge to deeply held intuitions that led Kant to predict that nations would not recognize the necessity of establishing the necessary 'world republic' and instead settle for the second best solution of establishing a voluntarist association or league of nations. In my view, this is why Kant argues that people will refuse to establish the only means through which rightful interactions are possible, because they find that it conflicts with 'their idea of the right of nations' or their idea of state sovereignty. "[C]onsequently", Kant continues, "they discard in *hypothesis* what is true in *thesis*" (8: 356f).[25] Treating the establishment of the international political authority as a voluntarist project is therefore a wise strategy, even if international political obligations in principle are non-voluntarist in nature.

Another reason why it is prudent to consider the establishment of a world republic a voluntarist project is, Kant argues, that a world republic would be practically unmanageable.[26] Kant therefore suggests that more limited, voluntary 'congresses' of states should be instituted to solve particular problems of interaction. The main idea, I suggest, is that geographically more limited transnational, public authorities, such as the European Union, can constitute both the first steps and partial means through which truly international and cosmopolitan co-operation is established.[27] So, premature, overly

---

[25] The full argument runs like this: "Reason can provide related nations with no other means of emerging from the state of lawlessness, which consists solely of war, than that they give up their savage (lawless) freedom, just as individual persons do, and by accommodating themselves to the constraints of common law, establish a nation of peoples (*civitas genitum*) that (continually growing) will finally include all the people of the earth. But they don't will to do this because it doesn't conform to their idea of the right of nations, and consequently they discard in hypothesis what is true in thesis. So (if everything is not to be lost) in place of the positive idea of a world republic they put only the negative surrogate of an enduring, ever expanding federation that prevents war and curbs the tendency of that hostile inclination to defy the law, though there will always be constant danger of their breaking loose" (8: 356f).

[26] Kant argues that "[o]nly in a universal association of states... can rights come to hold *conclusively* and a true *condition of peace* come about. But if such a state made up of nations were to extend too far over vast regions, governing it and so too protecting each of its members would finally have to become impossible, while several such corporations would again bring on a state of war. So *perpetual peace*, the ultimate goal of the whole right of nations, is indeed an unachievable idea. Still, the political principles directed toward perpetual peace, of entering into such alliances of states, which serve for continual *approximation* to it, are not unachievable. Instead, since continual approximation to it is a task based on duty and therefore on the right of human beings and of states, this can certainly be achieved" (6: 350).

[27] Textual support for this pragmatic reading seems given by Kant immediately after he mentions the problem with "vast regions". Here he emphasises the need for "continual approximation" to the "universal *association of states* (analogous to that by which a people becomes a state)" and he argues that the "*permanent congress of states*, which each neighbouring state is at liberty to join" (6: 350). He then gives an historical example to illustrate this point: "[s]omething of this kind took place (at least as regards the formalities of the right of nation for the sake of keeping the peace) in the first half of the present century, in the assembly of the States General at the Hague. The ministers of most of the courts of Europe and even of the smallest republics lodge with it their complaints about attacks being made on one of them by another. In this way they thought of the whole of Europe as a single confederated state which they accepted as arbiter, so to speak, in their public disputes" (ibid.). Viewing such more limited transnational efforts (as long as they do not unite into a superstate (8: 354)) seems like a reasonable interpretation of Kant's position.

ambitious, and coercive attempts at establishing an international legal framework might only add to the anarchy characterizing current international relations. After all, what we have a right to do is to establish a rightful legal order—not to dissolve all relations.[28] Nevertheless, these pragmatic considerations don't undermine Kant's argument that in principle the establishment of a public or international authority is constitutive of rightful international relations (6:311, 350, 8:310f, 356). Hence, it does not undermine the principled claim that only such an international authority can settle conflicts and rightfully exercise coercion in the international sphere. Only by uniting themselves can interacting nations "settle their differences legally" (8: 379) or interact rightfully.

If we contrast Kant to Hobbesian and Lockean conceptions of international relations, we see two main differences. First, Kant argues that international justice in principle requires an international and cosmopolitan authority. He challenges their claims that the main reason why we would want an international and cosmopolitan authority is due to considerations of prudence, since he argues that it is in principle impossible to establish rightful relations without also establishing an international authority. Second, Kant turns the claim around and argues that considerations of prudence make it necessary to proceed on a voluntary basis and in limited yet progressive steps as we seek to establish rightful international and cosmopolitan relations.

Kant's conclusion to the discussion of international justice in DR can be seen to affirm the interpretation I have proposed, namely that although international political obligations are non-consensual in principle, establishing a legitimate cosmopolitan authority must proceed with an eye to prudence and so voluntarily:

> [M]oral practical reason pronounces in us its irresistible *veto: there is to be no war*, neither war between you and me in the state of nature nor war between us as states, which, although they are internally in a lawful condition, are still externally (in relation to one

---

[28] Hence, in my view, those passages where Kant apparently argues that the international public authority should not have coercive powers must be read in light of pragmatic considerations. For example, in (8: 383f), we find, "[t]here can be talk of international right only on the assumption that a state of law-governedness exists (i.e., that external condition under which a right can actually be accorded man). For as a public right, its concept already contains the public recognition of a general will that determines the rights of everyone, and this *status iuridicus* must proceed from some contract that cannot be founded on coercive laws (like those from which the nation springs), but can at best be an *enduring free* association, like the federation of different nations mentioned above. For in the state of nature, in the absence of law-governedness, only private right can exist" (8: 384). True, this passage tempts us to conclude that Kant conceives of international authority in voluntarist terms. Nevertheless, we should resist the temptation to be too quick. Instead, we should interpret this (and similar) passage in light of Kant's general account of political obligations in combination with his prudential cautions. Thus, in this passage we must pay attention to how Kant argues that 'at best' the international authority is considered as a voluntarist project, where 'at best' is understood as referring to prudential considerations. Kant's reference to the talk of a 'federation' above fits this interpretation. Indeed, he speaks of the voluntary federation in (8: 357) just after he points out that people reject in "hypothesis what is true in thesis. So (if everything is not to be lost) in place of the positive idea of *a world republic* they put only the *negative* surrogate of an enduring, ever expanding *federation* that prevents war and curbs the tendency of that hostile inclination to defy the law, though there will always be the constant danger of their breaking lose". So again, Kant reiterates the strict necessity of the world republic, but emphasizes that people will proceed by voluntarist means.

another) in a lawless condition; for war is not the way in which everyone should seek his rights... we must work toward establishing perpetual peace and the kind of constitution that seems to us most conducive to it (say, a republicanism of all states, together and separate)... the condition of peace is the only condition in which what is mine and what is yours is secured under *laws* for a multitude of human beings living in proximity to one another and therefore under a constitution. But the rule for this constitution... must... be derived *a priori* by reason from the ideal of a rightful association of human beings under public laws as such. (6: 354f)

I have suggested that attention to the argument concerning Kant's nonvoluntarist conception of national justice as provided in the first parts of DR sheds much needed light on certain important features of his understanding of international justice. This passage is one place where those features are illuminated. First, we see that problems relating to assurance ('the condition in which what is mine and what is yours is secured under laws') and indeterminacy (the need for 'public laws') are essential to understand why the state of nature is a lawless condition or necessarily a condition of wrongdoing. It follows from this that no one can be seen as having a right to stay in this condition, as this would be to have the right to refuse to interact with others rightfully. The argument also explains why only a public international authority ('a republicanism of all states') can exercise coercion rightfully in international interactions. Any unilateral use of coercion will always involve committing wrongdoing in the highest degree, and often (if used against those who want to leave the state of nature) involve wronging others. Finally, considerations of prudence make it wise to seek the establishment of this authority by voluntarist steps, since this is the best way to realistically seek rightful relations—or perpetual peace.

3.   Conclusion

I have argued that the liberal ideal of political obligations in the international sphere is non-voluntarist in nature. I argued with Kant that the *impartial form* of the international authority is what gives it, and never anyone else, rightful standing to solve problems of assurance and application in the international sphere. The authority of the international and cosmopolitan power stems from how it represents each interacting states and private person and yet none of them individually. Any state that insists on providing assurance or applying international laws on its own, commits wrongdoing 'in the highest degree' on this account, since this fails to respect the sovereignty of other states and private individuals in the international sphere. It is due to the fact that international justice is possible only through the establishment of an international and cosmopolitan authority that it has a special status that individual states cannot possibly have.

Index

AMINTAPHIL: The Philosophical Foundations of Law and Justice

1. S. P. Lee: *Intervention, Terrorism, and Torture. Contemporary Challenges to Just War Theory.* 2007.   ISBN 978-1-4020-4677-3
2. D. A. Reidy, W. J. Riker: *Coercion and the State.* 2008.   ISBN 978-1-4020-6878-2

Printed in the United Kingdom
by Lightning Source UK Ltd.
130825UK00002B/58-294/P